Commendations

'*This Is My Body* is a book many of us have been waiting for. It grants space for trans Christians to give distinctive voice to theology grounded in particular and diverse experience, free from the often oppressive constructions of gender and identity imposed by 'The Church'. This book reveals the diversity of trans experiences and models hope, anger and grace in powerful ways. It announces the growing confidence of trans Christians and our refusal to be treated as second-class and welcome under sufferance.'
The Revd Rachel Mann, Poet-in-Residence, Manchester Cathedral

'I read these essays with a growing sense of excitement. Here is highly readable theology rooted in the experience and faith of trans people. It will encourage everyone who is part of a sex/gender minority, and to those within the majority with ears to hear, it will transform their understanding.'
Adrian Thatcher, Honorary Professor in the Department of Theology and Religion, University of Exeter

'We all desire to be whole and to belong, to know who we are and to be truly accepted. *This Is My Body* makes a simple but profound appeal for the voices of transgender Christians to be heard within the Church, the Body of Christ. Rooted in the pioneering pastoral and prayerful work of the Sibyls, founded to support trans Christian people, this is an important and timely work of theological resourcing. Thoughtful, accessible and honest, in giving voice to the faith stories and pilgrimages of transgender Christians it provides spiritual and theological nourishment for all.'
The Revd Duncan Dormor, Dean, St John's College, Cambridge

'*This Is My Body* describes a collection of personal accounts from a number of Sibyls members, past and present, reflecting on their personal journeys as transgender and spiritually aware, and managing to negotiate, for better or worse, the path to their authentic identity.

'The book also provides a wide ranging social history of a particular group of transgender Christians – in the broadest sense of the word – from a variety of churches, but mainly the Church of England. The Sibyls are inclusive and tolerant with a shared ethos of "love thy neighbor" and "do unto others ..." Members are mostly, but not exclusively transgender, and others with an interest in the issue are also welcomed. This includes myself.

'Miss Jay Walmsley, the 'founding saint' of Sibyls, gives a splendid and coherent account of how the organisation originated and grew, and continues to evolve under new leadership. As a group, Sibyls arrange weekend retreats, evening church gatherings at St Anne's Church in Soho, London, and summer garden parties, usually at Jay's home.

'One chapter, by co-editor Michelle O'Brien, delves in some detail into 'intersex', its relationship to and distinction from transgender (formerly termed transsexual) conditions.

'*This is My Body* makes understanding transgender easy and interesting. It should be mandatory reading for affected and interested persons; even for those of little faith.'

**Dr Russell Reid, consultant psychiatrist,
formerly of the London Gender Institute**

'Fifty years ago when the world was ablaze with family values, gays and lesbians emerged from the shadows to share their story. Since then knowledge has brought understanding. Now it is the turn of transgender people and this important book, edited by Christina Beardsley and Michelle O'Brien, will help everyone to understand their lives. It is a scholarly book but accessible to the general reader.

'The many contributors speak movingly of the way that until recently the churches have ignored the spiritual needs of transgender women and men. This will now change. The Sibyls, a support group founded ten years ago by Jay Walmsley, enables members to meet together and share their stories. We have much to learn from them.'

**The Revd Malcolm Johnson, former rector of
St Botolph's, Aldgate**

'"If I am not for myself, who will be for me? But if I am only for myself, who am I? If not now, when?" (Hillels, Ethics of the Fathers, 1:14) springs to my mind browsing through these chapters. *This Is My Body* is an account of a truly proactive, community-led and multifaceted approach to trans and faith issues. It is written from a Christian perspective and yet I experienced it strongly resonated with me as a Trans Jew. This book is truly inspiring for everyone!'

Surat-Shaan Knan, Liberal Judaism, Founder of Twilight People

THIS IS MY BODY

Hearing the Theology of Transgender
Christians

**Edited by
Christina Beardsley
and Michelle O'Brien**

DARTON·LONGMAN+TODD

First published in 2016 by
Darton, Longman and Todd Ltd
1 Spencer Court
140 – 142 Wandsworth High Street
London SW18 4JJ

Reprinted 2016

ISBN: 978-0-232-53206-7

A catalogue record for this book is available from the British Library

Designed and typeset by Kerrypress, St Albans AL3 8JL
Printed and bound by Short Run Press Ltd

Contents

Contributors

The Editors

The Revd Dr Christina Beardsley, a Church of England parish priest for twenty-two years, and a hospital chaplain since 2000, is Head of Multi-faith Chaplaincy at the Chelsea & Westminster Hospital, London, and a Visiting Lecturer in Healthcare Chaplaincy at St Mary's University, Twickenham. Co-founder (with Melanie Cherriman) of the Clare Project in Brighton & Hove for people dealing with issues of gender, and co-deviser (with Michelle O'Brien) of the Sibyls' 'Gender, Sexuality, Spirituality' Workshop, Tina has served on the Sibyls' Committee (2003-14) and as the first Changing Attitude, England Trustee for trans people (2006-13). A speaker, writer and activist for trans inclusion in the Church, she has authored several articles and chapters about trans people's spirituality, and Church policy towards trans people, healthcare chaplaincy and spirituality, and a biography of a Victorian preacher: *Unutterable Love: the Passionate Life & Preaching of FW Robertson*, (Lutterworth, 2009).

Michelle O'Brien has been an active member of the Church of England for most of her life, studied Philosophy at Bristol University, was a Franciscan novice in her early 30's, and then did a Masters degree. She was a server and member of the PCC, Deanery Synod, and Southwark Diocesan Synod, was involved with Inclusive Church, and was also involved in the Sibyls for ten years. Between 2003 and 2010, Michelle undertook post-graduate social research into the medical experiences of intersex and trans people (University of Surrey, Roehampton). During that time, she set up an online support group for people with Androgen Insensitivity Syndrome who were assigned male, was one of the early members of Organisation Intersex International (OII), co-founded OII-UK, and remained involved with OII and intersex advocacy for ten years. S/he continues to remain an ally to the Sibyls, although considers herself a lapsed Anglo-Catholic. Since moving to NZ in 2010, Michelle has focused on independent advocacy, research, lecturing and writing about intersex and trans issues; she runs her own website.

The Contributors

Ms Helen Belcher, a founder of Trans Media Watch, is secretary of the UK Parliamentary Forum on Gender Identity, a member of the

Stonewall Trans Advisory Group, and, prior to transition, was a cell-group leader in two Evangelical churches.

The Revd Dr Chris Dowd (formerly an MCC minister) is a URC minister in the north of England who has recently completed doctoral research into trans people's spirituality at the University of Birmingham.

Dr Susan Gilchrist, a retired academic, secretary of the Sibyls Committee, is a member of the LGBTI Anglican Coalition and an independent researcher.

The Revd Dr Mercia Josephine McMahon has served as a Changing Attitude, England Trustee for trans people and is an independent scholar and author with a background in theological education and formation.

Mrs Terry Reed OBE is the co-founder, with her husband, Mr Bernard Reed OBE, of GIRES (Gender Identity Research & Education Society).

Miss Stephanie Sheppard is a member of the Methodist Church and an Evangelical trans Christian activist

Miss Elaine Sommers, a retired surgeon, is Accepting Evangelicals Trustee for trans people.

Miss Jay Walmsley is the Founder of Sibyls.

Ms Jasmine Woolley is a Social Worker in the north of England.

The Trans Awareness Group: members of a local Church of England parish in a southern diocese (**Jean Boothby, the Revd Elizabeth Bunker, Morven Fyfe, Jen Lynch, Anne Passmore, Stephen Passmore**).

Thanks to the following members of **Sibyls** for personal testimonies:

Abigail
Ms Carol Nixon
Janet
The late Michelle Le Morvan
Raymus Bowerbank
Suzanne
'Jemma'

Special thanks to **Dr Susannah Cornwall** for writing a Foreword to the book, and to the **Revd David Horton** for his closing reflections.

Foreword by Susannah Cornwall

At the inaugural scientific meeting of the British Association of Gender Identity Specialists (BAGIS) in Exeter, UK in 2015, I was asked to speak about the faith and spiritual needs of transgender people. Those present, representing experts in gender medicine from several of the NHS gender identity clinics in England, as well as from the Netherlands, the USA, South Africa and beyond, expressed a desire to explore how spiritual and religious needs could be better integrated into trans people's care pathways, and acknowledged that this does not yet adequately happen. 'We feel ill-equipped to address spirituality', one attendee told me, 'but we're coming to realize that attention to religious and spiritual needs is a central factor in people's wellbeing and positive health outcomes. We can't ignore it any more'.

Of course, not all people with a trans identity choose to transition gender publicly, and neither do all – by far – seek surgical or hormonal intervention when they do so. Nonetheless, the fact that greater attention is now being given to spirituality alongside other elements of transgender people's identities even in medical contexts points to a shift in mood in recent years. At least part of this shift is due to the work of those who have long insisted that trans identity and religious faith need not be understood as incompatible, irreconcilable or contradictory. This book represents the fruits of conversations which have been taking place over a lengthy period, among those who have sought to build a safe space for Christian trans people and their families and friends as part of the Sibyls transgender Christian spirituality group.

When I began researching intersex and transgender theologies in the early 2000s, I soon came across references to work by the editors of this collection, Christina Beardsley and Michelle O'Brien, notably their text *The Transsexual Person is my Neighbour* (with an appendix on intersex), written for churches and distributed by the Gender Trust (Beardsley 2000, 2004; O'Brien 2004). At that time, Christina was also one of the only trans Christians to have publicly commented critically on the treatment of transgender in the Church of England's 2003 publication *Some Issues in Human Sexuality* (see Beardsley 2005). I have had the honour of working with Christina on several occasions since then, including a special issue of *Crucible: The Christian Journal of Social Ethics* on Sexuality, Otherness and Power which I edited in 2013; at the Centre for the Study of Christianity and Sexuality's conference Embodied Ministry: Gender, Sexuality and Formation at Ripon College Cuddesdon in 2014; and at a day workshop on Variant Sex and Gender, Religion and Wellbeing at the University of Exeter in 2015. She has proven to be a generous and creative interlocutor, and has given valuable input to my own continuing research on transgender spirituality and healthcare. Michelle's work on intersex was a stimulus to me to undertake both theoretical work on intersex theologies (which became my book, *Sex and Uncertainty in the Body of Christ: Intersex Conditions and Christian Theology* – Cornwall 2010) and research among intersex Christians reflecting on their own experiences (some of which appears in my edited book, *Intersex, Theology, and the Bible: Troubling Bodies in Church, Text, and Society* – Cornwall 2015).

What follows in this book represents a collection that is valuable for several reasons. First, it represents a broad historical sweep, including fascinating accounts from erstwhile members of Sibyls who have since died (such as Michelle le Morvan), and older members' reflections on their memories of negotiating trans identity from as far back as the early decades of the twentieth century (like that of 'Jemma'). This kind of social history is all too often lost, and its inclusion here is testament to the book's long journey to fruition and its thorough attention to the genealogy of Sibyls as a movement. Second, the book redresses an imbalance Mercia McMahon and others have noted, namely that much theology on transgender to date – especially outside the USA – has been written *about* rather than *by* trans people. Indeed, suggests McMahon in the chapter below, 'The driving force of trans theology should transfer to members of the community once there are sufficient trans identified trans theologians to sustain the sub-discipline'. This book represents a significant step in that direction. Third, it includes contributions both from people who have transitioned to living full time in their affirmed gender, and from those for whom cross-dressing is a significant but not sole aspect of their gender identity. It represents a mixture of lay and ordained people, and members of several Christian denominations alongside those who no longer identify as Christian and have found greater freedom and flourishing beyond the Church. It therefore represents at least some of the diversity of the inadequately-termed 'transgender community', as well as including contributions from non-trans allies including David Horton and Chris Dowd.

This is not predominantly an academic book, though several of the authors have also published (on transgender and other areas) in academic contexts. There is critical gender theory here, to be sure, but it is given second place to the foregrounding of testimony (in the broadest sense). The book seeks to root itself in the everyday experience of transgender Christians, reflecting not only on their tales of navigating gender clinics, churches and professional lives, but also on their more personal life stories: their relationships with partners, with children, and with God. In this sense, it is avowedly and unashamedly 'everyday theology', persuaded that reflection on real life and lived concerns is a central and legitimate starting point for talk about God – and that transgender experiences and body-stories are a specific and authentic site of divine blessing and revelation.

There are still voices in the community which remain to be fully heard. For example, readers will notice that the majority of the contributors here are trans women, many of them older. This may simply reflect the fact that, in Britain, there are approximately four times as many trans women as trans men, and that the median age of transition is 42 (Reed et al 2009: 4). It may also represent the fact that younger people are more likely than older ones to identify as having no religion (Office for National Statistics 2013), and less likely than older ones to attend a Christian church. However, the numbers of trans men, and people who identify as genderqueer, genderfluid or non-binary, are increasing rapidly, particularly among the younger generations. On-going conversations in this area, therefore, will need to pay attention to non-binary and otherwise non-mainstream voices, and to explore further what spirituality may look like, and how transgender people's spiritual needs may most effectively be met, beyond traditional expressions of faith.

Jay Walmsley, the founder of Sibyls, notes in 'The Story of the Sibyls' in Part 2 that the group now has fewer members than it once did, and suggests that this may be because, as society becomes more accepting of transgender people, the need for a movement such as Sibyls decreases. Indeed, says Walmsley, 'The hope is always that one day there will be no need for groups like this. If society were fully supportive, there would be help for all who need it. Our prayer is that someday, hopefully soon, we will not be needed and can disband'. However, as Walmsley goes on to acknowledge, Christian churches have, sadly, not always been harbingers of welcome or inclusion of variantly-gendered people. As with lesbian, gay and bisexual Christians, some commentators may ask why someone would wish to continue being associated with an institution which does not endorse one – and which may, indeed, tell one that one is peculiarly sinful, damaged, or disordered. But the message of Sibyls – and of the broader trans Christian voices which this collection engages – is that the Christian community is impoverished, and will become more so, if it ignores and excludes the trans stories already in its midst.

The editors of this collection have assembled and curated a series of narratives which testify to the breadth of experiences – some uplifting, some justly angry, some heart-breaking – of trans people navigating their relationships with the Christian Church. It is my hope that the book will become a landmark text and testify to the many theological possibilities that full acknowledgement of a diversity of bodies, genders and sexes brings to life together.

Dr Susannah Cornwall
Advanced Research Fellow in Theology and Religion, University of Exeter
Director, Exeter Centre for Ethics and Practical Theology (EXCEPT)

Introduction

Much has been said and written about trans people by theologians and Church leaders, including Pope Emeritus Benedict XVI in the Catholic Church, Professor Oliver O'Donovan in the Church of England, and Evangelical commentators Keith Tiller and Don Horrocks. Lesbian and gay Christians have spoken, although people with power often dismiss their views, while little has been heard from trans Christians. This book includes voices associated with the Sibyls, the UK-based confidential spirituality group for transgender people and their allies.

This Is My Body offers a grounded reflection on people's experience of gender dissonance that involves negotiating the boundaries between one's identity and religious faith, as well as a review of the theological, cultural and scientific literature.

The on-going Church 'debates' about sexuality – usually about homosexuality – often leave lesbian and gay people feeling excluded. Trans people tend to feel even further excluded from that debate, and from the lesbian and gay response to it. This book is written as a significant contribution to the debate by people coming forward within the only organisation in the UK established to support those who find themselves affected by these issues, regardless of whether they identify as transsexual, transgender, cross-dressers, or intersex.

To quote from the manuscript version of Helen Savage's PhD dissertation (see 2006: 254):

> The Sibyls bear witness to the vitality of engagement by transgendered and transsexual Christians with the Christian tradition. This is a good example of 'ordinary theology', but as such, risks being undervalued and even ignored by a Church that fails to respect all but the kind of theology forged in the limited context of academia. If the Church is to become more truly itself and to discover its own significance, it too needs to listen before it dares to speak. It too needs, in this way, to commit itself to its most vulnerable members in hope and expectation. This too is the only kind of community in which 'creative fidelity' to the biblical tradition can take place effectively.

The Sibyls

The main purpose of the Sibyls has been to support trans Christian people on their journey. Jay Walmsley, the founder, was for many years the key figure, as the first point of contact for enquirers, and a listening ear, not just in relation to people's experiences with their churches, but in navigating the impact of transition on their jobs, partners and families. Eventually, a group of Sibyls' listeners was formed to share this task.

Support has always involved a regular series of meetings, some held in members' localities, but the main focus being the two annual retreats, one held at a venue in the north of England, the other in the south. These weekends are based around the daily office, in its traditional or modern forms, and the celebration of Holy Communion. In the early days of Sibyls, Holy Communion was celebrated at most events, as it might be the only opportunity for those who had been rejected by their churches to receive the Sacrament.

Until the formation of the Sibyls Committee, twelve years ago, the organisation of these retreat weekends fell largely to Jay, who also liaised with national Church institutions, and with the British Government (e.g., during the public consultation on its Gender Recognition proposals). In such instances, individual Sibyls were encouraged to respond as well, but official Sibyls' submissions were drafted by Jay.

From the inception of the Sibyls' Committee, the tasks of pastoral and spiritual care, membership administration, publicity, finance and the Sibyls' interface with the churches and Government were divided among the Committee members. At this point the Sibyls began to engage with the major UK LGBT Christian organisations, including Changing Attitude (England), LGCM[1], Inclusive Church, the European Forum of LGBT Christian Groups, the Evangelical Fellowship of Lesbian and Gay Christians, and, more recently, the LGBTI Anglican Coalition and Accepting Evangelicals. These organisations demonstrated their readiness to welcome and include transgender Christian people, listen to their concerns, consider how they might fit in with, or differ from, their existing agendas, and to offer a platform to transgender Christians.

By 2005 the trans community had an – albeit imperfect – avenue for gender recognition, thanks to the Gender Recognition Act 2004.

1   Lesbian and Gay Christian Movement

Society was becoming more accepting. The churches, though, appeared less than whole-hearted in their welcome to trans people, and some remain uncertain. Once trans people became involved in Christian LGBT organisations, including board membership, their specific concerns began to be represented when those organisations met with church leaders. The 'T' in LGBT was no longer simply a letter, or an afterthought: trans Christian people had begun to speak for themselves in Church settings.

Partly, then, this is the story of how Sibyls members started to campaign, as well as offering support to members, a development that has led to an enduring tension within the organisation.

There is another narrative too, which interfaces with the Sibyls one: a developing genderqueer consciousness in one LGBT Christian organisation in particular, but to an extent in all of them. This factor in raising the profile of the 'T' in LGBT is the openness to trans people by those who, although primarily identified as, or perceived to be, lesbian or gay, have become increasingly aware of their own gender fluidity. A key figure is the Revd Shanon (formerly Sharon) Ferguson, the former CEO of LGCM. Shanon has co-led the Sibyls' Workshop in several settings in recent years, and the Workshop itself has demonstrated this synergy of trans and genderqueer insights.

The Book

An overriding reason behind the idea of a Sibyls' book was the feeling that conservative Christians, notably the Evangelical Alliance, were claiming to offer a definitive, biblical, and essentially negative theological perspective on trans people that totally ignored our experience as Christian trans men and women.

At the time Helen Savage was engaged in research on transsexuality and Christian ethics, and undertook several interviews with Sibyls members both for her doctoral studies and in preparation for the Sibyls book, which she hoped to edit with the late Michelle Le Morvan. Some of that material is included here but eventually, through pressure of work, Helen was obliged to hand over the editing to us. We wish to acknowledge Helen's initial role in collating contributions, and are also grateful to all those members of Sibyls who have contributed, supported and helped underwrite this project – especially Jay and Carol. All the chapters have been reviewed, edited and revised where necessary to meet the publisher's requirements and ensure consistency of style.

Working together on the book continued a collaboration that began in 2006 when we devised, and then, with Jasmine Woolley, developed the Sibyls' Workshop 'Gender, Sexuality and Spirituality' (See Chapter 1). Our approach to compiling and editing the book, like much of the content, reflects experiences in the Workshops, as well as Sibyls meetings generally. What connects the book's elements is that they are articulated by people who have wrestled with their issues of gender, sexuality and faith in deep and meaningful ways, rather than hiding from, and failing to confront them. People who are seeking integrity and wholeness: in their own bodies, with their peers, in their congregations and in their families.

The papers and narratives have been collected over the course of seven years, during which time at least one contributor, Michelle le Morvan, sadly died. The contributions represent a range of perspectives that will span nearly a decade at the time of publication. However, the delay in publishing some of this collection has been positive, because in the meantime, Sibyls have been exploring the issues by attending conferences, writing articles, booklets, poems, plays and prayers, or interviewing one another. More recently, the Sibyls workshop 'Gender, Sexuality and Spirituality' has emerged as a resource that we have been able to offer to the wider Church, and we are delighted at the opportunity the book offers to outline the contents of the Workshop, especially the triplet template devised by Michelle.

It was always the intention that the Sibyls' book should be grounded in the experience of Sibyls members, as well as exploring the more theoretical aspects of gender and transgender. That emphasis is retained, and clearly signalled, here by devoting Part 2 to people's recollections and testimonies, as well as the history of Sibyls as an organisation. Part 1 is more theoretical in character, but it too has an experiential focus, and considers a number of practical implications of trans identities and spiritualties.

This is not an academic book, but some chapters have academic content, which reflects the way some people have chosen to wrestle with the difficult questions life has thrown up for them, using the tools provided by their careers or vocations. For some, this has required a theological response, others have looked at the sciences and the humanities, while for others, a narrative or testimony has sufficed. The book very much reflects the concerns of the contributors.

Many of these chapters, like the lives of so many Sibyls, and other transgender people of faith, bear witness to the validity of accepting one's situation as part of that journey of faith, without necessitating a move away from faith; though some chapters explain why such a move seemed necessary. Here one encounters the voices that respond to God through the turmoil that being transgender can bring to a life, enduring the injustice experienced alongside those also oppressed, and through this drawing closer to God. Where there is disillusion with the Church, it is often because of the reaction of other people of faith who reject this part of the transgender person's journey.

Engaging with the narratives of trans (or intersex) people's experiences can be profound and moving: it is a privilege to have access to such intimate parts of people's lives, and is like walking on sacred ground. In some of the narratives, people re-trace the difficult paths they have travelled, and disclose parts of the self that might not otherwise have been told. In this respect, they resemble the Sibyls' Workshop, where people are able to expose vulnerable parts of their lives, and find a way of integrating some of what had seemed fragmented.

It is unfortunate that it was not possible to draw more material from trans men. The Sibyls has had difficulty in attracting, and keeping, trans men as members, in the past. This may have been because there were never enough trans men to encourage others to join and stay. Also, trans men are reputed to have a very good, and close, support network in the UK. As with intersex people, often the issues trans men are dealing with are very different from those of trans women. There are now a few long-term members of Sibyls who are trans men, but the response from trans men has been limited to what we have here.

The book is part of a larger project, which is about reconciliation, between individuals and the Church, and about liberation; the Sibyls has played a significant part in this.

A consistent theme of the book is the observation that the process of discussion about gender and sexual minorities within the Church, has tended to exclude LGBTI people themselves. It thus reflects many people's perceptions of how the Church treats LGBTI people, despite the call for discussion. The question is frequently posed, how can there be such a debate if the subjects of the debate are not allowed to participate? This book, along with the Sibyls and the Sibyls' Workshop, forms an important contribution to such a participative Church debate with LGBTI people, rather than a debate about them, a discussion that must involve the wider Church community in the future.

Part 1: The Workshop, Perspectives from Theology, Science, Social Science and the Arts

Section 1: The Workshop Chapters

The Sibyls' Gender, Sexuality and Spirituality Workshop

Michelle O'Brien and Christina Beardsley

> *The Sibyls' Workshop was devised by the editors and Jasmine Woolley, and its origin, content and evolution have been described elsewhere (Beardsley et al. 2010). This chapter contains further information about the Workshop, the theoretical background, its context in the Sibyls, and supplements the earlier narrative by incorporating developments in more recent workshops[1]*

Introduction
The Workshop has enabled trans Christians to articulate their religious faith, and the joys and complications it can add to their lives. It has also provided a forum for people of various religious backgrounds, diverse sexual orientations and gender identities to listen to each other, and appreciate commonalities and differences.

In the early days of the Workshop the original facilitators each offered a brief presentation at the start. These have expanded to form the three succeeding chapters (Chapters 2 - 4) of this book.

Origins
Looking back to late 2006, and the Workshop's origin, it is surprising that transgender people's perspectives were largely missing from LGBT Christian events. The organisers of an LGBT Christian day conference, held in January 2007 had not included trans issues, but responded positively to our offer of a trans-led session. Acknowledging their omission, they requested a workshop about

---

1   This chapter is derived in part from our 2010 *Theology & Sexuality* article, co-authored with Jasmine Woolley, published online on 21 April 2015 and available at: http://dx.doi.org/10.1558.tse.v16i3.259. It examines in more detail the theoretical background to the Workshops, as well as developments since 2010.

gender and sexual identity, arising from, but without being limited to, trans people's experience. During the early planning stages it was obvious – given the purpose of Sibyls – that spirituality would need to be added to gender and sexuality.

The triplet 'interplay' model 'identity, role, and presentation/attraction/practice' emerged at this initial stage.

Theoretical Background to the Interplay Model

John Money coined the term 'gender role' in 1955, to complement Robert Stoller's term 'gender identity' (O'Donovan 2007: 15):

> The term *gender identity* … refers to the mix of masculinity and femininity in an individual, implying that both masculinity and femininity are found in everyone, but in different forms and different degrees (Stoller 1985: p10)

Money developed theories about 'gender identity' which he used in his own work. Gender identity is an individual's understanding of their internal gender, which may differ from their external gender role, presentation, or biological sex.

> In 1955 I coined the term *gender role*. It is defined as *everything* that one says and does to indicate that one is either male or female, or androgyne. The other side of the same coin is *gender identity*. It is defined as the persistence of one's individuality as male, female, or ambivalent, as it is experienced in self-awareness and behaviour. Gender identity is the private experience of gender role, and gender role is the public manifestation of gender identity…

> Sexual orientation (or preference) and gender identity are frequently regarded as independent of one another, so that dirty sex doesn't contaminate wholesome gender (Money 1998: 347).

For Money gender role was socially engrained, through a series of learned behaviours, and includes mannerisms, ways of dressing, etc.

Michelle had encountered Money's theories while doing research into the medical experiences of trans and intersex people (and practices strongly influenced by Money). Playing with the ideas that Money developed helped look at phenomena differently, in the context of what adults actually do, and how they manage discordance.

As we developed the Workshop, it occurred to Michelle, that, while Money had noted a distinction between sexual and gender behaviour, and had distinguished between gender role and identity, there was room for a third aspect, that of actual behaviour. Nikki Sullivan identifies Money's gender role as being 'performative' in a Butlerian sense, as:

> an action or set of actions one articulates corporeally in the world of and with others, and, at the same time, it is constitutive of the self (Sullivan 2015: 22).

However, actual performance, behaviour or practice, seemed to us then to be located somewhere between identity, and one's role in life.

In terms of trans people and faith, there was an emphasis on people's gender role, and their gender identity, but often there was this third aspect, and when role/identity did not match, people engaged in a number of strategies to deal with this. In terms of expression of faith and sexuality, this seemed better described as 'practice' rather than 'role', although could be described as behaviour or performance; practice might not always align with internal identity or lived role.

For example, some trans people do transition, while others have a gender identity that differs from their birth/assignment (identity), and remain living in their original gender (role), and yet their behaviour may involve some degree of dual-role cross-dressing (practice) to avoid the conflict. As we developed the Workshop, it emerged that all the issues we were considering - sexual orientation, gender identity, and spirituality - could be affected by the three aspects: identity, role and practice.

The development of these 3*3 different aspects of human experience meant that quite a complex web of interrelations was possible. While the relations were straightforward for some people, for others they weren't, and the model provided a flexible framework that enabled people to reflect on their own experience. For some, this might be insignificant, but for others it could be significant.

The model emerged as an idea about how the intersections between the different aspects of faith, sexuality and gender could be mapped and discussed in a new way. Once we began to lead the Workshops, people seemed to find it helpful, with some gaining new insights and understandings about themselves. What stood out for

Michelle, and which seemed not to have been addressed properly before, was that while identity and role were well understood, what people actually did (behaviour/practice) might not neatly conform to either. It appears from subsequent Workshops that quite often they do not.

The importance of this third element was the opportunity that it gave people to reflect on and talk about the contradictions in their lives, which the dichotomous frameworks established by Money would not have allowed.

The model does not assume that 'identity', whether in terms of gender, sexuality or spirituality, is necessarily 'fixed' (although for some it may be). Nor has the Workshop been, primarily, a means of providing information about trans people and intersex people's lives, though it has served that purpose too. It has operated on the assumption that everyone experiences the interplays or conflicts to a degree, and has helped to situate trans people's experience alongside that of lesbian, gay, bisexual and heterosexual people and cisgender people.

The idea of using role-play, with hats and props, to prevent discussion becoming over-cerebral, was also present from the start and derives from Christina's experience of Diane Torr's 'Gender in Performance' Workshop (see Chapter 2). This 'physical' session has been included when the Workshop was delivered over a weekend and more time was available. It was also delivered, at their request, with a group of under-thirties LGBT Christians in 2008.

Development

The earliest versions of the Workshop served different purposes, depending on the backgrounds of those present. In LGBT Christian settings, trans people's life stories were told, and their faith journeys described, to a 'mixed' audience, some of whom were familiar with such narratives, while for others they were entirely new. When the Workshop was held exclusively with Sibyls members, it provided a unique opportunity for sharing in a large group setting, and strong emotions were expressed.

Initially facilitated by trans people, when it was held in a secular LGBT setting for the first time, in 2010, this was also the first occasion, but certainly not the last, that a cisgender gay man and a gender queer woman shared the facilitation. Those who did not identify as LGBT were also present in larger numbers than before at that event. The following year, the Workshop was delivered over the course of a day, with mainly cisgender and heterosexual identified participants, as part of the York Spiritual Directors course, and is now integrated into its programme, having been delivered again in 2013 and 2015.

Principles

According to the range of participants, different themes have emerged, but whatever the makeup of the group, speaking about one's own gender identity, sexual orientation and spirituality has been fundamental to the Workshop from the start. According to the late Marcella Althaus-Reid (Althaus-Reid and Isherwood 2009: 148) 'Queer theology is ... a first-person theology: diasporic, self-disclosing, autobiographical and responsible for its own words', and the facilitators attempt to model this openness in their introductions to the sessions, so that all the participants are encouraged to speak from their own experience.

Trans people, like LGB people, have been consistently problematized and objectified as 'other', by medicine, psychology, sociology, theology and the media. The slogan 'Nothing About Us Without Us!' or *Nihil de nobis, sine nobis*, is increasingly invoked to ensure that marginalised groups are recognised as the key 'experts', stakeholders and agents for change where their own experience is concerned, and in matters that directly affect them. This too is fundamental to the Workshop's ethos.

The Workshop has offered a space where trans Christians can articulate their experience of gender, sexuality and spirituality, framed around a structure that reflects the unique intricacies of transgender and intersex Christian's lives. Nevertheless, and intentionally, it has also been a conversation with those who are cisgender, and people of various sexual orientations and spirituality.

While people are left free to proceed at their own pace, there has been no scope for 'observers' in the Workshop. This has been problematic for those who are accustomed to the Church of England's tendency to conceptualise gender or sexuality as a topic for 'debate'. The Workshop, however, has never been a space for talking about others while remaining silent about one's own experience.

Outline (See Appendix 2)

Two or three people can facilitate the Workshop. Its strong, simple structure makes it easy to lead. The importance of confidentiality is stressed at the outset. If there are three presenters, in the introductory session they can each speak personally about one of the three main themes, gender, sexuality, spirituality, or about their interplay in their lives.

A facilitator starts by outlining their own self-understanding in terms of their gender, sexuality and spirituality. The participants then reflect alone on themselves in these terms. There follows an opportunity for people to discuss their personal reflections, first in small groups, then in the larger group.

The interplay model is then introduced (Appendix 2, Part 2.1), and one or more of the facilitators illustrates the model with examples from their own lives. Participants are invited to reflect alone on the model and how it relates to their lives. They are then invited to share what they have found in small groups, prior to feeding back to the large group.

The plenary session provides opportunities to summarise what people have heard and learned during the Workshop, note the key themes of the group work, and to prepare for the act of worship, if one is to follow. There can also be an optional 'movement' session, which uses mime, physical theatre, performance techniques, and visualisation to deconstruct the conventions of gendered movement. It is a space for the imagination, intuition and spiritual exploration.

Themes
Listening labelling, lamenting and longing
The Workshop calls for careful listening by both facilitators and participants, as each person describes their gender, sexuality and spirituality, and how they interplay in their lives. The narrating of personal stories offers insights into other people's identities and promotes mutual understanding among those divided by labels.

The effect of being labelled has been a consistent theme, as well as the fear of rejection, and the dynamics of exclusion and self-exclusion. The stereotyping that can follow if one is known to be gay has been mentioned, as was the fear that leads people to hide their relationship.

People have lamented that they lacked resources to inform their childhood self-understanding, or an appropriate discourse to frame understanding as they approached adulthood. Childhood memories of feeling and being different to others, of not fitting in and yet wanting to be 'normal', which is a prerequisite of spiritual growth (Stuart and Thatcher 1997: 237-38) were also mentioned.

People recalled being bullied, and the adult fear of homophobia that had led them to adopt masks to conceal their sexual orientation, or to engage in various smokescreen activities which had meant the avoidance, accommodation, suppression, and repression of their sexuality. For some trans women, the burden of trying to be male, or to fulfil other's expectations, had involved playing games, and presenting as male.

Such strategies overlaid a huge longing for self-understanding and self-expression which labels like LGBTI (or even, in some cases, male or female) were unable to encompass. It was noted that identity labels like LGBTI can shift, or function other than intended, and that while they can both stigmatise and empower, the spiritual dimension was ultimately more important; see Elizabeth Stuart (2007: 68) on the significance of baptism.

The psychological concept of the 'looking-glass self' developed by Charles Cooley (1864-1929) has been quoted by way of the summary attributed to Robert H. Schuller:

> 'I am not who I think I am
> I am not who you think I am
> I am who I think you think I am.'

The speaker then added, 'Thank goodness God knows who I am!'

Gender roles and expression

Participants have frequently expressed frustration with the gender binary (Mollenkott 2001: 17-37); for example:

- 'being female does not necessarily mean being a woman'
- 'does gender have to be so clearly defined?'
- 'are there really just two boxes, or is the reality more fluid than that?'
- 'why are people expected to compromise their gender due to lack of social acceptance?'
- 'men don't cry'

The status attached to gender roles was noted, including societal expectations of wives and mothers, and the fact of compromise. One could, for example, love being married while hating the role of wife. In some settings divorce has been discussed.

People have pondered whether any or all of the roles one plays are what one would wish, and that it is possible to lose oneself in a negative way so that 'the real me' is hidden.

The reality and impact of both patriarchy and matriarchy have been considered, and the continuing power of male over female, despite the impact of feminism. The issue of domestic violence has also been raised.

Society's perception that leadership is primarily masculine was apparently reinforced by a Church culture in which misogyny is rendered acceptable, discomfort with the Divine feminine is noticeable, and gender roles can be stifling. For example, the assumption that a married woman must be the minister's wife, rather than the minister; or the expectation that female clergy will be both 'the vicar's wife' as well as being the vicar; or that a woman vicar, who is a Mothers' Union member, will make the tea at the Mothers' Union meeting, whereas a male vicar would not be expected to do that. Gendered distinctions like 'male' nurse, 'female' minister were also questioned.

The effects of aging on gender have been explored. A single or widowed person, for instance, may have to play all the gender roles, otherwise stereotypically gendered tasks, such as DIY or home making, might remain undone. Retirement too can impact on people's roles, the fragmentation of former roles providing an opportunity to project into the community, adopt additional roles, and catch up on one's interests.

Gender variance, gender queer, gender and God

The label 'queer' is a classic example of 'reverse discourse' (Foucault 1998/1981: 101): formerly a term of abuse and insult, it has been rehabilitated and adopted with pride to convey sexual or gender variance. The emergence of 'queer theology' has even rendered it unexpectedly normative, as Christ's eschatological 'queerness' destabilises the unhappy 'norms' of 'culturally constructed identities' (Stuart 2007: 75).

The terms 'gender variant' or 'gender queer' have often emerged in the Workshop, with reference both to childhood – 'tomboy'; 'sissy' – and adult behaviours that reflect a dissonance with gender stereotypes that straight and cisgender people can experience as well as trans and LGB people. The painful childhood memories involved have also been explored in the movement Workshop.

Some people, intrigued by the theological question of the gender of the Godhead, have spent time considering whether God should be conceived as male, female, androgynous, un-gendered, and beyond gender categories.

Sexuality

The connection between love and sex has been an important topic of discussion. The double standard around sexuality, depending on whether one was a man or a woman, is still thought to exist. The greater availability of pornography was a new factor.

The sexually provocative clothing adopted by some trans women suggested they were compensating for a 'lost' (female) adolescence; while the hormone regimen of transition can lead to changes in sexual practice, including the gender of those to whom one is attracted, which requires negotiation by those in long-term relationships. Both these examples of the interplay of gender and sexuality appear to modify the claim that trans people's issue is 'exclusively' about gender, in contrast to lesbian and gay people, whose issue is said to be one of sexual orientation. Yet the overtly 'masculine' presentation of a butch lesbian, like the exaggerated 'femininity' of the drag queen, can function as codes for sexual orientation, and is another instance of the interplay between gender and sexuality.

Interplay and institution

Participants have noted that religion is only one aspect of spirituality, but have, more often, expressed dismay at what they considered the negativity of organised religion towards the interplay of gender, sexuality, and spirituality that many are seeking. There was disappointment that religious traditions rich in symbolism, imagery and theatricality, were sometimes reluctant to accept gender or sexual diversity, and that gender transition often meant toleration rather than acceptance, or even rejection from one's church.

A negative spirituality of expectations about gendered behaviours can reinforce the low self-esteem experienced by people with gender identity issues. Thus, spiritual identity can impact negatively on gender identity, which becomes confused with sexual orientation, due to the Church's current focus on homosexuality (Stuart and Thatcher 1997: 167), whereas some of its members are addressing gender issues. To 'escape' such dilemmas might involve being 'selfish' enough to break away from an existing religious practice, and walk a new spiritual path.

Participants discussed or told stories about the, often painful, interplay between an individual's gender, sexuality and spirituality and the expectations of institutional religion. Even in a supposedly secular setting people explored:

- 'The place of LGBTI people in faith communities'
- 'Opening dialogue between LGBTI people and faith communities'
- 'Connections – people and services'
- 'The use of Biblical texts as a form of homophobic/trans-phobic abuse '
- 'Is Deuteronomy 22.5 about trans?'

One person recounted how their same-sex relationship became unacceptable overnight at their church. With the arrival of a new incumbent, their 'lifestyle' was declared 'unbiblical' on the basis of Genesis 1.26-27, and 'natural law' arguments about male and female sexual orientation. In this instance the gender binary was deployed to inhibit sexual practice.

Individual Workshops have contained some of the grief, anger, and traumatic stress LGBTI people can feel, following exclusion from their family or church, or people's failure to show compassion to them, but participants have also considered their need to forgive the Church's leadership, and to release negative feelings they were harbouring towards the Church.

It was suggested that Church culture might be changing for the better, in that the era of knowing a priest was lesbian or gay, but never mentioning it seemed to be drawing to a close. Others though highlighted the problem of so-called open churches that are not really open, and how Church 'acceptance' could turn out to be conditional in practice. There was also unhappiness at celibacy being presented as the only alternative, due to teaching about the weight of sin attached to extra-marital sex.

Heartening stories about the inclusion of LGBTI people in local churches have also been told. Many, though, reported the problems created by the tension between 'muscular' and 'feminine' spirituality in Church culture, or the pressure to lead a double-life due to hostile Church attitudes to homosexuality, based on the frequently quoted 'seven proof texts' (Stuart and Thatcher 1997: 180) from Scripture, that are said to condemn it.

Some people expressed a vocation to change the Church from within by overturning the message that 'homosexuality is wrong', but the current precariousness of the clergy role for LGBTI people was also acknowledged.

Wholeness, interiority and exteriority

People reflected that spirituality is often misinterpreted as soul searching, whereas its many facets include:

- 'the visual, vision, beauty, the veil (clothing), mystery'
- 'thinking, teaching, liberal, personal experience, family, pro-life/pro-love'
- 'love, friendship, companionship, whole personhood'
- 'how God is for all, depth of love, acceptance'

A few people recalled early awareness both of their sexual orientation and of faith in God/Jesus' love, but usually people have described experiencing a process of self-discovery, self-awareness, and self-acceptance, in which unhealthy coping strategies were overcome, and sexuality or gender identity came to be seen as a gift. This discovery had often involved turning inwards, which might appear self-centred. However, this process was not simply about self-realisation, but involved awareness of others ('relationship with another' emerged as a key spiritual practice for one group), including God or even the experience of death and resurrection. 'Coming out' [as LGBTI] too was said to entail recognition by others, and a process of 'naming and claiming' which could entail significant loss as well as gain.

For some participants, whether through personal or societal change, gender, sexuality and spirituality had combined and intertwined, leading to an overwhelming sense of being whole, or a readiness to express who they really were (for example, 'godly and gay'). In certain cases former 'outsiders' had become 'insiders'. Others expressed a desire to live beyond boundaries, especially the gender binary's restrictions, in the belief that expanded choices and greater freedom would help to reconcile their gender and spirituality.

At one Workshop the question was posed 'what is spirituality for LGBTI people?' There were three responses. That love and respect are at the core of most religions, albeit overlaid by dogmatic, institutional, or superficial differences. That being human transcends gender and sexuality. That the constant wonder of the universe, the earth, and the human project - including advances in modern technology - is inspiring.

Transgender Christians noted that being trans can involve serving God in specific ways, and may be a unique or particular calling; see Mollenkott (2009: 46-58) on the lessons congregations can learn from trans people. People have also talked about liminality, about intersex people, and the role of the shaman

Many participants spoke of God being in the journey, and of exodus, or rescue.

Conclusion

A reaction, in part, to a Church culture dominated by discussions about sexuality, particularly the acceptability of homosexuality, the Workshop has added gender and spirituality to this conversation.

Applying the triplet of 'identity – role – presentation/practice' to each of the three domains of gender, sexuality, and spirituality, produced an interactive model that has enabled participants to examine their own lives in some detail. People have traced the tensions, conflicts, correspondence and interplay between different aspects of the self, and their impact on one's inner and outer worlds.

The confessional style that was readily accepted by LGBTI groups has required additional facilitation when transferred to more general settings. Many heterosexual and cisgender people seem less accustomed to speaking about their gender and sexuality in group settings, yet this is a crucial feature of the Workshop. The honest telling of people's stories, in a safe confidential space, has proved therapeutic for individuals, and has promoted communication across a range of gender, sexual and spiritual identities.

The Workshop draws on trans experience, queer theory, social theory, history, (and occasionally dance and drama), to highlight various powerful inhibitors to the spiritual journey of many LGBTI people, and has proved a flexible resource for mutual listening, exploration and, in some cases, personal integration. For some it has opened up 'the amazing spectrum of gender and sexuality'.

The Workshop was offered to the Church of England as a resource for its Shared Conversations on human sexuality. Had the offer been taken up, it would have enhanced the process by ensuring that it also encompassed gender and spirituality.

Chapter 2

Acting like a man – playing the woman: gender in performance

Christina Beardsley

The Western tradition of gender and sexuality is more diverse and complex than recent Church statements about marriage, or the male-female dichotomy, would suggest. Historical examples indicate a resemblance between pre-modern and post-modern perceptions of gender as a socially constructed performance.

Introduction

My research background is church history so I tend to approach gender, sexuality and spirituality historically. Having prepared for gender transition via mime and physical theatre, I find connections between drama and gender fascinating. The two combine in Shakespeare's plays, as discussed in this chapter, based on my short (illustrated) talk from early versions of the Sibyls 'Gender, Sexuality and Spirituality' Workshop.

Diversity and Christian tradition

The idea that transsexualism is a twentieth-century innovation was stated by Oliver O'Donovan (1982/2007:3) who describes transsexualism as 'a condition with no known history before its sudden emergence into public notice a quarter of a century ago, with no known cause and no known treatment'. However, the medical treatment of cross-gender identity and behaviour with surgery and hormones is almost a century old (Meyerowitz 2002), (though the ancient world knew of the feminising properties of mare's urine), and a huge literature (e.g. Gilbert 1926, 1932; Durova 1990; Green 1998; Farrer 1992) confirms the existence of pre-modern people who lived between male and female, or at variance with their birth gender.

Christian dismissal of transsexualism is often accompanied by a-historical appeals to 'traditional' Christian teaching about marriage and the family, or the fixity of male and female (House of Bishops 2003: 244-50) and their complementarity (House of Bishops 2013a: 4, 9-11; 2013b: 33-4). This polarised, complementary two-sex model of male and female dates largely from the Enlightenment, but as Adrian Thatcher (2012: 8f) notes, contemporary Christianity often reads its own tradition through this latter-day lens, even though the more fluid, one-sex model of the human person prevailed for much of Christian history.

Diversity on these topics is present in the New Testament. Jesus' teaching in the gospels includes sayings that imply the indissolubility of marriage (Mark 10:2-9; cp. Matthew 5:31, 32)[1] alongside passages about leaving family for the gospel's sake (Matthew 10:35-38; Luke 14:26-27; Luke 12:51-53), becoming eunuchs for the kingdom of heaven's sake (Matthew. 19:12), and, tellingly, that in the kingdom of heaven they neither marry, nor are given in marriage (Matthew 22:30; Mark 12:25; Luke 20:35); while imminent expectation of the last days demoted marriage for St Paul and his contemporaries (1 Corinthians 7:25-31). Early Christian monasticism, like recent 'transgender' readings of the Cappadocian Father, Gregory of Nyssa (House of Bishops 2003: 201-3; Cornwall 2009: 25-8), prefigure an enduring 'transcending' of sexuality and gender in Christianity that appears hospitable to some gender variant people (DeFranza 2015: 14).

Theoretical presuppositions

The French philosopher and architect of knowledge Michel Foucault (1926-1984), himself a member of a sexual minority, developed extensive insight into power dynamics, and an acute sense of sexuality as 'an especially dense transfer point for relations of power' (1998: 103).

Volume 1 of Foucault's *History of Sexuality* (1998: 63-73, 101-102) traces a process that began in the nineteenth century. Initially, the medical profession categorised people as 'inverts', 'transvestites', etc. to rescue them from penal systems that criminalised their behaviours, but this exchange reduced sexual and gender variance to pathology or illness. The second stage began when those who had previously accepted medical/technical labels as self-descriptive adapted them as a means of self-empowerment – Foucault describes

---

1   See Jo Ind (2003: 82-3) for a feminist reading of Matthew 19:5 as protective of women rather than a timeless model of matrimony.

this as 'reverse' discourse. A third, post-modern, stage arrives when these same groups of people – increasingly empowered and accepted by society – question the labels' sufficiency.

As Christian transgender people we have adopted labels to express our gender identity. We also appreciate their limitations, given the fluidity or complexity of our experience, and their frequent use by others, including fellow Christians, to deny or obscure our humanity. Conscious of our gender identity, particularly clinicians' assessments of us, and, to a lesser degree, of our sexuality, our Christianity is integral to our lives. Historically, spirituality has appeared more significant than either gender or sexuality, but the impact of feminism and sexual liberation make these categories impossible to ignore. Earlier centuries used the term 'gender' in this context,[2] but 'a difference of sex' was more common. This can confuse modern readers, for whom 'sex' tends to imply physical attraction and behaviours, not gender identity.[3]

The remainder of this chapter considers historical examples of gender variant behaviour, highlighting power relationships in the construction of gender, and the role of drama in its deconstruction.

Sex in the ancient Greek city

The television series *Sex and the City* offers a female perspective on love, relationships, and sexual encounters, in a culture shaped by feminism and the contraceptive pill. It contrasts sharply with the 'man's world' of Ancient Greece. Some women in the ancient world exercised power, but strictly within the household, with their husband's consent, though mutuality between husband and wife was possible (Foucault 1992: 154-165; 1990: 147-9).

In ancient Greek society, mature married men could also engage in relationships with younger men, but Foucault (1992: 187-225) explains that, especially in the (earlier) classical period, careful protocols and disciplines – '*askesis*': from which the word 'ascetic' derives – protected the young from exploitation, and reveal various assumptions about male power. For instance, good management of one's household, and of a relationship with one's lover,

---

2   *Oxford English Dictionary* gives examples from the fourteenth – nineteenth centuries (1979: 1126; [1971 Vol. G: 100]).
3   Marilyn Thomas (2008: 261) mistakenly claims that F.W. Robertson regarded the Virgin Mary as 'the sanctity of sexuality' whereas he meant she was the ideal of her 'sex', i.e., her gender.

demonstrated fitness for civic responsibility. However, a mature man who perpetuated the youthful phase of being 'the beloved' was considered shameful, as he should have become the lover, initiating a youth into public life. 'In the eyes of the Greeks, what constituted ethical negativity par excellence was clearly not the loving of both sexes, nor was it the preferring of one's own sex over the other; it consisted in being passive with regard to the pleasures' (Foucault 1992: 85-6). Such 'passivity', i.e. immoderation, or lack of self-control, whether in relation to women or boys, was considered 'effeminacy', but having previously played 'the role of passive, obliging objects' of desire to other men could undermine one's future political prospects (Foucault 1992: 219-20).

The exercise of erotic power over other men as a disqualification for political power is a demarcation of beauty/intimacy from civic office/politics experienced by women in the modern era. The normally, and ideologically, placid Stoic philosopher Epictetus (1928: 5ff) harangues an epilated, coiffed and finely attired pupil, in an attempt to restore his rationality and fitness for civic society. Yet, just as 'effeminate' men today can arouse both unease and fascination, the ancient world was also beguiled by the combination of male and female in a single individual, as the many classical statues of Hermaphroditus, depicted with both breasts and a penis, show. According to the one sex model that prevailed then, physiologically, male and female are not very different; but their social status differed, and hence the anxiety when the two were blurred.

Renaissance 'man'

A Renaissance writer, William Shakespeare was indebted to classical literature. His play, *A Midsummer Night's Dream* echoes the Latin novel by Apuleius, *The Transformations of Lucius* or *The Golden Ass* which, incidentally, satirises the effeminacy of the Galli (Apuleius 1950: 199-211), priests of the goddess Cybele, whose initiation included castration.

A married man, Shakespeare wrote love poetry to another, younger, male, and to a female: continuity with the classical tradition of a man with a male lover that, far from undermining his masculinity, demonstrated his social status. Shakespeare's plays are full of gender transitions, rendered yet more complex by the conventions of the Elizabethan stage, where a boy actor played the part of a girl, who may pretend to be a boy, and then offers to act the role of a girl, e.g. *As You Like It*. Note Shakespeare's ability to light-heartedly explore gender, and its power dynamics, uniquely facilitated by an all-male cast, with female roles played by boy actors.

Once women began to perform female roles,[4] the art of young men playing female roles was almost lost in Western professional theatre. Today, the closest approximation to Elizabethan theatre is Japanese Kabuki Theatre, where the onnagata (male actors playing female roles) tradition is strictly maintained. However, all-male theatrical productions never quite disappeared in England, due partly to the persistence of single-sex education. Peter Farrer considers the amateur boy actor Maurice Pollack (1885-1914), who specialised in female impersonation, 'the nearest equivalent to an English onnagata that I had yet come across later than the seventeenth century' (Farrer 1998: 10). Yet photographic illustrations in Farrer's other books depict young men convincingly portraying women in Victorian, Edwardian and inter-war theatrical productions (Farrer 2000: Illustrations 1-15).

As well as a recent revival of all-male productions of Shakespeare's plays, directors have been casting women in male roles in mixed-sex productions. Notable examples include Adrian Lester as Rosalind – 1991/1995, Mark Rylance as Cleopatra – 1999 and Olivia – 2002/2012; Fiona Shaw as Richard II – 1995 (Shaw 1998: xxiii-xxv), Kathryn Hunter as Lear – 1997 ('Designing Shakespeare' no date) and Vanessa Redgrave as Prospero – 2000. However, modern productions usually fail to recreate the effect of the Elizabethan boy player, choosing instead to emphasise the comic, rather than depictions of erotic power, by casting mature men as leading ladies (Nicol 2002).

When youthful, androgynous actor Eddie Redmayne[5] was cast as Viola in the Globe's 2002 production of *Twelfth Night*, David Nicol noted that his 'performance demonstrated that boy actors in cross-dressing comedies may be convincing as women – although paradoxically, they are more convincingly 'female' when wearing male costume'. This was also true of Tam Williams as Viola, 'cross-dressed' in grey jacket and trousers as the male page Cesario, in the 2007 production by all-male Shakespeare collective, Propeller. Nicol explains this phenomenon: 'When the actor performs the role of a woman, it may not be easy to forget that he is a man; but when the

---

4   The film *Stage Beauty* depicts the impact of this change on actor Edward Kynaston, a famed female impersonator of his day, described by Pepys as 'the prettiest woman in the whole house'.
5   Redmayne portrays Lili Elbe, who transitioned in the early twentieth century, in the 2016 film *The Danish Girl*.

same actor performs a woman who is learning to replicate the codes of masculinity, the focus on the artificiality of those codes means that the actual gender of the actor becomes obscured, and indeed irrelevant'.[6] This deconstruction of gender, which made sense in terms of the one-sex model, where male and female are on a sliding scale, contrasts with the more recent and restrictive two-sex model, which regards male and female as fixed and gender transition as impossible.

Anthony Dawson (1997) sees the transvestite actor in Shakespearean England as 'a polyvalent sign: on the one hand, he is a conductor of cultural anxiety about powerful, desiring women; but he also represents and enables the potential masculinity of women, thereby helping to empower them by showing the value of 'acting like a man''. The latter is easier to depict, as eroticism requires androgynous beauty and a subtlety absent from contemporary all-male performances (Nicol 2002). However, men performing, and thus defining, femininity (albeit female 'masculinity'), is problematic, and women today can play powerful roles, male or female, like the all-female Get Over It Productions' *Macbeth* at the Round House in 2009. This is not new: Sarah Siddons and Sarah Bernhardt both played Hamlet, but in the early seventeenth century women struggled for the right to play even female roles. The period 1580-1620 also saw a steady attack by preachers and polemicists on women who dressed as men in public (Howard 1998: 47).

Marriage in the Molly Houses
In the Classical-Renaissance paradigm, women and boys share a similar lack of status compared with men, who may be paramour to someone of either sex, or both sexes, without compromising their masculinity. The late Alan Bray (1982) believed that this changed at some point during the late seventeenth . Hitherto, those engaged in sexual relations with members of their own sex could reconcile themselves to their behaviour, despite religious and ethical prohibitions, largely because their actions were inconsequential in terms of their (gender) identity. The arrival of the two-sex model, which polarised male and female, seems to have altered that.

---

6   A similar point is made – through the lips of Kynaston – in the film *Stage Beauty*.

In north-western Europe, from about 1700 onwards, a group of adult males emerged who were attracted to other males, and whose behaviour, speech, mannerisms, and dress were considered effeminate by their contemporaries. 'They were neither male nor female but a third gender that combined some characteristics from each of *what society regarded as the two legitimate genders*' (Trumbach 1998: 16, my emphasis).[7] Here gender roles and behaviours are becoming exclusive compared to the earlier one-sex paradigm. Female cross-dressing in this era, Trumbach (1998: 17) notes, was about passing safely in male occupations (social power), rather than being sexually attractive to other women (erotic power).

Rictor Norton's book, *Mother Clap's Molly House* (1992), offers a detailed impression of life in the Molly Houses, the male brothels of eighteenth century London, where male prostitutes took female names, dressed in female clothes, enacted marriages with clients, and even simulated giving birth. Sexual relationships with other males had rendered the mollies ('molles' being Latin for soft) feminine. Their cross-gender behaviour – like the femme names for 'unmanly' schoolboys in Victorian children's fiction,[8] and, until recently, among some gay men, including ordinands at certain theological colleges (Coles 2014: 253-4) – had become transgressive.

Writing of the seventeenth-century theatre, Garber (1998: 177) claims that 'Transvestism was located at the juncture of 'class' and 'gender', and increasingly through its agency gender and class were revealed to be commutable, if not equivalent.' The mainly working–class mollies assumed titles like 'duchess': an enduring aspirational aspect of gender transition; for example, April Ashley's marriage to a member of the English aristocracy, the Honourable Arthur Corbett (Ashley 2006: 159-98). Ashley, a glamorous model, had erotic power, Corbett, social status. He achieved the annulment of their marriage in 1970, when the judge ruled that Ashley (and thus other male-to-female transsexual people) was male; a ruling that only makes sense under the two-sex model and not overturned until the passing of the Gender Recognition Act 2004. Corbett was himself a cross

---

7   Carter (1997: 38-40) critiques Trumbach's focus on the private and sexualised world of the mollies and the Molly Houses rather than the public and social world of the fop and the coffee houses.

8   I am grateful to Dr Julia Courtney for alerting me to this phenomenon in Charlotte M. Yonge's Clement Underwood ('Tina') in *The Pillars of the House* (1893: 7) and Clarence Winslow ('Miss Clara') in *Chantry House* (1905, i:18).

dresser, and Ashley's description of his covert cross-dressing in male brothels in the 1960s resembles the eighteenth-century Molly Houses (2006: 160,180). Ashley's own early career as a female impersonator suggests that theatre has remained socially accommodating to gender variance.

Drag/drab

The use of the word 'drag' to describe female impersonation is thought to be an acronym for 'dressed as a girl' and to derive from Elizabethan theatre. The modern term 'Drag King', for male impersonators, is preferable to 'dressed as a boy', which would contract as the unflattering 'drab' – which is hardly the effect.

As an art form, drag seems to have occurred among all social classes in Britain. In 1880s London, Boulton and Park (Farrer 1987: 5-9), and most of their circle, were middle-class young men, with the exception of the aristocrat, Lord Arthur Clinton, who did not cross-dress, unlike the fictional Lord Southdown, who performs the female roles in the second charade-tableau in Thackeray's *Vanity Fair* (Farrer 1992: 168-70). My nineteenth century namesake, the artist Aubrey Beardsley, wrote ambiguously of 'going to Jimmie's [St James's Restaurant, Piccadilly] dressed up as a tart' (Maas, Duncan, Good 1970: 53), and drew himself as a wide-hipped Pierrot, while his actress sister Mabel appears in Sir Oswald Birley's portrait dressed as an Elizabethan pageboy. Virginia Woolf's novel *Orlando* (1928) was inspired by the androgynous appearance and cross-gender behaviour of her upper-class lover, Vita Sackville-West. The eponymous hero/heroine, introduced as a young man in the Elizabethan period, changes gender during the eighteenth century; unconscious recognition, perhaps, that a significant shift in the construction of gender occurred then.

Might there be continuity between the working-class drag performances of the mollies, and later pantomime dames like Dan Leno (1860-1904), or the principal 'boy' played by a young woman? What about the female and male impersonators of the music hall era (for example, Rex Jameson, 1924-1983, who performed as the char, 'Mrs Shufflewick', and Vesta Tilley, 1864-1952), and the drag queens and drag kings of today's pubs and clubs? Or even the cross-dressing at the stag night or rugby club dinner (Gill 2007: 4)? If so it probably stems from social anxiety at the fixed roles and presentations of men and women in modern society imposed by the two-sex model of gender.

Popular performance

Camille Paglia's *Sexual Personae: Art and Decadence from Nefertiti to Emily Dickinson* (1991), documents the West's enduring fascination with androgyny (from the Greek words for man and woman). Conceiving Western perception as primarily visual, related to what she calls the 'pagan western eye' (Paglia 1991: 33-5) that would reach its apotheosis in cinema, she revels in similarities across the centuries. Androgyny has been pervasive in recent popular culture, including musicians like Marc Bolan, Mick Jagger, David Bowie, Boy George, k.d. lang, Annie Lennox, and Grace Jones. This 'camp' approach to gender, where one can experiment without being labelled, is where the pre-modern world of Shakespeare's theatre resembles the post-modern theory, expounded and developed by Judith Butler (2008 [1990]: 185-93), that gender is performative, or acted out; the notion that female, feminine, male, masculine behaviours are learned rather than innate, and consolidated by practice and repetition.

When I was considering transition in 1997 I found an experimental space at the five-day 'gender in performance' Workshop led by Drag King, Diane Torr (2010). It was a safe place to explore my gender, working from the inside outwards, from the unconscious, and emotions, through visualisation and physical workouts, to outward expression in posture and movement, and only then, through make-up, clothes and image. During the Workshop I became acutely conscious, and said so, of having lived much of my life in the head rather than in the body; presumably because to have fully inhabited my body would have exposed its lack of congruity with the way I felt 'inside'.

Fleshing it out

Some forms of spirituality encourage the splitting of mind and body; even Jungian idealisation of androgyny as an internal balance of masculine and feminine can encourage avoidance for transgender people. Before accepting that I ought to transition, this psychic androgyny seemed attractive. Hearing someone had transitioned, I recall exclaiming: 'they should be resolving this in their inner world.' Gender, though, is not just about our inner world; it involves embodiment and relationships. Historically, this has entailed negotiating power dynamics and changing constructions of gender. The rise of the two-sex model, and its increasing and unthinking endorsement by Western Christianity, has made such negotiations exceptionally challenging for gender variant people. Transgender people highlight the limitations of that model, and the theological and counter-cultural importance of Christianity's focus on being human, rather than male or female.

Chapter 3

The Social Construct of Gender

Jasmine Woolley

> *This chapter is a reduced version of text resulting from a dissertation for a Masters in Social Work which involved interviewing transgender people living in the North West of England in 2006. Their voices are not included, but their opinions are reflected within this chapter.*

Trans (transgender) people are at an interface between two perceived genders, and challenge the way society deals with people who do not fit the gender stereotypes. Challenging the gender construct is not a new phenomenon, as feminist perspectives evidence, but the way the gender construct is challenged by trans people is evolving, as awareness and visibility of trans people within society increases.

Western society seems to expect people's gender role performance to fall within accepted boundaries. The way trans people challenge such boundaries varies, and whilst some within the transgender community challenge the expectations of society in their gender expression, many conform to society's expectations of their chosen gender.

I would like to offer two definitions:

- **Social Construction:** Within society a spectrum of behaviour is defined for each gender to which people are expected to conform. This is reinforced by carers, peers, books, advertising and television. It includes what is permitted or legally accepted behaviour.
- **Gender:** There is a distinction between sex and gender. Sex is founded on a biological basis, whereas gender is broader than just female and male (Butler 1999). Gender is associated with behaviours, and expression of femininity or masculinity.

During childhood children are taught to embody male or female roles appropriate to their physical presentation. This construct is taught to children to respond appropriately, through literature and stereotypes from media sources, family and friends. How and why children become masculine and feminine is studied by Davies (2003), who suggests children must learn maleness and femaleness and they must get it right. Children quickly learn there are set gender rules and conforming to these artificial boundaries is expected. Davies says, 'everyone 'knows' that the world is divided into males and females' (2003: xi) and thinking otherwise is an 'incorrigible proposition within Western thought'.

Davies suggests this is a learned response to social conditioning, and while she does not explore a 'third gender', in chapter six she proposes movement beyond the male-female binary. Thorne (1993) shows children segregate themselves into appropriate gender patterns at meal times or when forming queues. For Thorne there is significant social pressure preventing boys and girls segregating from their own peer groupings. Some children manage to successfully cross the gender boundary during play, by abiding by rules of the other gender. Thorne finds girls who crossed gender lines received admiration from other girls, but this is not the case for boys.

The way people across the transgender spectrum respond to society varies, and whilst people who cross dress can remain hidden from society, Califia (1997) believes transsexual people need to transition and would not go through gender reassignment without exploring cross-dressing and homosexuality to see if these offer relief without a shift in identity or painful and expensive medical treatment.

Mallon (1999) finds non-conformity to gender leads to low self-esteem, mental health difficulties, substance abuse or suicide attempts because of internalised negative attitudes and often personality disorders or psychiatric difficulties amongst transgender youth. Tanis (2003) says that all adolescents search for identity, but trans adolescents often face additional challenges, violence or rejection at home, school or church.

Many trans people fear that their adolescent children may themselves have transgender tendencies, but Assalian (2002) finds this is rarely the case. The participants, aged between 3 years and 20 years, have other concerns such as,

I am going to miss calling her 'mom'; I am simply going to have to adapt; I still worry about who will walk me down the aisle (Assalian 2002: 1).

Research by Atchison (1998; cited in O'Keefe 1999), reveals the response of partners can be worse if the trans person is denying their behaviour, leading to the partner being deeply disturbed. If they are living secretly there is added pressure and relationship breakdown is more likely. Bolin (1990) finds trans people 'must learn to come out. The closet for them is as real as it is for gay men and lesbians' (cited in Herdt 1993: 473). She says for transsexual people there are two closets, one before they admit their transgender nature, and the other after full transition and gender reassignment. Following surgery they 'deny their pasts and their transsexualism. [This] makes them vulnerable to outing' (Herdt 1993: 473). Green (1998; cited in Whittle 1999) indeed finds this to be the case from her experience, '[I] inched my way out of the transsexual closet with considerable trepidation', but does not disclose her past now.

Bolin (1990) feels in the past trans people had no choice but to blend back into society, but:

it has become possible to have a public identity as a transsexual and still have a reasonably normal life (cited in Herdt 1993: 473).

There is more acceptance of not conforming to the gender system, it is acceptable to be transgender now and 'you no longer have to fit in a [gender] box' (Herdt 1993: 475).

Bolin (1990) finds in her research with trans people that society is becoming more tolerant of them, and they hope there could be established 'not just a third gender but the possibility of numerous genders and multiple social identities' (cited in Herdt 1993: 447). However, it is difficult to challenge the gender system when transsexual people try so hard to fit gender ideals, reinforcing the gender binary system.

The Gender Recognition Act 2004 (Crown 2004) shows that politically there is acceptance of trans people within legislation, which has implications within society as it challenges discrimination, and by the Equality Act 2010. One result is in the response of the police. They have introduced procedures for dealing with hate crimes against trans people, and policies for responding to trans people who come into contact with the police (Sexton 2005), and have undertaken diversity training with trans people.

> Their duties must ensure that they are treated with the same level of respect and dignity as any other member of the public (Sexton 2005: 2).

Bornstein (1994) makes a claim that gender does not exist, but is nothing but a social construct, and Califia believes that it is acceptable to 'straddle the gender line and … create a new social category' (1997: 188). Mollenkott feels that transsexuality is a construct of the gender binary and says,

> this binary gender construct has outrun its usefulness because of the massive damage it is doing to real human lives (Mollenkott 2001: 7).

Growing-up, childhood and adolescence

Often trans people recall instances in childhood where they had thoughts or feelings of a transgender nature. This can be positive affirmation of future gender expression, or a strong sense of gender boundaries they refused to cross. Davies (2003) in her research finds this is common in children of three or four years old, and finds that 'sex/gender-role socialisation theory' (Davies 2003: 5) is the reason children take on gender more enthusiastically than adults expect, and there is usually one central adult, with the support of a multitude of others.

Rogers (1988) finds no evidence that '"male" [or "female"] behaviour follows from having male [or female] genitals, hormones or genes' (Cited in Davies 2003: 10). Califia (1997) comments that without sex-roles, infants and toddlers are believed to be in danger of being in a genderless state and therefore are perceived to need adult intervention.

Young people probably have more information now, and while more work needs to be done with transgender youth it is still a hard journey to enable them to accept a transgender nature. Mollenkott (2001) feels that it is terrifying for trans youth, and remaining invisible is often necessary. Transgender youth often have difficulty mixing with their birth gender and find more affiliation with the other gender, but is this because of social construction, as masculinity and femininity are not inherent properties of individuals (Davies 2003)?

Thorne (1993) feels that at the level of social situations, gender has a fluid quality, and believes there are important implications for social change. Deconstructing gender in young children (3-4 years) seems an almost impossible task, as parents who have tried to teach alternative narratives, such as a pro-feminist standpoint, will be familiar. However, if as Thorne suggests gender has a fluid quality, it may be possible to deconstruct gender at a later stage (6-7 years).

Developing a cross-gendered identity

In the early stage of cross-dressing a person may have a mixed sense of emotions. This could be trepidation, fear or anger, but enmeshed with a feeling that although strange and unfamiliar, they feel comfortable or acceptable in their own mind. Many trans people start cross-dressing in their childhood or teenage years to different extents. They may be private about it, blend genders or even leave the house cross-dressed, and this varies. Bornstein comments:

> when I was growing up, people who lived cross-gendered lives were pressured into hiding deep within the darkest closets they could find (Bornstein 1994: 8).

There is more information about being transgender now due to the Internet. Historically trans people struggled to get support, often felt very alone, but this appears to be changing. Developing a new sense of self is an important aspect of being transgender, and discovering their true identity can lead to a sense of freedom not previously experienced, as reflected by Morris, who says transsexuality

> is one of the most drastic changes of all human changes… but it seemed only natural to me, and I embarked upon it only with a sense of thankfulness, like a lost traveller finding the right road at last (Morris, 1986: 104).

Overcoming personal or internalised oppression

Overcoming personal barriers often prevents trans people from accepting themselves and experiencing this sense of truer identity. Many people take years to allow themselves to become transgender and have to come to terms with it over a long, drawn-out process. The small steps they take can feel increasingly more natural, as they overcome their internalised oppression.

This slow process to self-acceptance can be unconscious or definitely chosen, and trans people report that the decisions they make involve acting on how they feel, rather than actively choosing a path to take. People may live for many years in a dual role; for some this is sustainable, but others have need to transition because they cannot live this dichotomy.

Bornstein faced her own fear:

> as I got over that internalised phobia of my transgender status, I began to get curious about the nature of desire, sex and identity (Bornstein 1994: 38).

Mollenkott says,

> unless you face your feelings, denial will cause frustration, anger and depression (Mollenkott 2001: 60).

Some trans people cannot fully accept themselves unless other people accept them, and are bound up in how they relate to other people and the importance of relatives' and friends' attitudes towards them. They make decisions of who to tell, and how much to tell them. Accepting yourself as being transgender can be the hardest part, as Glenn (cited in Mallon, 1999) links this with inner guilt, and being successful to oneself was most important.

Some trans people cannot live with the secrecy of their transgender nature, and contemplate extreme actions as a response, which can include suicidal thoughts, but often coming out takes a lot of emotional strength.

The internalised pressure to accept your birth gender can be very great and there can be significant trauma in accepting a trans identity. The role that social conditioning adds to this can cause further complications. For example, once someone comes out as transgender they may need to transition quickly because having an in between identity leads to confusion for others, and to less acceptance longer term. Herdt (1993) says that once a transsexual person lives in their new gender role and has gender reassignment surgery there is a temptation to deny their transsexual past. Green (1999) agrees:

> in order to be a good - or successful - transsexual person, one is not supposed to be a transsexual person at all (cited in Whittle 1999: 120).

This level of secrecy is a burden on the transsexual person, for whom:

the most intimate and human aspects of our lives are constantly at risk of disclosure… and must consciously be on the guard against discovery (cited in Whittle 1999: 120).

Some trans people are determined not to do this, but whether they do in reality varies. As transsexual people choose to self-identify in ways that names their history, this enables the binary gender construct to be challenged.

Overcoming cultural oppression

When overcoming social oppression, trans people have different reactions. Those who are transvestite have the option to remain more hidden whereas transsexual people have to tell their relatives and friends. The response from them may be inconsistent, at times they can appear to accept it, but at other times be more dismissive, thereby sending out mixed messages leading to further confusion. Relationships with work colleagues can be difficult, and many trans people change jobs or careers at the point of transition.

However, responses from partners can be critical. Many trans people find their partners cannot accept their acquired gender, leading to a higher rate of family breakdown. Even within families there can be mixed responses from different family members and it is often difficult to predict who may accept or reject the trans person's identity. There can be conflict within families of who to tell, and families are reluctant to tell children, and try to keep it hidden from them, maybe trying to protect them from questioning their own identities, in case they explore alternative gender narratives themselves.

For some trans people there is nobody within their circle of family and friends who is prepared to accept them, and they may change their entire network of friends as a result. This radical change could lead to emotional problems that leave long standing scars.

Even people who are not 'out' may have difficulty with family, because things they do seem out of the stereotype for their gender, leading to rumours and gossip within families. Constructing new friends who are sympathetic can still be difficult, because there is not always the understanding towards trans issues, even within the lesbian, gay and bisexual sphere. However, Prosser (1999) feels questions of gender identity are not exclusive to transgender people as they do not 'have a monopoly of gender dysphoria, and that the grounds of any distinction between transsexual and butch are contestable' (cited in Whittle 1999: 85-6).

A transvestite identity can enable keeping cross-dressing a secret from wider family and friends, and for some people this is preferable to confronting other people with their identity. Keeping such a secret could lead to emotional distress, whereas disclosing emotionally significant aspects of one's self concept to others has long been suggested as contributing to mental health (Nuttbrock 2002).

The experiences of trans people have few common threads across the categories within the transgender spectrum, with transvestite and transsexual people having very different experiences. Nuttbrock (2003) finds that sifting through friendship networks, avoiding those who may be critical towards their core gender, is a process within transitioning, until new friendships are developed.

Overcoming structural or societal oppression

Within the trans world, there is a feeling that society is more tolerant than previously, as transgender issues are now more broadly addressed in Western culture. However, trans people are concerned they might continue to experience abuse: hearing society's messages that being transgender is increasingly acceptable may not match people's personal reaction to having a trans neighbour. Conversely they may accept trans people they know personally, who pass well in their acquired gender, but struggle with the broader transgender movement.

The change over the last decade has been that there is more tolerance of trans identities, but deconstructing the gender binary is necessary. A significant amount of positive education is still needed to enable trans identities to become more mainstream. Following initially quick changes, it may take a long time to happen; there are more trans people in the media now, but structural issues make it hard for society to change. Mollenkott (2001) suggests removing female and male boxes from documents such as passports and driver's licenses would be acceptable.

Some organisations have tried to introduce flexibility within gender check boxes on equality monitoring or other questionnaires (i.e. male/female/transgender), but opinion is divided within the trans community as to whether this is positive or whether this reinforces the gender binary. Consideration is needed of whether a separate question would be necessary to capture this information should it be needed (i.e. is your gender the same as that assigned at birth?).

Bornstein (1994: 58) questions why the bi-polar gender system is important and what keeps it in place, 'Why do we have to be gendered creatures at all?' However, Califia feels that erasing the dividing line between female and male is not going to achieve the desired outcome, but says that

> I'd love to live in a society where I got to emphasize other aspects of my personality more than gender, or could move back and forth between gender identities (Califia 1997: 272).

The trans community is still causing difficulties for society, and there are similarities with what happened fifty years ago within the women's movement, although there are significant differences. The acceptance of trans issues has been to some extent embraced, compared to when people like April Ashley were undergoing transition and gender reassignment. Burns (2004, cited in Savage 2005:68) argues that society has not yet become that accepting,

> the single most terrifying force in the lives of the average transsexual person is the British press

Savage continues,

> the transsexual community still experiences much that is written about them in the British press as hostile, discriminatory and misleading (Savage 2005: 68).

Some trans people feel there is a third gender category, for transgender, but many trans activists reject this as a solution to the gender binary. Bornstein feels that transsexual people perceive that there is no in-between ground and most opt for maintaining the binary gender system:

> I saw myself as a mistake: some*thing* that needed to be fixed and then placed neatly into one of the categories (Bornstein 1994: 64, emphasis in original).

Many transsexual people find it hard to understand transvestism as this confuses society, but within the trans community there are different needs and focuses for different strands of transgenderism. But does transsexualism challenge the gender binary, or does it reinforce it? Opinion within the trans world is divided. Many transvestite people do not conform to either gender role, and this can bring more disapproval and hostility. Califia (1997) finds that the visibility of the transsexual community does question the binary gender system, but those who cannot 'pass' in their acquired gender have little choice but to become gender activists and fight the oppression.

Within legislation, significant changes were made with the Gender Recognition Act 2004 (GRA) in conjunction with the Equality Act 2010 and the Marriage (Same Sex Couples) Act 2013. This legislation confers transsexual people the rights as if they had been born with their 'acquired gender', such as marriage rights, social security benefits and adds transsexual people to the list of people protected. This includes those assumed to be transsexual by association. Transsexual people are allowed new birth certificates in their 'acquired gender' under strict criteria, irrespective of any surgery that they have undergone. This legal protection is reflected in the way the police force now deal with both the reporting of hate crimes on trans people and in dealing with trans people who are detained.

Challenges presented by the medical model

For transsexual people, there is a mixed response to the intervention of the medical profession. On the one hand many transsexual people want medical intervention in order to bring their bodies into line with their social expression, but there is disagreement on classifying gender dysphoria as a medical condition. The medical profession stands as gatekeeper to what transsexual people say that they want, which is often gender reassignment of some sort. However, some trans people have rejected this as an option. Califia (1997) comments that gay men and lesbians do not need doctors or psychiatrists in order to come out, or hormones to be comfortable with their own bodies.

Lesbian, gay and bisexual people broke the link with the medical model and Stryker (1997; cited in Whittle 1999) presents the same challenge to transgender people, that activists need to do for gender dysphoria what gay liberation did for pathological homosexuality, rather than relying on self-appointed clinical caretakers.

Bornstein says that

> we're taught that we are literally sick, that we have an illness that can be diagnosed and maybe cured (Bornstein 1994: 62).

needing the medical seal of approval for gender reassignment surgery. Although Savage says that amongst health professionals there is widespread acceptance that

> gender dysphoria is not an 'illness', mental or otherwise, and that once apparent, it is a permanent, persistent condition (Savage 2005: 59).

There is growing awareness within the medical profession of the issues faced by trans people but there is still a lack of understanding that cuts across all areas, from General Practitioners to psychiatrics. Many trans people report losing control of the management of their 'condition' because of the way they are treated by gender identity 'specialists'.

However, Stryker (1997; cited in Whittle 1999) feels that trans women are treated better than trans men, as the clinic system works better for trans women, as does the surgery - cosmetically and functionally - and trans men may forgo genital surgery altogether.

Mollenkott (2001) feels that transsexual people are often assumed to have a personality disorder, psychosis or mental illness and need to convince professionals they need access to gender reassignment. For transgender people to be liberated from a medical approach, access to services only once a diagnosis of gender dysphoria is established needs to end. Tanis says that,

> the double bind of proving that we are sane enough to have surgery but crazy enough to need it is demeaning and ultimately unhelpful, placing gender transition squarely in the category of pathology rather than as a process of wholeness and transformation (Tanis 2003: 175).

Challenges presented by religious institutions

There are many different experiences of trans people of faith; some are forced to leave their place of worship, whereas others find some degree of acceptance. Some Christian communities accept them, and they become confident in their faith, often after years of struggling to reconcile their trans status with their faith.

Often trans people describe times when their difference has led to extreme reactions including some churches trying to 'cure' transsexuality by exorcism or prayer sessions. However, for those who find churches that accept them, the trans person gains much strength and sense of belonging. Highly conservative elements among the Christian churches and other faiths do not accept expressions outside the socially constructed norms. There are different conditionings, through childhood, social, family and friends, but those who experience religious conditioning believe that this is the strongest, and much more intense.

Mollenkott says that if religious people knew of the plight of trans people, 'they will repent of their oppressive attitudes and open their hearts to a transformation' (2001: 82).

Conclusion

Developing an alternative gender narrative that opposes the gender binary is important to many groups within society (e.g. feminists, gay people) as well as trans people, but the question remains to what extent trans people challenge this binary or reinforce it. There has been significant movement on this question over the last twenty years, but the way that gender clinics operate within the medical model does not always allow dissolution of the gender system.

As evidenced in this discussion, I believe that the way that people learn how to do gender is embedded within society, and that this is a social construct that causes people to accept or reject it, often without considering it to any great extent. The phenomenon of transsexuality is a real reaction to this construct, but people who experience its oppression need to be able to be accepted by society without fear of rejection, prejudice or ridicule. Trans activists are seeking to ensure the future freedom for people, irrespective of their gender presentation.

Welcome to the *genderevolution*, indeed (Califia 1997: 277, my emphasis).

Chapter 4

Intersex, Medicine, Diversity, Identity and Spirituality

Michelle O'Brien

> *This chapter draws on my writing over the past twelve years,*
> *supplemented with reflection: a talk given in Paris in 2006 (O'Brien*
> *2006), my research dissertation of 2010, my talks in the Workshops*
> *(Beardsley et al. 2010), as well as papers, talks and writing on my*
> *website (O'Brien 2015).*

Background

My journey has led me to understand that there were things that
happened to me in childhood that I would now describe as treatment
for an intersex condition. Much of my self-realisation was thanks to
the early work of ISNA, AISSG(UK), DES-Sons[1], Suzanne Kessler,
Anne Fausto-Sterling, Morgan Holmes, Alice Dreger, Sharon Preves,
amongst others. I was fortunate, through online groups, to get
to know Dana, Scott, Tom, Yann, Curtis, Sophie, Gina, Jim, Chris,
Sally, Peter, Hannah, Maria, some of whom, and others, whom I
met face-to-face in the UK and France. I became an early member of
Organisation Intersex International (OII), and a founder member of
OII-UK. This led me to conduct post-graduate research into intersex
and transgender issues from 2003 to 2010, where I got to know
Del LaGrace Volcano and others involved in the London Critical
Sexology meetings.

---

1   ISNA was the Intersex Society of North America, the first major generic
intersex advocacy group, founded in the early 1990's. AISSG(UK) is the
Androgen Insensitivity Support Group, the first condition-specific intersex
advocacy and support group, founded in the UK. DES-Sons, and its spin-off
DES-trans, were an international support and advocacy group for people
affected by diethylstilbestrol, which was given to many expectant mothers
during pregnancy between the 1940s and 1970s.

I now understand that some people are born different from the way people usually expect males and females to be. Male and female are treated as two distinct categories in our society, although there is a range of people who are born somewhere in between. This phenomenon has been accepted and accommodated within different cultures, such as some First Nation American, Polynesian, and Hindu groups. In the book of the Acts of the Apostles, Philip is directed to talk with an Ethiopian eunuch (Acts 8:26-40), and his eligibility on the path to salvation is acknowledged, with no judgement passed on his status as a eunuch; Jesus makes clear there are two types of eunuchs (Matthew 19:12), those who are born (intersex), and those who are man-made (castrated). Nothing in the New Testament appears to suggest that being a eunuch is a barrier to entry to the Kingdom.

I lived as a Christian for most of my life, but I was also influenced by the teachings of the Buddha, and other great teachers from other faiths such as Lao-Tzu and the Sufi mystics. I entered a religious community in my early thirties to explore asceticism and discipline. This experience helped me understand the 'Middle Way' between denial and decadence, like the path that Jesus took between living under the Law and license.

I was not cut out for a life in religious community, but still followed this middle way with the understanding that I did not have to 'get it right', simply to walk the path.

This balancing act between my faith as a Christian, and my understanding as a philosopher who valued Oriental traditions, was reproduced in how I was to deal with the discomfort I felt about the gender I had been assigned and had reinforced on my body and mind, both medically and socially. The issue became so strong in my consciousness that it became hard to function.

I was married for a while, and my spouse was aware of these issues, I was involved in the local church, but my work suffered, my relationships suffered, and my health suffered. I knew that there was much to be done for the Kingdom of God, and that time was limited, but my gender dysphoria lay in the way of my progress. I realised that accepting, rather than denying, the situation might be the only way to resolve it.

The process of changing my gender took place over more than a decade, starting in my thirties. Through snippets of information from doctors, supplemented with my own research, I began to unravel things about my childhood that turned my world upside down. I realised that I was not the person I had always thought I was. The more I learned, the more I felt torn in two. I am not sure how I survived that time. What I came to understand was that I was born with intersex characteristics, and had at least two gender reinforcement surgeries to make me appear more masculine, as well as psycho-social gender-reinforcement.

When I changed my life by living as a woman rather than as a man, not much about me was different, although the way I was treated certainly was! I was the same person I had always been, and it was not that difficult a change to make. I am not sure how anybody could have related to me as a man; as I began to see men through a different lens, I realised I was never quite like them. In hindsight, I can see that there are many differences, but these are external, social, and to do with people's perceptions: I am treated very differently when seen as a woman compared to when seen as a man.

I soon realised that just as I had not been a man, I was not a woman either, nor could I ever be: I could live and perform as a woman, in a similar way to how I had lived and performed as a man. I found myself living as a woman, accepted that way, more comfortable that way, and decided to stay like that; I did not know then that I could be anything else. The determinism of the meta-narrative of women trapped in men's bodies, of a social female-gender being hard-wired into the brain of somebody with a male body (or vice versa) was meaningless to me.

I would have preferred not to have a gender, but I lived in a society where binary gender is compulsory, so chose that which was not chosen for me.

Eventually, I found the two models of gender difficult to understand, because people are not always as clear-cut. I found it increasingly difficult to make the effort to give out the signals that denote female rather than male. These days I can be referred to as male by one person, and female the next. I don't correct people, because they are not wrong.

I have come around full circle through transition. I started out with some genital ambiguity, nowadays known as 'XY-DSD', of uncertain aetiology, and my male assignment was reinforced surgically and socially. I went through adolescence as male, and spent part of my adult life living as a man: when I transitioned to female, it was to discover I was intersex all along, and I decided that intersex was a truer reflection of my identity.

Where did this fit in with my faith? My relationship with the religion I grew up with and participated in during my adult life has become tenuous since I 'came out' as intersex. I don't believe that G*d makes mistakes, nor that original sin would make a child the way I was born, and when I read the account in Genesis 1, I believe that in terms of sex and gender, it is we who have misunderstood. I am not a literalist, I believe that the Bible is mainly myth, metaphor and analogy; having studied social anthropology, I can give no more literal credence to Christian Scripture than the creation and genealogical narratives of indigenous people; each has something that speaks to our common human experience. So, when I read that we humans are made in the image of God, and that we were created male *and* female, not male *or* female; there is no disjunction there, only a conjunction (Gen. 1:27). According to Susannah Cornwall, Sally Gross explained this in 1998:

> Sally Gross suggests that although many people appeal to Genesis 1:27 to 'prove' that people were designed to be male *or* female, it can also be interpreted as suggesting that all humans are (or were, in the primal creation) *both* male *and* female (Cornwall 2015: 12).

The image we were created in is male *and* female, reflecting a G*d who is both male *and* female; we can see aspects of this in every human, where parts of male anatomy resemble 'female' anatomy (men have nipples) and parts of female anatomy resemble 'male' anatomy (the clitoris). We reflect G*d, and exist between male and female; as an intersex person, I am more a mixture of both than usual, and just as reflective of the God who is both male *and* female. Unacknowledged in much of Judaeo-Christian-Islamic theology, this is not alien in other cultures, nor in some strands within Judaism.

When I am rejected by those in the Church for being who I am, or when I reject the Church for rejecting my brothers and sisters in the LGBTI community, I am not rejected by, nor do I reject G*d. I reject a human construction of G*d - an idol made in the form of a man - rather than G*d as G*d is in G*d's self (as Meister Eckhart could have said).

Intersex
The word 'intersex' is, and has been, used in used in different ways. Intersex replaced 'hermaphroditism' to describe a set of medical

conditions where certain aspects of a person's physiology lie between what is typically expected for males and females. These signs can be chromosomes that are not XX or XY; reproductive organs that are neither fully male or female; sex-reversal (where somebody's primary and secondary sex characteristics are not what is usually expected with XY or XX chromosomes). In the 1990s intersex also became the preferred term for use by activists in the early intersex movement; for some it became an identity. There is often a difference between medical understanding and that of people who identify as intersex. Some intersex conditions can involve serious, and in some cases life-threatening, medical problems beyond the configuration of genitalia, but many of those who identify as intersex tend to regard non-conforming genitals as not being a medical problem per se. Instead, they argue that medicalising non-conforming intersex genitals is unnecessary and pathologising, that these procedures have lifelong consequences, yet are carried out in early childhood without the individual's informed consent.

It is difficult to discuss intersex without referring to the medical conditions that produce intersex; yet there is a tension between viewing intersex medically and as a social phenomenon. Genetic or other congenital factors can give rise to intersex characteristics, but those characteristics themselves are not necessarily problematic. Medicine has historically regarded intersex characteristics as defects, which needed fixing surgically. This was my experience. I have written about what intersex is, and what it is not, in Christina's Gender Trust booklet (O'Brien 2007).

It is difficult to generalise about how intersex conditions present themselves, because individuals' experiences vary, even within the same condition.

Intersex is about differences in physical characteristics, and is different from trans. For some individuals there may be 'gender dysphoria' as well (as in my case), but for most there isn't. Even the idea of referring to the discomfort some may have with their original assignment as 'gender dysphoria' is problematic. Intersex people usually identify as male or female, remain in their assigned gender from birth, but quite a few transition as adults, or identify as intersex per se. In a recent study, around 25% of people with intersex experience were found not to identify with the gender they were assigned (Schweizer et al. 2014).

Uncommon Realities

The issues around sex/gender tend to be viewed through a polarised lens: 'man', male', 'XY', 'masculine' and 'penis' tend to be seen as in some way opposite to 'woman', 'female', 'XX', 'feminine' and 'vagina/uterus'. The legacy of Cartesian dualism in body and mind persists in the way sex and gender are viewed in Western culture (Hird 2002a; Wilton 2000).

Whether sexuality or gender is fixed or fluid is a reflection of this dualistic approach, and reflects debates about nature versus nurture (Colapinto 2001; Hird 2000; Lancaster 2003; Weeks 1991), the medical versus social construction of transsexualism (Billings and Urban 1996) and transgression versus transcending a mis-gendered body (Hird 2002b; Van Lenning 2004).

Common myths about sex and gender include that 'man', 'male', 'XY', 'masculine' have some universal equivalence and that any one of these implies the others; similarly for 'woman', 'female', 'XX', 'feminine'. Trans people most defy this, as do feminine males and masculine females. Some intersex people's histories and experiences disturb this dichotomy too (Chase and Hegarty 2000; Fausto-Sterling 1985; Halberstaum 1998; Harding 1998; Liao 2005; Meyer-Bahlburg 2001; Migeon et al. 2002; Tauchert 2002; Van Lenning 2004).

Uncommon realities that don't fit assumptions about how people are include: people born with XY chromosomes who at some stage in their lives transition from male to female, or people born with XX chromosomes who transition from female to male. They become identified as men or women, despite having XX or XY chromosomes. There are males who can be feminine, and females who can be masculine.

Intersex conditions are seen as rare, less common than transsexuality; but, although contested, the numbers of people affected by intersex conditions is now considered to be 1-2% of the population (Diamond 1999; Diamond 2002; Diamond and Beh 2000; Diamond and Beh 2006; Diamond and Kipnis 1998; Diamond and Sigmundson 1997; Fausto-Sterling 1985; Fausto-Sterling 2000; Sax 2002; Vilain 2002; Vilain 2006; Vilain 2008). Many people do not know that they are affected, as this was kept from people for many years.

Many children with Congenital Adrenal Hypoplasia and XX chromosomes have been operated on to remove or reduce the size of their clitoris because it looked more like a penis (Lee and Witchel 2002; Minto et al. 2003; Sultan et al. 2002). People with Androgen Insensitivity Syndrome have XY chromosomes, often appear female, and are raised as such, and as they grow older develop similarly to other women, until their periods fail to start and it becomes clear they cannot give birth; many have their gonads removed before adulthood (Creighton and Minto 2001; Cull 2002; Hughes 2002; Minto et al. 2003; Wisniewski and Migeon 2002; Wisniewski et al. 2000). People with mixed XX/XY chromosomes can have a combination of 'male' and 'female' features; traditionally doctors would assign them as female, with surgery to conform their bodies to their assigned gender (Adams et al. 2003; Hrabovszky and Hutson 2002; Kim et al. 2002; Lerman et al. 2000).

The idea about the universality of women having XX chromosomes, or men having XY chromosomes, and that masculinity is a male attribute, or femininity is a female attribute is more simplistic than the complex reality. Most men have XY chromosomes, and most women have XX chromosomes, but not all: having XY or XX chromosomes is not what makes people male or female, and does not automatically result in male or female development, although it usually does. While medicine views an XY person developing as female, or an XX person developing as male as a disorder, the individual affected may not see themselves this way. Some would say that XXY is intersex, but I have limited space to describe all the different possibilities.

Gender is a social, not a biological reality; the significance placed upon chromosomal sex is socially constructed. The power to control intersex people's sex and gender rests with those who construct the discourse used to talk about intersex (or transgender). Whether people are intersex (or trans), the discourse they use about themselves tends to be drawn from medical-scientific explanations: chromosomes, hormones, surgery, sex characteristic, sex, and gender.

Intersex people
Most intersex people tend not to be concerned about the appropriateness of their sex assignment, but many of those who experienced early childhood surgeries are often concerned about surgeries carried out to 'correct' atypical genitals, the lack of consent by the affected individual, and the legacy that carries through to adulthood. Not all intersex people experience such surgeries. It is becoming more accepted that non-consensual surgical intervention should be avoided where possible, but those who manage intersex people's health seem slow to embrace this.

Research that has been carried out suggests that the numbers of intersex people who go on to reject their birth-assignment is more than transsexual people in the general population. Intersex is more common among the general population than transsexuality, but less open.

Reflection on the terms we use and on experience

We can define our terms, it is not possible to define people in the same way. Throughout my research, I was struck by how the terms we use can be liberating for some, and oppressive to others. Even to discuss words like intersex, transsexual and transgender in the same sentence is seen by some as being offensive. People come in many different forms, and their life-trajectories bestow unique experiences that the fixed categories derived from the nineteenth century may not encapsulate.

Even if our sexual and gender identities could be defined through biological and psychological essentials, they cannot be understood that way. Where it may be possible to explain the brain and what it does, descriptions of neurological mechanism and activity cannot inform what it means to have a conscious life (McCulloch 1994). Sartre appreciated that understanding people and their world is a different exercise to an objective study of nature (Sartre 1958/2003). Similarly, the lived-experience of people in the context of sexuality and gender-identity cannot be understood through empirical investigations either. The lived-experience of intersex people must be approached existentially and phenomenologically, rather than just through science and medicine.

The way we are, in our bodies, and the mind that is an integral part of them, is our being, our existence, our essence, and our spirit. This cannot be encapsulated in the dry categories of academia: this is the living flesh of which we are made. We become what others see in us. The role of medicine has been to categorise, define, dissect and describe us – to take us apart, reduced from the whole. Intersex has been defined as something alien and other, something to be studied, modified, corrected, and conformed. This approach of defining terms and allocating categories, then applying them as if they in some way define who one is, strips people of their humanity; it is dehumanising, and rests on an a priori premise that intersex people are in some way intrinsically deficient, deformed and wrong.

Yet, intersex people exist, and do so in ways that defy the rigid constraints that professionals might seek to impose upon them through the arbitrary definitions of binary sex, gender and sexuality configurations. There is no comfort in holding on to these standardised notions of how people should be, because their existence from birth as people who have not developed in ways that 'should' be, exposes these definitions for the inadequate representations that they are. The protocols of 'experts' who experimented with their lives can seem like a conspiracy to make them conform to their notions of how men and women should be, and what it is to be human; failure to live up to those standards can prevent such people from being full members of society.

These definitions and protocols do not serve intersex people at all – they serve those who create them, and becoming free, involves self-liberation from the definitions imposed by others. Professionals have sought to define people through terms like transsexual, intersex, hermaphrodite, transgender, and now seek to codify intersex further using 'Disorders of Sex Development'. Submitting to these terms colludes with the on-going process of oppression that has been perpetrated against intersex people. This is the essence of our being – we are human beings, and it is as human beings that we need to be defined.

The process of definition becomes a channel through which intersex people can be assessed, judged, manipulated, and coerced. Experts become assessors, seeing how well individuals correspond with their definitions, and put them through tests, in order to see how well they can fit within the categories deemed as acceptable (even to see if some can pass as 'transsexual'). Intersex people have not been listened to, allowed to describe themselves, or consulted on what is best for them. This is because the expert is the 'objective observer', while the 'observed subject' has been regarded as inferior, not fit to judge what is in their own best interests. The evidence is clear – children have been assigned and treated in certain ways, without asking what they themselves might want. Adults have been given a limited range of options, and limited ways of pursuing them. Theory, and the evidence selected to justify theory, is asserted as being more significant than the experience of those subjected to the practical consequences of theory.

In these situations, what is expected is that the individual will conform to what society expects them to be, not to what or who they actually are. The definitions that affect intersex people are definitions about society, and social expectations, not about the individual themselves. Having defined the way people should be, the individual has to conform, and their own interests have been deemed secondary to those of society as a whole. Defining people in terms of sex and gender role, identity and identification is about social control and policing the boundaries of sex and gender.

Because of this limitation in labelling, I find myself increasingly reluctant to say 'I am a man', 'I am a woman', 'I was a man', 'I was a woman', 'I am transsexual', 'I am transgender', 'I am gay', 'I am lesbian', 'I am queer', 'I am straight', or even 'I am intersex' – because none of these descriptions adequately define who I am. They are ways of categorising me in order for others to have power over me. This power is so significant that the state and the medical profession become involved in enforcing conformity.

Intersex disturbs our notions about fixed, discrete, binary opposites in gender, just as much as transgendering the boundaries between male and female can. For those who have had some of these experiences, and who find it difficult to clearly identify as male or female, the need for a space in our society that is 'other' than male or female is obvious. Sadly, it is the legacy of Church teaching that there are two inflexible sexes that cannot be changed or intertwined that has prevented society from achieving such a space in the way some traditional cultures have. Rather than embracing the 'other', those outside the constraints of sex and gender, the Church still seems to want to pretend that those who are different do not exist. Denying that people exist erases their humanity.

Intersex as a way of being

I have come to see walking a middle way between the sexes as my path. It is a path between the two compulsory genders, another way, a narrow way, a difficult place, but the only place I can genuinely be. It is like living in a crack in the world from which comes a specific type of knowledge and power. But, as a realisation, it is not about what I have become, but the way I am, the way I always was. It is how it has always been for me, physically, mentally, and emotionally, and reflects things about me from when I was born, before somebody decided to correct the ambiguities in me. Finding and being myself is like a religious calling, because this is how it was meant to be. This middle way between genders should sit comfortably within any spiritual path or discipline, drawing strength from both genders, instead of just one, not as a third, but as a path between genders, knowing gender is illusory, socially constructed.

Concluding comments

I have explained that medical conditions can give rise to intersex characteristics, but those characteristics are not always in need of medical correction, and that intersex can mean different things to different people: some restrict its usage to a very narrow set of conditions and signs, others broaden it to include any form of sex and genital ambiguity somewhere between that normally expected in male and female human beings.

I have explained what the implications for a strict binary approach to gender are, for intersex and other people, and how that approach is unscientific, and that it is reinforced by Scripture through an erroneous interpretation of Genesis 1:27. I have also clarified that intersex is different from transgender, although for some individuals, there may be overlap.

I have a more Foucauldian understanding that rejects these medical conditions as in some way defining us, and see intersex as part of a person's life-history, and being; something that is not disordered in its own right, but an aspect of human variation. Medical treatment of underlying conditions may be necessary where there is a risk to life or health, but there is no need for cosmetic change to fit social expectations of how men and women should be. I seek a space within society for those unable to identify as, or commit to, either of two exclusive genders, which would include those who would prefer to identify other than the way they were assigned after birth. I choose to be intersex, because that is how I was made, and what I am.

Section 2: Theology and Trans Chapters

Chapter 5

Trans Liberating Feminist and Queer Theologies

Mercia McMahon

The title deliberately has a double meaning of both trans people being liberated, and in true Liberation Theology method, that theology being written by trans theologians. The author investigates the contributions that could be made to both feminist and queer theologies if trans people write theology, rather than having theology written about their experience. The chapter centres on a critical conversation with the trans-inclusive contributions of the liberationist, feminist, and queer theologian, Marcella Althaus-Reid [1952-2009].

The subject area of trans theology took a major step forward in 2009 with the publication of *Trans/Formations*, a collection of essays about either the personal experience of being a trans Christian or theological reflections on the existence of trans people (Althaus-Reid and Isherwood 2009). It was edited by Marcella Althaus-Reid and Lisa Isherwood, but Althaus-Reid's role was limited because she became seriously ill as the editorial process began and died before its publication. In this chapter I will address her legacy and the extent to which it could help in the further development of a trans theology.

Althaus-Reid was a Professor of Divinity at the University of Edinburgh, but her theology remained grounded in her background in Argentina. This geographic focus is especially true for her allusions to trans people, which relate to poor Latin American trans women (e.g., Althaus-Reid 2000: 79-83; 2003: 9-10; 2004a: 166-168; 2008b). Her background is in Latin American liberation theology, but she engages in limited discussion about liberating trans people. Rather, she analyses the experiences of transvestite women in order to explore the boundary-breaking nature of their existence (e.g., Althaus-Reid 2000: 198-199). Due to her untimely death it is unclear what future steps she hoped to inspire by co-editing

Trans/Formations. Nonetheless, elements of her theological project offer a useful model for the development of a trans theology. Those elements are her encouragement for theologians to engage with the sexual and gender variant side of human life (Althaus-Reid, 2000: 87-89) and her theological model of see, discern and act (Althaus-Reid, 2000: 126).

It is from the sexual and gender variant side of human life that Althaus-Reid drew both the name for her theological method and the title of her first book, *Indecent Theology* (Althaus-Reid 2000). She defines this as a theology that challenges the Latin American axis of decency/indecency that, even in liberation theology circles, is used to suppress both female and queer voices (Althaus-Reid, 2000: 22-23). She calls for personal sacrifice from closeted theologians: 'God cannot be Queered unless theologians have the courage to come out of their homosexual, lesbian, bisexual, transgender, transvestite or (ideal) heterosexual closets' (Althaus-Reid 2000: 88).

That the call to open closet doors is made in relation to gender identity as well as sexuality was ground-breaking, especially within the context of feminist theology. Not that gender identity and sexuality are completely separate, as the sexual nature of trans and intersex bodies is something that should challenge present categorisations of sexuality (Reay 2009: 164-165). Nor is sexuality limited to questions of physical intimacy, as it also involves a feeling of being outsiders in a culture defined by heterosexual lifestyle (Althaus-Reid 2004b: 106).

Althaus-Reid wanted to move Christianity and theology away from a dependence on a heterosexual ideology that silenced other perspectives (2003: 2). The trans voice in theology is among those that need liberation from such silencing. She located that silencing within an 'axis of decency/indecency' that was used to regulate the lives of others, especially women (Althaus-Reid, 2003: 172n1). That challenge to the axis of decency/indecency is a reminder for any trans theology to be inclusive of all aspects of gender variance. Transsexual people who transition from one side of the gender binary to the other are often accepted in Church communities, so long as they are heterosexual or celibate in their new gender. Althaus-Reid's legacy reminds such transsexual people to reject the temptation to sacrifice the full acceptance of all trans people for the sake of limited acceptance from Church cultures that still value decency. To accept Althaus-Reid's call to challenge the decency/indecency axis would require any trans theology to be inclusive of all gender variant identities and the variety of sexual identities that those individuals possess.

Such inclusivity would require a clear understanding of who belongs to the trans community. Althaus-Reid noted (2000: 115) that her students queried why middle class people are excluded from popular Bible Studies. Trans theology could benefit from a similar exclusion of those who want to show their support, but the imprecise nature of gender variance would make such exclusion difficult to achieve. The question of 'Who is in insider?' is an on-going debate within gender variant communities and the imprecision of those boundaries is something that any trans theology needs to address.

The ideal trans theology is one that is written by members of trans communities, but with so few trans identified theologians this is a long way from becoming reality. Due to this situation those who engage in trans positive theology as outsiders need to be careful that they are fully engaging with the community and not making assumptions about what trans people experience. Althaus-Reid gave an example of the danger of not engaging with the community in her account of a discussion group she ran for poor Buenos Aires women in 1987. When asked if they identified with the Virgin Mary in their sufferings, one woman responded, 'No, because she has expensive clothes and jewels, she is white and she does not walk.' (Althaus-Reid 2004a: 30)

From an outsider's perspective Mary might seem a good symbol; she was a poor Palestinian woman ruled by an oppressive military dictatorship. This proved not to be the case for these poor Argentine women just four years after the end of military rule. Instead they interpreted Mary as rich via the local culture of processional statues. Likewise, a trans positive theology should check the interpretations with the trans community and not just source its experiential data there.

Theologians should be encouraged to write trans positive theology, and to maintain contact with members of trans communities who are also members of faith communities. As more trans writers of trans theology become established those outsider perspectives would take on a different function: acting as a critique of debates that have become too insular. Nonetheless, the driving force of trans theology should transfer to members of the community once there are sufficient trans identified trans theologians to sustain the sub-discipline.

To date much of the theological use of trans experience has been to provide illustrations to deconstruct gendered views of God (Althaus-Reid 2000: 79-83; Quero 2008: 112). Other uses argue for trans acceptance (Mollenkott 2008: 98-99) or freedom from violence (Althaus-Reid 2004a: 166-168). Those last two are concerns shared by trans communities, but they are not the sum total of insider trans concerns. Lack of engagement with the community could lead to a similar mistake to Althaus-Reid's assumption that poor Argentine women would relate to Mary, or what might be described as the theologian having a rich virgin moment.

This brings us to the other main resource that Althaus-Reid could provide for trans theology: the liberation theology paradigm of see, discern, and act (Althaus-Reid 2000: 126-132).

Seeing involves the observation of the lived situation of the community that the theology is addressing. In the case of liberation theology this involves the lives of those experiencing poverty, and for trans theology it would consist of the lives of gender variant people. This begins with how existence is seen by the oppressed community and suggests that they should reconsider their seeing in order to begin to liberate themselves from oppression (Althaus-Reid 2000: 126). The mixture of chapters in *Trans/Formations* could be classified from this seeing context: the personal trans testimonies are giving the primarily outsider theologians the material to work with. Yet it is only in Krzysztof Bujnowski's testimony chapter that we see something that goes beyond the tropes that outsiders tend to assume make up the sum total of a trans-focused theology. In 'Through the Wilderness' (Bujnowski 2009) he explores his personal experience of isolation of growing up secretly transsexual until a transition in his fifties. This fits in with the outsider trope of gender identity, but explores it through the decades-long experience of living in an incongruent gender role, rather than the more stereotypical narrative of what changes were made in transition.

As community insiders write more trans theology, I would expect themes such as those explored by Bujnowski to become increasingly evident. Examples of wider topics would include the inter-section of trans and bisexual identity, the insider-outsider relationship that trans women have with feminism, the ambiguity over sexuality experienced by many post-operative transsexual people, the place of trans people within wider queer networks, resisting the sexual objectification of trans women, the differing perspectives of trans men and trans women, the distinct needs of transsexual and gender queer communities, and relating to controversies within trans activism.

Over the last decade there has been a welcome increase in non-condemnatory theological attention to gender variant people and *Trans/Formations* is a good example of that. However, it is also a telling example of how the agenda for trans theology continues to be set by outsiders, who focus on gender identity, transition journeys, surgery, discrimination, sex work and violence. To restrict trans theology to those subjects is as inadequate as limiting feminist theology to women's ministry, violence against women, and motherhood, because they are the issues that some male allies think sum up women's concerns.

In terms of published trans theology, the seeing moment has so far been disappointingly narrow in its focus. This hampers the move to the discerning stage, because the subject-matter continues to be limited by those dominant outsider perspectives. It is important to note, however, that the insider perspective is not limited to the seeing phase. In Althaus-Reid's expression of the liberation theology method the voice of those in poverty should remain dominant even as the Bible and theological tradition are introduced to the process (Althaus-Reid 2000: 129). That would mean in trans theology that the trans voice is still driving the discernment phase. In that regard, *Trans/Formations* was remiss, with an exception being Lewis Reay's 'Towards a Transgender Theology: Que(e)rying the Eunuchs' (Reay 2009).

The voices of outsiders are still very important due to the paucity of trans theology written by trans people, but the discerning phase requires trans input. Without some trans involvement we are back in the territory of mistaking a rich virgin as a good symbol for the poor. As more trans-identified theologians come forward there will be a need for the non-trans facilitators to step back and allow as much of the conversation as possible to be guided by members of trans communities. Given the low numbers of trans people it is likely that trans theology will never be as exclusively an insider task as feminist theology, but outsiders should still aim for a policy of self-moratorium.

An example of a rich virgin moment from an outsider can be found in Althaus-Reid's own work. In 'Mutilations and Restorations: Cosmetic Surgery in Christianity', she entitles the concluding section 'Transsexualities', yet the section is devoid of any reference to transsexual experience, beyond the sentence: 'Yet transsexualism and transgenderism remind us that sexual identities can only be found grounded in earthquakes: their only commonality in their continuous and slippery *différence'* (Althaus-Reid 2008a: 78).

Even that differentiation is coloured by the preceding paragraph asserting that gender is performative and cosmetic surgery is something of which Pelagia, the fifth century transgender saint and subject of the chapter, might be guilty. This leaves the impression that Althaus-Reid may be uncomfortable with transsexuality, maybe even accepting the criticism that it is conformist and decent. This is in contrast to her various explorations of cross-dressing themes, which appeal to her as being both transgressive of societal norms (2004a: 165) and found among the most economically excluded in Latin American society (2008b: 86). Her lack of comfort with transsexuality is suggested in her using the term to mean something completely different from its use by trans people: 'Finally, we need to reflect on Queer theology and its transsexual acts through which it problematizes the call to restore an original woman's body and also insists on the right to disrupt women's bodies' (Althaus-Reid 2008a:74).

That she is much more comfortable with gender variant people who are not transsexual is evident in her statement that 'Following Queer theory, genders are performative acts which depend on cosmetic excesses, including tattoos, bird masks, leather, S/M vinyl clothes, imposing high heels. They can also be supplemented with fake breasts or alterations in voice tone' (Althaus-Reid 2008a: 78).

Therefore, this section called *Transsexualities* in a chapter on cosmetic surgery only mentions gender variant experience through those who temporarily alter their bodies (i.e., they would not normally be defined as transsexual). This is a puzzling omission for a trans-positive theologian, who has criticised the making invisible both of the poor (Althaus-Reid 2004a: 130) and women (Althaus-Reid 2000: 37; 2008a: 72). Her early death leaves unresolved this question mark as to whether she was trans-positive or simply liked using the gender variant as theological illustrations. Co-editing *Trans/Formations* did not clear up that issue as it is mostly outsider perspectives with insider testimonies to provide further illustrative resources. This definitely constitutes a rich virgin moment for her, but that does not detract from her liberation model being a worthwhile model for a nascent trans theology.

The discerning phase involves bringing together trans experience from the seeing phase with ideas from the Bible and Christian tradition. It is preferable if primarily members of trans communities undertake this, as they are better equipped to weed out rich virgin moments. Such insider prevalence would broaden the subject-matter from the seeing phase beyond the standard canon of outsider perspectives. Yet this engagement with tradition, and more particularly Scripture, will be limited for a similar reason to the inherent contradiction at the heart of Althaus-Reid's theological project. She holds on to her liberation theology roots, updated via post-colonial reflections, while bringing feminist theology into the equation. Yet when it comes to an engagement with Scripture there is a chasm between those strands in her work. The Biblical theme of the exodus from slavery into freedom in a new land can provide a rich seam to be mined for liberation and post-colonial theologies, but feminist theology has struggled to discern an equivalent resource for women.

The Bible is an even worse resource for trans people than it is for feminist theology. The aspect that has attracted most trans theological interest is in the re-examination of eunuchs (Kolakowski 2000; Reay 2009). Seeking a link between eunuchs in ancient near eastern culture and transsexuality on the basis of body modification is, however, problematic from an exegetical viewpoint. There is no evidence that the castration of eunuchs came from a desire to be seen as a different gender from that assigned at birth. It involved a way of gaining access to power through being less of a rival to the ruler than a non-castrated male and being trusted as a go-between with the ruler's harem (Llewellyn-Jones 2002: 24). Reflection on eunuchs might open up some avenues for finding scriptural warrants for the acceptability of body modification, but any stronger link between eunuchs and trans women appears to be reading too much into the text. The other main Biblical focus for trans theological reflection is the negative one of Deuteronomy 22.5, which outlaws cross-dressing. However that cannot provide a resource for the discernment phase of a liberative theology, as it provides nothing positive to say about trans people, beyond the acknowledgment that gender variant behaviour exists.

Another possible resource for discernment is the history of cross-dressing saints, such as St Pelagia, who is the focus of the article in which Althaus-Reid has her transsexual rich virgin moment (2008a). However, those historical/mythical figures present a similar problem to eunuchs. There is no evidence that their cross-dressing is anything other than a means to power or safety in a man's world. In the case of cross-dressing female saints the motivation appears to be a strategy for participating more fully in a patriarchal society. As a consequence such cross-dressing saints provide less of a resource for trans theology than it does for feminist theology; the context in which Althaus-Reid was using Pelagia.

Trans theology is left with little from the Christian tradition that can be used directly as a resource. It can take Biblical and traditional elements that have resonances for trans people, such as eunuchs or cross-dressing saints, but with the acknowledgment that these are all rich virgins, i.e., they do not fully equate to the experience of trans people. Some of these eunuchs or cross-dressing saints might have been trans, but there is no greater likelihood of that than for the wider population, as the primary reason for their gender non-conformity appears unconnected to a notion of gender identity.

This does not leave trans theology bereft of a discernment phase, as trans theologians and popular study groups can analyse non-trans specific parts of the Bible and tradition and assess them from a trans perspective. This was hinted at by Althaus-Reid in her example of a gay man re-interpreting the raising of Lazarus in a homo-erotic fashion. She concluded by noting that a person who is transvestite might provide a different reading again, inspired by the initial homo-erotic interpretation (2000: 130). A possible example of this would be the story of the eunuch Hegai being in charge of the king's harem (Esther 2:15) re-read by a transsexual woman to relate to the experience of being given access to women-only spaces, but continuing to be treated as if she had a privileged access to male power. As another example, if a discussion was taking place on powerful women contrasting the gender non-conforming Deborah and the gender-conforming Jael (Judges 4), then a trans man might explore the interpretative boundary lines between reading Deborah as a woman who refused to accept patriarchal restrictions on access to power and an alternative reading of Deborah as someone engaging in traditionally male roles because she did not identify with his/her birth gender.

The final stage of this liberative trans theology is to act, although action is constrained by the limitations of access to power of the community in question (Althaus-Reid 2000: 129). For example, among the Argentine transvestite community there are severe financial limitations, due to poor employment opportunities and very low social status (Althaus-Reid 2004a: 167). There are (at least) two further inter-related trans limitations on access to power: numbers and stealth. These limitations can be summed up in the concept of invisibility (Green 2006). The low incidence of trans people who are visible (e.g., transsexual people, people who cross dress and others involved in the queer scene) reduces the numbers who are available to engage in public action. For transsexual people this number is further reduced by those who retreat from prior political activism into stealth, i.e., living incognito in their non-birth gender. So the invisibility begins with low numbers making it hard to get politically noticed and then some of those who are politically active retreating into a self-embraced invisibility.

That action will also be limited by the legal and cultural framework within which trans communities find themselves. The United Kingdom in the twenty-first century has witnessed a vastly improved set of legal protection for transsexual people, and by extension some protection for other gender variant people, but cultural levels of discrimination remain rife, especially in relation to faith-based transphobia. Since the 1990s there has been a slowly increasing level of trans activism, which has become much more evident since the rise of social media. That latter style of activism has focused on direct action, especially small demonstrations, while the older style of working the corridors of power has continued. A liberationist model of theology would need to engage with the concerns of all strands of trans activism or it would be guilty of merely appropriating trans experiences.

Returning to seeing after carrying out the action is an important element of following this model for theology. It is needed to make the process a hermeneutical circle by never finishing the cycle of creative engagement and action (Althaus-Reid 2000: 129-130). This would include raising community consciousness about what action has already taken place. The community may respond that they do not see the benefits of these past actions in their lived experience. That would necessitate a re-working of the previous action, as the purpose of a liberative theology is to facilitate improvement in the lives of those in the various trans communities.

The publication of *Trans/Formations* was an important milestone in the journey towards a trans theology, but it also revealed its limitations, especially with regard to the theological contributors being primarily non-trans. Trans theology remains in its infancy and it is unclear whether Althaus-Reid would have made a lasting contribution to its development, given her primary focus on transvestite people as exemplars of the intersections between queer lived experience and economic deprivation. Nonetheless, her inclusion of some sections of the trans community in her indecent theology brought trans theology within the ambit of mainstream academic debate. The full impact of her plan, alongside Lisa Isherwood, to bolster the development of trans theology is not yet clear, but *Trans/Formations* will remain as Althaus-Reid's legacy to this nascent discipline.

It is, however, within Althaus-Reid's wider theological project that I see her most telling legacy. Without her indecent theology, there would be less room for the wider gender variant community to be engaged by, and to engage in, theology. For without the openness to the sexually indecent, trans theology would be reduced to the tiny community of heterosexual post-operative transsexual people who appear acceptable to prevailing Church cultures. The see, discern, act model from liberation theology also provides a firm foundation for discussing how to do trans theology. Althaus-Reid was not very good at giving trans people their own theological voice, but she left a legacy with which trans people and non-trans facilitators can take that project forward.

Chapter 6

Taking Issue: The Transsexual hiatus in 'Some Issues in Human Sexuality'

Christina Beardsley

This chapter is a revised and updated version of my article[1] critiquing 'Transsexualism', Chapter 7 of the House of Bishops' document Some Issues in Human Sexuality. As in the original version (2005), I note its lack of engagement with transgender people, their clinicians and the relevant scientific literature. I also discuss more recent developments, including the discovery that, in 2003, the House of Bishops agreed that belief in the legitimacy of a change of gender is a theologically acceptable position in the Church of England. Their decision is not widely known and was omitted from Some Issues.

For some believers, the Bible and the Christian tradition possess a timelessness and certainty denied to scientific research, with its dependence on shifting theories which are likely to be disproved or overtaken. What if new learning were to lead into an intellectual cul-de-sac rather than a genuine advance in understanding? Such caution is apparent in *Some Issues in Human Sexuality* (House of Bishops 2003). Bishop Richard Harries, Chairman of the House of Bishops Working Group, explains in his Foreword that the document 'works within the parameters' of the 1991 House of Bishops document, *Issues in Human Sexuality* and was not intended to alter the position taken there (House of Bishops 2003: ix).

Despite this limitation, the authors made an ambitious attempt to review some of the relevant theological literature on sexuality and gender that had appeared in the intervening years. They also acknowledged a societal shift from a concern with the special needs of lesbian and gay people, to the broader spectrum of lesbian, gay,

---

1   First published in *Theology* (2005), CVIII, 845: 338–46. Revised, updated and reproduced here with permission.

bisexual and transgender (LGBT) people, by including chapters on Bisexuality and Transsexualism. This chapter focuses mainly on the discussion of 'Transsexualism' (Chapter 7), but begins with some general observations, and briefly comments on 'Homosexuality and biblical teaching' (Chapter 4) and 'Gender identity, sexual identity and theology' (Chapter 5).

General observations

Although the document engages with what it describes, uncritically, and with little explanation, as 'traditional' and 'revisionary' approaches, it tends to 'reply' to the latter in an attempt to 'settle' the arguments. However, authors like Boswell (1980), Countryman (1988) and Vasey (1995) – self-identified gay men, writing from personal experience, as well as scholars – produced some of the more creative theological work in the area of sexuality at that time, and the literature has grown enormously since then.

It is, in any case, difficult to achieve closure in historical research. As *Some issues* observed (House of Bishops 2003 185-6), Alan Bray had noted the anachronism, both of Boswell's study on Christian same-sex liturgies, and the arguments of his critics; but Bray's own research on this topic, which took it to another level, appeared as *The Friend* (2003) in the very same year *Some Issues* was published. The appeal to history is important but the document appears unbalanced, in Anglican terms, in the weighting it gives to Tradition, which is so notoriously difficult to 'pin down' historically: as mid-nineteenth century Tractarians and Evangelicals discovered when both appealed to the Patristic period and the English Reformation in their controversies only to reach different conclusions.

It is also less certain than the document assumes, that the recent 'tradition' of the Church of England has been negative to homosexuality. Rather, the Church as an institution has chosen to ignore, or suppress, a more sympathetic episcopal and parochial pastoral policy that found expression in two Board of Social Responsibility Working Party reports, published in 1970 and 1979. The former was not widely circulated; the latter is known as 'the Gloucester Report', after its chairman, the then Bishop of Gloucester, John Yates. Both are discussed by Coleman (1980: 215f, 265-272). Like 'the Osborne Report' (1989) – named after the Revd June Osborne, (now Dean of Salisbury) who chaired the working party – which was prepared for the House of Bishops prior to the 1988 Lambeth Conference, and adopted a generous approach, they are evidence of an affirming strand within the modern Anglican 'tradition' that has been deliberately obscured. Indeed, the Osborne Report was immediately embargoed and only made available twenty-three years later in January 2012 (Thinking Anglicans 2012).

Another imbalance is the document's apparent preference for Scripture and Tradition as its twin building blocks. 'Reason' too has carried significant weight in Anglicanism, particularly in ethical discussions in modern times, where openness to scientific truth and research has been especially valued. However, there is in this document – or perhaps this is due to its 'fairness' to all shades of opinion – a distinct obscurantism with regard to the prevailing medical and psychological verdicts on homosexuality and transsexuality.

The document has a frustrating circularity, partly stemming from its attempt to apply the Bible passages that supposedly refer to homosexuality to the current situation. The document regards the Bible as a record of the gracious love of God, and a guide for life for human beings in the light of that love. However, the Broad Church tradition, stemming from Coleridge, shattered the illusion of the Bible as a prescriptive book containing detailed instructions. As F.W. Robertson (1874: 114-115) wrote in 1852 'Christianity is a spirit – it is a set of principles, and not a set of rules… A principle is announced; but the application of that principle is left to each man's (sic) conscience.'

The document claims to be 'a guide to a debate'. Yet what it portrays as genteel discussion was one of the most painful episodes in recent Anglican history, and there is scant recognition of the anger, anguish and turmoil spawned by Church of England (and Anglican Communion) policy in this area as recounted by Johnson (1994: 152-167) and evidenced by Fletcher (1990). The Church of England has made up its mind about its gay clergy on a number of occasions, but prior to the Marriage (Same Sex Couples) Act 2013, did not act publicly on those decisions, leading to a sense of paralysis and hurt on every side of the argument. Nevertheless, this impasse suggested unease with the idea of the Bible as a moral rulebook, and its misuse for homophobic and transphobic purposes, combined with unwillingness to confront such usage.

In spite of greater openness since the General Synod debate of 1987, it remains problematic for LGBT clergy, in particular, to speak from their own experience without risking censure. The foreword contains a quotation from an Anglican statement on the nature of dialogue (House of Bishops 2003: x), but genuine dialogue on these matters seems rare and is only now being addressed comprehensively by the Church of England through its Shared Conversations, and the diocesan meetings that began in 2015. *Some Issues* lacks the diocesan level engagement envisaged by *Issues*, and is thus yet another document 'about' LGBT people. Its effect has been particularly disempowering for LGBT people, and it was troubling to learn that the working group chose not to consult several people with relevant experience and knowledge – including eminent medical practitioners – even though commended by fellow bishops.

Despite these faults, the document continues to be cited in relation to the current context, notably by the *Report of the House of Bishops Working Group on human sexuality* (House of Bishops 2013) – 'the Pilling Report' named after is chairman, Sir Joseph Pilling – which states (**38**) that the 'important theological and pastoral issues' raised by transgender and intersex people were beyond its remit, and referred readers to *Some issues* where it claimed some of these are outlined.

Homosexuality and biblical teaching

It is unhelpful to say that the consensus among biblical scholars favours a 'traditional' and negative estimate of homosexuality in the standard biblical texts without stating the background of the authors concerned. The writers' own perspectives would seem to be relevant in weighing this claim.

The most startling and significant omission in this section is any reference to Jesus' own interpretation of the meaning of Sodom – Matthew 10:14, 15; 11:24; Mark 6:11; Luke 10:10-12 – which, according to Boswell (1980: 93ff), following Bailey (1955) and others, and assuming Marcan priority, is more to do with *hospitality and welcome* than sexual misconduct. Even Coleman (1980: 102ff) – who is more cautious, having reviewed inter-testamental interpretations – acknowledges that Jesus' focus in these passages is the rejection of the message. It is puzzling that our Lord's own words on this subject were ignored in this chapter: 'And whosoever shall not receive you, nor hear you, when ye depart thence, shake off the dust under your feet as a testimony against them. Verily, I say unto you, it shall be more tolerable for Sodom and Gomorrah in the day of judgement than for that city' (Mark 6:11).

Further information was also required to support the assumption that the Church's blessing of same-sex couples would undermine its teaching on marriage (**8.4.63**), a view that the Church of England has continued to maintain into the new era of same-sex civil marriage, without Synodical debate, and with serious repercussions for its LGBTI clergy and laity.

Gender identity, sexual identity and theology

This is the most satisfactory section of the document, partly because, as a historical survey, it feels more grounded than the other chapters. It might have been richer still had the authors consulted *How Sex Changed* (2002) by Joanne Meyerowitz which describes, not merely the social challenge to the rigid binary concept of gender prevalent in the nineteenth century, but how research into genetics and the development of the human foetus began to reveal the bi-gender potential of each person. These scientific advances made it possible for gender therapists like Harry Benjamin and others to persuade the medical profession to intervene with hormones and surgery in cases where people's bodies showed no evident pathology.

The authors are aware that gender – 'masculine' and 'feminine' characteristics and behaviour – is increasingly perceived as culturally and socially constructed (**5.3.21**) and that biological sex too has a history (**5.3.30**). Like Meyerowitz, they describe the historical shift from the idea of the female as an inferior male (the one sex model) to the Enlightenment vision of two distinct and complementary sexes (the two sex model), which increasingly confined middle class women to the private sphere, and its subsequent erosion by women's emancipation and the rise of feminism. However, Meyerowitz emphasises that research on the human body paralleled these social changes, and affected concepts of gender identity, as increasing numbers of scientists challenged the idea of separate and opposite sexes. Male and female began to be seen as ideal types, with actual men and women somewhere in between, and it was gradually acknowledged that every male has aspects of the female, and every female aspects of the male, not just in terms of masculine and feminine traits, but on the basis of biological sex.

> In its earliest stages the human embryo did not manifest its sex, and in its later development its sexual differentiation remained partial. The similarities of male and female reproductive organs seemed to reveal their common origins: testis resembled ovary, and penis resembled clitoris. All males maintained vestiges of the female (nipples and rudimentary breasts), and all females

retained vestiges of the male. The embryonic Müllerian duct, which developed into fallopian tubes, uterus, and vagina in the woman, remained undeveloped in the man, and the Wolffian body and duct, which developed into the vas deferens, seminal vesicle, and epididymis in the man, remained undeveloped in the woman. These were not 'dead vestiges', one scientist noted, but 'latent dispositions' (Meyerowitz 2002: 21-23).

Transsexualism

Chapter 7, like the other chapters, begins with quotations from those affected but they are incorrectly referenced.[2] These are said to be authentic voices 'from the debate', assuming that there is a debate on transsexualism as a condition, as distinct from the question of its acceptability amongst Christians. That this is a doubtful assumption is demonstrated by the next section, **7.2**, 'The nature of transsexualism' which is mainly a summary of the views of moral theologians on this subject, rather than what it claims to be. It has no accounts of the experiences of transsexual people; nothing from the practitioners treating them; nothing about the role of Gender Identity clinics; and there is no mention of the American Psychiatric Association's *Diagnostic and Statistical Manual Volume* (then in its fourth, currently in its fifth edition), and its role in the diagnosis of Gender Dysphoria. There is no reference to the Harry Benjamin Guidelines, now renamed the WPATH, World Professional Association for Transgender Health *Standards of Care*, and only one, oblique, reference to the 'Real Life Test' or 'Real Life Experience', but nothing about its significance for transsexual people. There is no indication of the numbers of people affected; no statistics on success outcomes; and little information about research into a physiological cause of transsexualism (except by way of the Evangelical Alliance report at **7.2.13**).

Nor does the chapter refer to *Transsexualism: The Current Medical Viewpoint* (1996a) produced for the Parliamentary Forum on Transsexualism in 1996 by Dr Russell Reid of the Hillingdon Hospital, Dr Domenico di Ceglio of the Tavistock Clinic, Mr James Dalrymple of London Bridge Hospital, Professor Louis Gooren of the University of Amsterdam, Professor Richard Green of the Gender Identity Clinic, Charing Cross Hospital and Professor John Money of Johns Hopkins

---

2   The fourth quotation, by Georgina Everingham (2000: 4), is misattributed to Parakaleo Ministries, and the third, by Parakaleo Ministries, is misattributed to Georgina, something neither would welcome.

Hospital, USA, which states that 'the weight of current scientific evidence suggests a biologically-based, multi-factorial aetiology for transsexualism' (Reid et. al 1996a: **6.7**). A further serious omission is any reference to the article 'A sex difference in the human brain and its relation to transsexuality,' by J N Zhou, M A Hofman, L Gooren and D F Swaab, (1995: 68-70) which 'shows a female brain structure in genetically male transsexuals and supports the hypothesis that gender identity develops as a result of an interaction between the developing brain and sex hormones.' Nor is there mention of the article, 'Male To Female Transsexual Individuals Have Female Neuron Numbers In The Central Subdivision Of The Bed Nucleus Of The Stria Terminalis' (Kruijver et al. 2000).

Given that it lacks the grounding of transsexual people's experience it is hardly surprising that it feels somewhat disembodied. It is ironic therefore that it should reproduce Oliver O'Donovan's belief that there is a parallel between the claims of transsexual people and Gnosticism, on the grounds that both share a similar misguided philosophy of the material creation (**7.3.10**). The similarity between Gnosticism and transsexualism is repeated at **7.4.10** and **7.4.22**, and there is something disturbing about this attempt to identify a contemporary 'issue' – to use the document's terminology – with an ancient 'heresy', as it immediately imputes 'error' to the transsexual person. Gnosticism was a notoriously varied and complex phenomenon but one common feature was its adherents' claim to possess a secret or esoteric knowledge, or 'gnosis,' into which neophytes could be initiated by various rituals. This is hardly a helpful parallel to what is essentially a matter of individual consciousness, namely the transsexual person's unease with their assigned gender.

This unease, or gender dysphoria, more accurately describes transsexual people's experience than the notion 'that they have a body of the wrong biological sex' (**7.3.7**), albeit some transsexual people's narratives have spoken of feeling 'trapped in the wrong body'. The transition journey, in which the subject's body is subtly, or dramatically, changed by hormones and surgery, is not a Gnostic rejection of the body, or denial of its importance, but a quest for fuller embodiment. Indeed, after starting on hormones, people frequently say things like, 'It was as if my body had been longing for these and was at last being satisfied.'

What is apparent is that transsexual people may be tempted to deploy the negative effects of the mind/body dualism, prevalent in

Western society, to live in the mind rather than the body, as a way of avoiding or denying their situation; a tendency reinforced by the lack of embodiment in certain Christian attitudes to sexuality.

One of the biblical passages that the document considers relevant to transsexualism is Genesis 1-2, but handled in a manner that has prompted Adrian Thatcher (2010: 22-3) to argue that verses are being forced to bear a weight of interpretation never intended by the original writers. The circularity of the report's method is particularly apparent in the pivotal role accorded to Genesis 1.26-27, whose reference to 'male' and 'female' is assumed to denote self-evident concepts that support the authors' preconceived ideas about marriage and gender. Thus, the apparently open 'Questions about the Bible' at **7.4.8** have already been firmly closed at **7.4.4** to **7.4.6**. The biblical material on eunuchs is mentioned briefly (**7.3.3**, **7.3.28**, **7.4.8**), but more could have been said about why transsexual people have identified with it, and its message of inclusion.

One of the most damaging aspects of Chapter 7 is when it reproduces the views of those who deny that people can change gender, and who maintain that the person concerned must continue to be referred to by their birth gender. In therapeutic terms this is recognised as completely undermining and was the principal medical reason for the campaign to allow birth certificates to be changed. To quote psychiatrist, Dr Russell Reid (1996b: **5.3** & **5.4**):

> Quite simply, the lack of an appropriate legal status means that the patient is in the constant situation of having to believe two quite opposite things about themselves at the same time, that on the one hand they are female and that on the other hand they are male. This is a massive assault on their sense of self, their well-being and, potentially, on their mental stability... To be constantly reminded of one's past history and diagnosis is therapeutically counterproductive and militates against the acceptance of body image and the resolution of their new gender role. Possible consequences are distress and despair, leading to clinical depression, with social withdrawal, diminished self-worth and self-esteem.

The assumption at **7.3.16** that a transsexual person 'chooses' his or her gender identity is ill-conceived. As far as the person is concerned their gender identity is perceived as given (even God given, see

8.6.11); the problem is that the development of their body (especially at puberty) has not conformed to their identity.

The emphasis on the body as the God-given element in gender identity in the document – which quotes the Evangelical Alliance report, Oliver O'Donovan's booklet and a letter by the Roman Catholic ethicist Luke Gormally – means that transsexual people would be encouraged to marry and have children, even though the intransigent nature of their condition can result in the future breakup of marriage and family, and is one of the most painful possible outcomes of transition.

As many transsexual people have married, and some remain with their life partners after transition, it is untrue (and offensive) to suggest, as George Woodall does, that a transsexual person 'is not adequately integrated to the minimum degree necessary to be capable of living out a married life' in their acquired gender (**7.3.46**). A similar argument is put forward at **8.6.13** with regard to the ordination of transsexual people, whereas, in fact, in terms of treatment, the supervising psychiatrist is looking for psychological integration and stability to ensure that the individual can handle the rigours of exchanging one gender role for another. To quote Russell Reid (1996b: **5.2**) again:

> The success rate for treatment of transsexualism is very high and the medical treatment which they receive enables the majority of individuals to live an otherwise quite normal, unremarkable life... The typical patient works through this difficult and lengthy medical agenda with courage, patience and dignity.

As this quotation illustrates, the psychiatric perspective on transsexualism can highlight the spiritual dimension of gender transition, a topic that is also missing from Chapter 7. To negotiate and cross a gender boundary involves not only 'transcending' certain aspects of physical reality, but exploring a frontier or edge of life where, as in other instances, the numinous is often encountered. After decades of social exclusion, transsexual people are finding their voice and articulating the spirituality of their journey. Some relate to the growing number of historical and cross-cultural studies of 'third-gender' people, which the document alludes to when it mentions the Indian Hijra – 'male eunuchs who live as women ... and often thought of as possessing supernatural powers' (**7.2.9**) – but does not pursue further.

Some transsexual people with a mental history of depression and suicidal tendencies, who then transition, go on to enjoy productive employment and a stable social life in a transformation that corresponds remarkably to baptismal language of rebirth and resurrection. Most transsexual people also choose, or are 'given,' a new name to match their gender identity, which has parallels to Scripture and the religious life, where a person's name is changed to signify a fresh start. These themes could have been explored. It is also disappointing that the document omitted to mention the role of the Sibyls in promoting Christian spirituality amongst transgender people, and its valued programme of retreats and pastoral care.

Although the Sex Discrimination (Gender Reassignment) Regulations of 1999 improved the employment rights of transsexual people, those who transitioned prior to that date risked unfair dismissal, and gender reassignment can still involve rejection by family, friends, churches, colleagues, and, even now, employers. Similarly, although the mass media have greatly encouraged acceptance and understanding, through well-researched documentaries and sympathetic storylines, some transsexual people retain a sense of living on the margins.

One might have expected some reflection on the impact of social exclusion in a chapter on this subject, especially as it was to feature prominently in the parliamentary debate on the Gender Recognition Bill in 2004. In that forum the scientific arguments were eloquently presented by Lord Winston, and a huge majority gave transsexual people in the United Kingdom the right – following a due process of recognition of their 'acquired' gender – to change their birth certificates and to marry someone of the opposite sex.

In contrast to its response to the Marriage (Same Sex Couples) Bill, the Church of England did not object to such marriages taking place in its churches. In this instance the House of Bishops was publicly divided, though only fairly recently has it emerged (Beardsley 2013: 18) that in 2003, the House not only discussed a draft of *Some Issues*, but ruled on the dilemmas posed in Chapter 7. This decision, which is still not widely known, states that, among the range of views in the Church about transsexualism, two positions 'could properly be held'. One was that 'some Christians concluded on the basis of Scripture and Christian anthropology that … 'gender reassignment' and 'sex change' were really a fiction', and the second was that 'others were persuaded' in response to 'profound and persistent' indications 'that medical intervention ... was legitimate and the result could properly be termed a change of gender.'

It is regrettable that this decision was not communicated in Chapter 7 of *Some Issues*, which gave the impression of a theological impasse over transsexualism, whereas both, albeit contrary, theological positions had been approved by the House of Bishops. Meanwhile, the House initiated the discussions with the Lord Chancellor's Department which eventually secured the exemption that clergy with conscientious objections need not celebrate a marriage if they 'reasonably believe that the person's gender has become the acquired gender under the Gender Recognition Act 2004.'

Chapter 7 of *Some Issues in Human Sexuality* signalled an end to 'the transsexual hiatus' that had prevailed in Church discussions of sexuality and gender, but its emphasis on Scripture and Tradition, and neglect of Reason, precluded consideration of transgender people's experience, and a growing body of scientific and historical evidence in favour of its validity.

Chapter 7

Trans Awareness Group Discussion and Report, May 2008:
A response to 'Transsexualism' (Chapter 7) in the House of Bishops' discussion document 'Some Issues in Human Sexuality'

Participants/Authors: Jean Boothby, Rev Elizabeth Bunker, Morven Fyfe, Jen Lynch, Anne Passmore, Stephen Passmore

In 2005 a local church ran a series of 'hot topic' discussions, one of which focussed on transgender issues. A group was formed from those attending that discussion in order to explore the issues further. This is a re-written summary of their report, produced by the editors, in liaison with the group facilitators.

Introduction

A transsexual person is someone whose gender identity is different to that of their biological sex. Transgender is an umbrella term covering a range of gender variant behaviour, ranging from someone who cross-dresses occasionally through to the transsexual person who undergoes gender reassignment and lives as a member of the sex opposite to their biological birth sex. Gender reassignment is a complex process involving legal changes and medical treatment. Some people who undergo gender reassignment prefer to refer to themselves as transgender rather than transsexual to indicate that the main issue is about gender not sex.

The primary aim of the Group was to raise awareness and understanding of transgender issues among its own members with a view to becoming an awareness raising resource in the parish and, ultimately perhaps, the deanery and diocese. As a starting point the Group explored the 'Critical questions raised by the debate about transsexualism' (House of Bishops 2003: 243) in Section 7.4 of Chapter 7 'Transsexualism' of *Some Issues in Human Sexuality*. After that, the Group considered related topic areas.

The reporting in this chapter reflects the order of *Some Issues in Human Sexuality* to assist cross-referencing and the development of the discussion in the Group's meetings. The summary of discussions has been kept brief.

Discussion of Questions from Some Issues in Human Sexuality

What it means to be a person (paragraphs 7.4.2 – 7.4.6)

The Group agreed there were many aspects to being a person: spiritual, physical, mental, emotional, interdependency on others. Being made in the image of God encompassed qualities and characteristics rather than mere physical characteristics. God is multi-faceted and so embraces all aspects of what is found in humankind.

It was agreed that Western society emphasises conformity to bi-polar gender roles, which results in children making the distinction at an early age, but that this rigid expectation also creates suffering for trans children.

Initial discussions clarified that the terms 'sex' and 'gender' had different meanings and should not be used interchangeably. Exploratory debate suggested that 'sex' relates to biological characteristics, such as genitalia, chromosomes and physical appearance, while 'gender' relates to definitions of masculinity and femininity; gender being more behavioural than biological and related to societal roles. Intersex is a term describing people whose biological sex is ambiguous.

The Divine Order (paragraph 7.4.7)

In considering 'What constitutes the sex given to us by God?' (House of Bishops 2003: 244) the Group looked at a summary of work done in the 1950s and 1960s by Dr John Money, showing variables in sex and gender (Money and Ehrhardt 1972). It was noted that while sex was biological, gender was related to a person's role in society and that gender identity was an issue of self-perception.

Genesis 1.27 asserts 'Male and female he created them' (RSV). Given current medical understanding, the presentation of Adam and Eve as examples of male and female perfection seems over-simplistic today. Seeing everybody as a blend of male and female is still consistent with the concept of the image of God, and with Genesis 1.27. Sex and gender variation is a form of natural diversity rather than an illness.

Because intersex and trans people exist, they have been created by God, and it is important for trans people to be true to their God-given gender. Treatment to align the body to one's gender identity can be compared to repairing a heart defect to improve the quality of life.

Gender dysphoria was not a consequence of the fallen-ness of creation. Medical evidence suggests that it is part of the natural diversity of creation. Society's inability to accept and embrace diversity is a consequence of fallen-ness.

There was concern that the questions in the Bishops' document were framed to invite a negative response rather than open exploration. It was noted that Chapter 7 had been written without medical references and was not appropriately contextualised.

The Bible (paragraph 7.4.8)

Chapter 2 of the document was seen as densely written in a way that did not encourage open debate. In studying the Bible it is important to have a consistent approach, taking into account both the original meaning of the text and its interpretation for today's society.

The context of Bible passages is relevant when considering transgender issues and attitudes. The dimorphic distinction in Genesis 1-2 was offering an ideal and predates modern scientific understanding of reproduction or genetics.

The cross-dressing prohibition in Deuteronomy 22.5: 'A woman shall not wear anything that pertains to a man, nor shall a man put on a woman's garment,' (RSV) was intended to distinguish the Israelites from other tribes who practised cross-dressing fertility rites and temple prostitution (Brown 1990: 104). The rule is located within a collection of laws, including a prohibition on the use of wool/linen mix cloth for ordinary people (Deuteronomy 22.11 RSV). Few would consider this binding today, when mixed fibres (e.g. polyester/cotton or wool/lycra) are commonplace and accepted. Similarly, it is acceptable for women to wear trousers in most cultures today

Eunuchs were originally despised because of their inability to procreate, but by the time of Isaiah eunuchs were included in the worshipping community. Just as the Ethiopian eunuch was seen as a Christian once he had submitted to baptism (Acts 8), so too should transgender people be welcomed equally.

The healing of lepers and their restoration into the community, at a time when lepers were segregated out of fear, has parallels with transgender people, as well as people with HIV.

Trans people themselves had different perspectives about their own situation.   Some see themselves as a biological error or a 'mistake of nature'; while others feel that their transgender status is intended by God:

> For thou didst form my inward parts,
> Thou didst knit me together in my mother's womb.
> I praise thee, for thou art
> Fearful and wonderful.
> Wonderful are thy works!
> (Psalm 139, 13-14. RSV)

Medical Intervention (paragraphs 7.4.9 – 7.4.15)

The lack of understanding shown in the Bishops' document about medical treatment, with its implication that this is a one-step change by a single operation, is a cause for concern. Gender Reassignment is a process, involving legal changes (of name and gender), as well as medical treatment (including lifelong sex hormone treatment and surgery).

No reference was made to intermediate treatments such as electrolysis and speech therapy, which are usually essential for trans women. Although there is often a single (major) operation for trans women to reconfigure the genitals, for trans men there are three distinct stages of surgery: mastectomy, hysterectomy and phalloplasty, which itself requires a number of distinct operations. It is worth noting that while most trans women do want genital surgery, for trans men the situation is different. Most trans men want mastectomy but many decide not to proceed with phalloplasty, either because the end product is not satisfactory, or for ideological reasons: 'I don't need a penis to be a man' (Lee Gale)[1].

The Bishops' document seems to imply that the only permissible psychological help that should be available would be to condition the person to live as a member of their biological birth sex. The Group

1   'Love It' magazine, 12-18 June 2007, p24-25

argued that a holistic approach to treatment is necessary, including counselling to identify the appropriate path for each person on an individual basis. Some trans people need counselling to come to terms with past bad experiences to do with being trans (i.e. psychological healing to enable the trans person to live successfully in their realised identity). Such counselling may be beneficial either before or after transition. Concerning the ethics of surgery, comparison was made with people who suffer psychologically because of prominent ears, for example, for whom corrective surgical intervention is regarded as acceptable.

In deciding whether it is appropriate to use NHS resources for transgender surgery, the key criterion is post-operative quality of life. Medical opinion is that treatment by hormones and surgery is for many people the best option:

> Studies which have been carried out indicate that a treatment model using the principles described above is highly successful, with some suggesting up to a 97% success rate (Reid 1996: 6).

The Bishops' document stated that transition 'destroys the capacity of the post-operative transsexual to have children' (House of Bishops 2003: 247). That the loss of reproductive capacity is a problem assumes that the transgender person would have become a parent had they remained in their birth sex, but the ability to bear/father a child is not guaranteed. If the loss of eggs or sperm is the issue, medical technology can now harvest these for use by the self or others.

There were concerns about the impact on children whose parent was 'persuaded' to remain in their birth sex, marry and reproduce as a 'cure'. The cure approach is adopted by Parakaleo Ministry whose mission statement reads: 'The ministry mentors those seeking to re-establish their God given gender identity and destiny' (Parakleo 2008). Although this appears to be welcoming, and to support open exploration, the organisation's focus is to encourage people to remain in their birth sex and to actively discourage them from exploring all options available, as the Parakaleo ministry equates 'God given gender identity' with birth sex and asserts on the *Frequently Asked Questions* section of its website that: 'Christians should be willing to support in every possible way the struggles of transsexual people to accept their true birth sex'.

In many cases, people who have attempted such a 'cure' have sought reassignment later, with consequently greater disruption and distress to their spouses and children, than would have been the case had they not been persuaded to marry and have children.

Marriage[2] and Birth Certificates (paragraph 7.4.16)

The Gender Recognition Act 2004 became law after publication of the Bishops' document, and the Group reviewed a summary of its provisions, noting the opt-out clause permitting Church of England clergy to refuse to marry anyone they suspected of holding a Gender Recognition Certificate (later extended by Statutory Instrument 2005 No.54 to cover ministers of all religions) (Crown 2005). The Gender Recognition Certificate (GRC) gives full legal status in the 'acquired gender' and the replacement birth certificate issued is in the standard format.

The Bishops' document talks about the 'pre-operative transsexual'. It was felt that this terminology was unclear, as it seemed to be used by the document only to refer to a person living in their birth gender, but the term could equally apply to a trans person with a GRC who had not undergone any surgery. Surgery is not a mandatory condition for the granting of a GRC.

The Bishops' document suggests that a Christian marriage is only valid if it can produce children, which is a concern. While children are one aspect of Christian marriage, they are not an inevitable consequence and the emphasis on procreation has shifted in modern society. This belongs to a much wider debate, and such a view would also militate against the marriage of the elderly, infertile men, and women who have had a hysterectomy; the Group did not consider this was what the Bishops' document wished to imply, and thus its argument seemed to start from a false premise.

Transsexual People in the Life of the Church (paragraph 7.4.17)

A guest speaker who was a trans priest was invited for this section. The difference in protective legislation for religious and secular employees was highlighted. The Church of England claimed exemption from compliance with equal opportunities legislation, which permitted it to dismiss an employee on grounds of sex, marital status, disability, race, colour, nationality, ethnic origin, religion,

---

2   Superseded by the Marriage (Same Sex Couples) Act 2013.

sexual orientation or age, all of which would be illegal for a secular employer. In secular employment, decisions made by civil courts create binding precedents on other courts, whereas decisions made by a Bishop are not binding on other Bishops.

The Evangelical Alliance's position, that trans people could not be priests because their lifestyle set a 'wrong' example for their congregations seemed incomprehensible to the Group. It appeared to be linked to the Old Testament requirement of priestly physical perfection (Leviticus 21:16-24), which is at odds with modern attitudes to clergy with physical disabilities. Indeed, a trans priest could be seen as a positive role-model to other trans people.

The baptism, confirmation and communion status of trans people was also raised, and has parallels with the status of divorced people within the Church. It is important to recognise the love of God in the situation and to value the person as an individual and for what they have to offer the Church. Debarring trans people who are leading a devout Christian life from the sacraments seems un-Christian, and contrary to Acts 10:15: 'What God has made clean, you must not call profane' (NRSV).

To support pre- and post-operative transsexual people three concepts were identified:

1. Willingness to listen
2. Recognising the person's need to talk about their situation
3. Emphasising loving and caring for one another at all times (e.g. respectful use of the correct gender pronoun).

Transsexual people pose a challenge for churches seeking to support them, as do congregation members who are uncomfortable with something outside their own experience (and perhaps wanting to leave the Church), who may need pastoral support themselves.

Discipleship (paragraphs 7.4.18 – 7.4.22)
'What does it mean for a transsexual person to live in obedience to Christ?' This is the same for all Christians, whether transgender or not:

1. Love God
2. Love your neighbour
3. Prepare to be changed (2 Corinthians 5.17) 'So if anyone is in Christ, there is a new creation;' (NRSV)

The document considered whether obedience involving accepting a given biological identity or whether seeking a 'new post-operative identity', (House of Bishops 2003: 249) was acceptable, thereby ignoring that surgery was not the only change in external appearance, and failing to acknowledge that gender identity is retained after transition, with the body altered to address social perceptions and expectations.

In terms of what constitutes our God-given identity, the document's assertion that 'our bodies are part of who we are,' (House of Bishops 2003: 249) appears to imply that a psychological male in a female body is a valid identity. Unfortunately, society cannot accept the dichotomy, and an insistence on conformity to a male or female identity limits an individual's response to God's creative potential.

The Group also queried the ultimate relevance of the body to identity.

Any consideration of theological grounds for accepting the incongruence of mind with body needed to be rooted in an understanding of the medical issues.

Topics discussed by the Group, not addressed in 'Some Issues in Human Sexuality'

Stages in the Trans Journey

Transition is a process with several stages:

Social change: telling family and friends of the decision to transition and asking them to use a new name and appropriate pronouns.

Legal/official change: formal change of name, registration with official bodies in the post-transition gender (Inland Revenue, Passport Agency, DVLC, work records, pensions, banks etc.).

Medical changes: may include hormones and/or surgeries.

Gender and sexual orientation are not interchangeable, nor are they interdependent. Gender is whether one identifies as male or female, while sexual orientation is whether one identifies as heterosexual or homosexual. Sexual orientation may change with transition, or it may stay the same but be defined differently. E.g. a biological male with a female gender identity may be sexually attracted to women and pre-transition would be defined as a heterosexual male but post-transition as a homosexual female.

Partner Issues

This meeting was led by the wife of a trans man. A number of statements from partners of trans people were presented, and how these might be responded to, was discussed. The following issues can arise for partners of trans people.

Partners are not prepared for the demands the transition process makes on them or their relationship, even where they have always recognised the core gender identity. They may not expect they will need support, but they may find that they do.

The change can be too great for some to adapt to, causing the relationship to break up.

Accepting there is a journey to be made by the partner and by the relationship itself helps some survive. This can apply whether in same-sex or opposite-sex relationships.

Lesbian partners of trans men often find their own identity threatened by being seen to be in a heterosexual relationship.

Survival may mean clinging to everyday things and going through the usual motions.

An unexpected transition, can lead to a sense of betrayal by the partner.

People whose transition involves changing home and job to start a new life can isolate the partner because of the secrecy involved.

Children

Two aspects were considered: 'trans children' (children having gender identity issues) and children in families with a parent who has transitioned.

- Trans children

Dr Domenico di Ceglie at the Portman Clinic in London runs the only clinic in the UK dealing with childhood gender dysphoria. Few children who have gender identity issues go on to transition as adults (not all tomboys are trans, so caution is needed). It is more common for children seen at the clinic to become homosexual or bisexual. Dr di Ceglie's approach to exploring gender issues with the child and its family and school was seen as positive.

Among children dealing with gender dysphoria 'suicide attempts in adolescence are frequent' (di Ceglie 2000), and this concerned the Group, because in modern society male/female gender roles were no longer rigid. Some families still have very rigid gender expectations and the issues are not entirely to do with role.

Material from the Sci:dentity project being undertaken at Goldsmiths College, University of London was also reviewed (Rooke and Gooch 2006a; 2006b). Some children do not identify as specifically male or female, but as 'gender queer': either a blend of male and female or alternatively neither male nor female. The key factor in offering support is to encourage an environment of conversation and openness

Support for trans children and their families is provided by the organisation *Mermaids*.

- Children of trans parents
An excerpt was watched from the documentary *My Mums used to be Men*, about a 9-year-old girl, Louise whose father had transitioned and was now living as a woman, and raising her, supported by a partner who was also a trans woman (Beanland 2007). The programme tried to address the bad publicity given to the family by lurid newspaper reporting. Louise seemed happy, outgoing, confident and well-adjusted, and did not see her family as 'weird' until the press intervened. Louise was not disadvantaged by having trans parents but was adversely affected by bad publicity.

Pastoral Issues within the Church
Pastoral issues were raised for trans people as well as other congregation members. The booklet *The Transsexual Person is My Neighbour: Pastoral Guidelines for Christian Clergy, Pastors and Congregations* (Beardsley 2007) was seen as useful and based on common-sense. It is helpful that such resources are available.

It is important to befriend the trans person and their family, as it is easy to overlook partners, children, etc., all of whom are affected by the transition process.

Regarding the name which should be recorded on the electoral roll: was this required to be the legal name or the baptismal name, as these would differ if the person transitioned post-baptism?

Raising awareness about transgender issues is relevant even when no trans person is known to the congregation, because it might encourage those who were afraid of their status being known to come out, or improve the welcome trans people who do come forward will receive. There can be a fear in some congregations of saying the wrong thing, or asking intrusive questions. Raising awareness to create an open environment for discussion would minimise this. Leaflets or articles in church magazines might help promote awareness of the issues and make people feel less awkward.

The Department of Health (DoH) bereavement booklet (Whittle and Turner 2007) was reviewed, and a similar set of church guidelines would be useful. The DoH guidelines raise specific issues and highlight the extra sensitivity needed:

1. A trans woman with no Gender Recognition Certificate (GRC), living as female and all other documentation female: the guidelines to mortuary staff and the coroner are to record the death as female. This may create issues if the wife has never accepted the transition and is organising the funeral and wants the trans woman referred to by the former male name. Does the officiant at the funeral use male or female name? Special pastoral care would be needed.
2. A trans woman with GRC: her death must be recorded as female and her trans status cannot be disclosed because of the legal protection surrounding GRC.

Clergy need to be clear when taking a trans person's funeral whether this can be referred to in the address. The law protects people who have a gender recognition certificate: their previous gender is confidential so that revealing it, if learned in an official capacity, is a criminal offence and carries a heavy fine (Crown 2004). However, some families will feel the trans-status is integral to the person and that it should be mentioned – this can vary from person to person. For their own protection, it was felt that clergy should obtain agreement in writing.

The group recommended the appointment of a diocesan expert who is aware of support networks and legislation and can provide advice where situations that involve trans people arise.

Recommendations

1. Religious debate needs to be in the context of modern medical and psychological understanding.
2. Willingness to be open about the issues and to encourage supportive debate.
3. The appointment of a diocesan expert with knowledge of support networks and legislation, available to advise when

situations involving trans people arise, within the legal framework of the Gender Recognition Act 2004.

4. If a member of the congregation transitions, confidential pastoral support should be offered to the individual, if required. Expertise on trans issues was less important than someone non-judgemental, open-minded and willing to listen. Such support should also be available to the partner and family (ideally with a different pastoral worker).

5. Clarification whether Church authorities require legal or baptismal name to be used on the electoral roll.

6. A guidance leaflet for clergy about the funerals of trans people.

7. Transgender issues to feature in the pastoral training of clergy and Readers.

Conclusion

While the House of Bishops' document raised a number of key issues, it had adopted a very literal view of Biblical texts without taking the historical and social contexts into account. No consultation with medical or psychological specialists to try to understand their insights into the issues appeared to have taken place. Nor was there evidence that the Bishops' working group had spoken to anybody actually affected by these issues. The document was written in a way that encourages a negative attitude to transgender people. It also failed to address issues about the pastoral care of those affected, including families and congregations.

It was recognised by the group that there had been a number of legislative changes since the House of Bishops had produced their document and further debate was still needed.

Section 3: Scientific and Other Perspectives

Chapter 8

Gender Incongruence in the changing social and medical environment

Terry Reed (Gender Identity Research and Education Society)

> *The expression of gender characteristics ... that are not stereotypically associated with one's assigned sex at birth, is a common and culturally diverse human phenomenon [that] should not be judged as inherently pathological or negative.*

This quote from the World Professional Association for Transgender Health, *Standards of Care,* Version 7 (WPATH 2012: 4) reflects the rapidly changing perceptions of what it means to be trans, non-binary or non-gender in an essentially binary, cisgender world. The discomfort experienced by those in this situation is known as 'gender dysphoria', which is described in the UK Good Practice Guidelines as *'the distress associated with the experience of one's personal gender identity being inconsistent with the phenotype or the gender role typically associated with that phenotype'* (RCPsych 2013). So, the dysphoria may be generated by the unwanted physical characteristics (phenotype) associated with the sex assigned at birth, as well as the gender expressions and social attributes commonly associated with that sex. One or both these factors come into play, to different degrees in different individuals.

Arguments continue about whether gender is a social construct or, alternatively, biologically inspired. This is to misunderstand the interface between different aspects of gender. Gender role and gender expression are certainly constructs that vary with time and place, depending on local cultural norms and mores; the social construct is alive and well. The gender identity however, is an internal matter; where this sense of self conflicts with societal norms, and remains repressed, there may be personal psychological turmoil and pain; when the gender identity is publicly expressed, the apparent conflict with the socially constructed framework may cause the individual to become stigmatized by prejudice, targeted for ridicule and vulnerable to hate crime; the individual taking this step risks losing close relationships and employment. Yet, for some it is not just a better way forward, but the *only* way forward. Suicidality is common – a conservative estimate is that 34% of trans people have attempted suicide at least once (Whittle et al. 2007). In societies that are more accepting of gender diversity, it is argued that the psychological distress of gender variant people is lessened (Connolly 2003).

So why are growing numbers[1] of people revealing that they cannot live comfortably within the binary, man/woman construct, as predicted on the basis of their birth sex? (Clark et al. 2014; EU 2014; Glen and Hurrell 2012). Until quite recently, such personal experiences were 'diagnosed' as psychiatric in origin, leading to a medical approach that was paternalistic at best, but ultimately undermined personal autonomy and, for many years, imposed an inflexible linear progression through a medical system that recognised only binary outcomes. Access to the system necessitated making prior social changes which threatened to destabilise the family, social and working lives of trans people. Yet a statement published in 2008 in the Department of Health documentation prepared by GIRES said:

> some people will regard themselves as neither man nor woman … they may regard themselves as 'gender queer' (any gender experience that is not recognised as 'typical') … clinical responses should be flexible and should recognise the personal need for some feminising or masculinising treatments, without the need to follow any one particular pathway or arrive at one specific destination (Reed et al. 2008).

---

1   The Equality and Human Rights Commission found 1% of the cohort (n=10,000) met the criteria for protection under the Equality Act 2010, (Glen and Hurrell 2012). Although these figures cannot necessarily be extrapolated to the whole population, they are supported by figures from New Zealand, where 1.2% reported being transgender (Clark et al., 2014); and the European Agency for Fundamental Rights, The Netherlands: ambivalent gender assigned male: 2.2%, assigned female: 1.9% incongruent gender identity: assigned male: 0.7% , assigned female: 0.6%; and Belgium: ambivalent gender identity: assigned male: 4.6%; assigned female: 3.2% incongruent gender identity: assigned male: 1.1% assigned female: 0.8 (EU 2014).

Nothing changed as a result of these words at that time, but over recent years the gender landscape has developed in positive ways: UK equality and human rights legislation supports transgender people, including in the delivery of treatment; the current NHS constitution emphasises patient choice, equity of access and equality of outcomes; there has been a steady liberalisation of protocols within the clinics specialising in gender treatments. The UK has not yet adopted an 'informed consent' model, but there is a better understanding of the wide variety of gender experiences outside the binary model, and more attention is now paid to the individual medical needs of trans people, including those with non-binary and non-gender identities. Crucial to the changing attitudes among providers, is the proposed revision of the International Classification of Diseases (ICD10), in which all conditions and illnesses, requiring treatment, must appear (WHO 2006).

Currently, the outmoded term 'transsexualism' still appears in the Mental and Behavioural Disorders section of the ICD, so it is categorised as a psychiatric disorder or mental illness. However, the Executive Board of the publishers, the World Health Organisation, was advised by its Working Group on LGBT service users, in May 2013, to *'abandon the psychopathological model, in favour of one that reflects current scientific evidence and best practice'* (WHO 2013). The upcoming ICD11 will re-classify and rename the condition, possibly as 'gender incongruence'.

The role of science is therefore important in enabling trans and non-binary people to access treatment, without the disempowerment of the current mental illness diagnosis. Understanding the biological correlations with gender dysphoria overcomes the dangerous myths that abuse or parenting is to 'blame', or that this is a 'lifestyle choice'; it also invalidates 'reparative therapy' approaches which endeavor to train gender variant children into social conformity – a practice now recognised, as not only unethical, but also as unsuccessful. Rather than 'correcting' the gender identity, it merely serves to heighten the dysphoria, and lower self-esteem. As mentioned above, the opposite approach, demonstrated in cultures where binary models are less rigorously followed, is seen to lessen the dysphoria.

The clearest indications that gender identity depends more on brain development, than it does on sex assignment at birth, or social influences thereafter, come from the experiences of infants whose genitalia at birth are neither clearly male nor female, owing to genetic and hormonal anomalies. These, and other cases of accidental damage to the penis, were subjected to early surgical 'correction' of the genitalia, typically achieving female appearance, regardless of karyotype (chromosomal configuration: XX female, XY male). However, children raised as girls following these surgeries did not always develop a congruent gender identity, despite the best efforts of their families and doctors to make them conform to societal norms. Their gender identity resolved independently of genital appearance and the imposed gender role, in spite of the persuasive power of these two factors (Dessens, et. al. 2005[2]; Diamond and Sigmundson 1997; Hines 2004[3]; Kipnis and Diamond 1998; Reiner 2004).

This supports the view that pre-natal sex hormones (Bao and Swaab 2011), and/or direct genetic effects (Dewing et al. 2003), have an indelible impact on brain development. Consequently, the practice of surgical intervention, in these cases, is now less often undertaken in infancy and is subject to legal challenge.

Studies on twins and on other family co-occurrences of severe gender dysphoria indicate that these are unlikely to be random, and the potential for a genetic link in a subset of these individuals is postulated (Diamond and Hawk 2003; Gooren et al. 2013; Green 2000). The comparison between monozygotic (identical) and dizygotic (fraternal) twins is especially informative, since the former have a much higher degree of concordance for permanent transition of the gender role: 33% in male monozygotic twins and 23% in female monozygotic twins, even when reared apart, compared with dizygotic twins where concordance is essentially zero. Thus a strong genetic influence is inferred. A genetic anomaly of repeat polymorphisms in the gene coding for the androgen receptor has been found in two studies on different populations of individuals identifying as women, in contradiction to their male phenotype and karyotype (Hare et al. 2008; Henningsson et al. 2005). An atypical response to testosterone in these individuals is therefore inferred.

---

2   Dessens found a much higher frequency of individuals within this group who identify comfortably as men: of 250 raised as girls, 13(5.2%) experienced female to male gender dysphoria; of 33 raised as boys, four experienced male to female gender dysphoria; therefore, it appears that of the total 283, 42 individuals must be living comfortably as men or uncomfortably as women. (These figures do not represent the whole XX, CAH population and, therefore, although interesting should be viewed with caution).

3   A very small minority of female individuals with congenital adrenal hyperplasia, who have been raised as girls, choose to live in adulthood as males (estimates range from about 1% to about 3%).

Certain chromosome disorders, for instance XXY, and XYY, in those with male phenotype, are associated with a raised incidence of individuals who identify as women (Diamond and Watson 2004; Snaith et al. 1991). Additionally, low androgen input to an XY fetus associated with medication to the pregnant mother, is linked with a raised incidence of individuals assigned male at birth, later identifying as women (Dessens et al. 1999).

Hearing in the cis male and female populations is hard-wired differently: male hearing has distinct right ear advantage, whereas female hearing has left ear advantage, but is more balanced between the left and right ears, than male hearing. A study on hearing in trans individuals found that trans women's hearing, despite being assigned male at birth and usually raised as boys, is significantly different from cis males and, in fact, resembles the cis *female* pattern (Govier et al. 2010). The same study also confirmed previous studies that demonstrated a marked correlation with non-right-handedness in both trans men and trans women (Green and Young 2001; Zucker et. al. 2001). In addition, trans women have been shown to have physiological responses to specific odours that reflect their gender identity, in contradiction to their male karyotype and sex assigned at birth (Burglund et al. 2008).

Three post-mortem studies have been carried out on small cohorts of individuals who, in life, had experienced their gender identity as being incongruent with their phenotype. In these individuals, unlike the control subjects, small nuclei in the brain, known to be sex-dimorphic, have been shown to have neural differentiation in opposition to genital and gonadal characteristics (Garcia-Falgueras and Swaab 2008; Zhou et al. 1995; Kruijver et al. 2000). Professor Louis Gooren, in his affidavit to the court in the Bellinger v Bellinger case in 2000, argued that the Zhou et al. brain studies cited in the peer-reviewed journals, *Nature*, and *Clinical Endocrinology* 'substantiate the hypothesis' that people experiencing gender dysphoria are 'intersexed at brain level and deserve the same medical care as other intersexed patients' (McNab 2000; Thorpe and Walker 2001: paragraph 30). Recent scans of the white matter of the brains of untreated trans men indicate that their neural patterns are masculinised, and appear male in three of the four levels scanned (Rametti et al. 2011a): white matter in the brains of untreated trans women, is shown to be feminised and significantly different from both male and female controls at all four levels scanned (Rametti et al. 2011b).

In sum, the science indicates that the binary sex and gender models are far from universal. Nature loves variety, and variations in the brain are just a small part of human diversity. It is clearly demonstrated that, in a few individuals, some aspects of brain development are not consistent with genital appearance, or with the gender of rearing, although these factors, and the resultant social pressures, undoubtedly shape and modify final outcomes. The likelihood of such inconsistency is shown to be enhanced where, for whatever reason, there are unusually high levels of testosterone in utero, in those assigned female, or diminished uptake of testosterone, in those assigned male. There appear to be many potential biological pathways, and these are likely to vary between one individual and another, yet it is safe to say that the condition does not result from psychopathology, nor is it a life-style choice, or some kind of whim or fantasy.

It is important to understand that the correlations outlined above, while indicating a neurobiological basis in the development of gender dysphoria, may not be used diagnostically. There will be different etiologies in different people, and there would be a risk of finding false negatives because our knowledge is still not comprehensive, and may never be. The only safe way of understanding who a person is, is to listen to them. Trans, non-binary and non-gender people are entitled to respectful and equitable treatment, regardless of their biology.

Once trans people have adjusted their lives, with or without medical assistance, they may identify as just ordinary men and women, albeit with unusual medical histories. It is surely the measure of a grown-up culture that we celebrate the diversity of our society, and support and encourage trans people, wherever they may identify on the gender spectrum, to contribute as family members, employers, employees, artists, artisans, teachers, doctors, lawyers, professionals, in all walks of life – ordinary people leading ordinary lives.

Chapter 9

Five things cis folk don't know about trans folk because it isn't on trashy TV - my right of reply

Chris Dowd

> *This contribution has arisen from many conversations with many people over the past few years. As a researcher writing his doctorate on the experiences of trans folk, I have been the recipient of lots of opinions, really weird questions and the bizarre assurance of people who have seen one trashy documentary about a sex change and feel they know everything that there is to know about trans folk. As I normally bit my tongue (although occasionally I did get on a soapbox with some socially awkward results) this is my right of reply to all of you …*

To those of us who are cisgender, we have grown up in a world where there are two loo doors marked 'men' and 'women' and we are sure which one we should use. Because we are never challenged on this assumption, we don't think there is another alternative. This system is so deeply engrained in our society that people will voluntarily queue for one loo while the other is empty because it is the 'wrong' gender.

Our assumptions have been reinforced by the Genesis creation story and by a society which teaches us that there are clear differences between men and women. One of the greatest shocks I received in my early research was that this 'normal' system isn't normal at all. The Berdache, Hijras, Sworn Virgins of Bulgaria, *Fa'afafine*, *Xanith*, Muxe are all examples of variant genders in different societies all over the world. The problem is that those of us who benefit by this binary system don't seem to question it, even when we see ourselves as radical in other respects.

Trans folk disrupt our comfortable assumptions about gender. They teach us that gender is more fluid than we would like to admit.

For many, whether a Christian is seeking to uphold a traditional interpretation of Genesis, an essentialist feminist is arguing for the uniqueness of female identity or a social conservative who believes the social advances towards the equality of women and sexual minorities are to be regretted, trans folk pose a threat to a cherished worldview. There are many unfortunate and regrettable attacks by these groups against trans folk simply because they (i.e. trans folk) exist. For many of us, it simply is that we haven't thought about gender much and respond to trans folk with curiosity tinged with a vague sense of threat.

One of the ways we have attempted to understand trans folk is to medicalise them. On many occasions I have heard gender dysphoria described as a birth defect where 'people are born in the wrong body'. After treatment the trans person is cured and they are safely on the other side of the gender binary (reaffirming that there is only male and female) and there is a happy ending to an awkward story.

Like most simplistic statements this obscures more reality than it admits. From my research I learned that transitioning isn't primarily a medical procedure but a psychological and spiritual one. All of the hard work leading up to gender transition surgery is about the trans person learning to become themselves after many years of self-repression and hiding. Most studies show that trans folk are aware of their gender dysphoria sometime between the ages of 2 and 7 (Conroy 2010; Dietert and Dentice 2013; Forcier and Johnson 2013; Futty 2010; Grossman and D'Augelli 2006; Kennedy and Hellen 2010). That means that these young people have learnt all sorts of coping strategies to avoid addressing their own feelings and hide themselves from others before they have even reached puberty. This leaves emotional wounds to be healed and behaviours that need to be changed so that an individual can thrive in their new reality.

The trans folk I interviewed went through a complex process of reconciling who they were to themselves, their families and to God. All of them had begun this process of transition long before they ever went to a gender reassignment clinic. Medical treatment was simply a physical manifestation of a change that had already happened. While transition is an important change, it was not the most profound one. Finding out who you are, resolving guilt and shame, confronting the past and starting to envision a better future are far more difficult and profound changes to personhood. The blade of a scalpel or a shot of artificial hormones can't do this.

Many of the folk I interviewed continued to heal psychologically and spiritually for many years after medical treatment concluded. Once freed, they were able to heal and create a new life. This wasn't a mechanistic medical process but rather a journey of identity. Sexuality needed to be explored and re-evaluated, previous relationships renegotiated, the past integrated and the wounds created by living a life with gender dysphoria needed to be healed. This is the work of years.

My particular research interest, the faith lives of Christian trans folk, showed that faith was also re-evaluated. My research showed an almost universal shift in religious outlook from a literalist and often narrow viewpoint to a much more expansive and generous view of God and others. A gentler, all-embracing and all loving deity replaced an angry Father God over the course of years. One of the striking findings of my research was the almost universality of forgiveness. Many of the interviewees spoke about a process of forgiving themselves and also forgiving others for the hurts incurred in the past. Many of the interviewees had recognised that the only way to completely free themselves of their pasts was through both extending and receiving forgiveness.

My other concern about medicalising trans folk is that their embrace of surgical procedures is not universal. Not all trans folk want to move from one restrictive gender identity to another. Some (particularly the younger trans folk I met) wanted changes that freed them to be the physical person that matched their identity. Some were happy to express their gender variance in non-medicalised ways or ways that did not require what we would see as full physical gender transition. Restricting a trans identity only to aspiring transsexual people or transsexual people doesn't really give a full picture of gender variance.

Closely related to this is the assumption that trans folk change gender. The original assumption of my research was that trans folk had a unique contribution to understanding the dynamics of gender. This, I assumed was because they had experienced both genders within the Church and therefore would be able to compare and contrast their experiences. What became obvious as the research progressed was that this was incorrect.

Trans folk could not tell me about the cisgender places because they were never cisgender. While they may not have recognised or accepted that they had gender dysphoria, it had always been there.

This means that their experiences were always different because their gender was never cis male or cis female.

While I completely accept that some people transition physically, I believe it is simply folk becoming who they are. What changes is the potential to express physically the spirit that already lives in a not particularly satisfactory natal body. If the aim of the gender journey is to resolve this gender dissonance, it is logical to argue that the person and their preferred gender identity pre-exists. This means trans folk don't change their gender but rather manifest their pre-existing but obscured gender.

While this may seem an excessively subtle point, I believe it is an important one. Recognising that the identity of trans folk pre-exists reframes their gender journey from becoming another identity to fully becoming themselves. This also takes out the idea that gender transition is a choice but simply a process of finding and claiming oneself. The only choice is between integrity of identity and continued disassociation from selfhood.

One of the other assumptions I frequently encountered was that trans folk always liked drawing attention to themselves. In many minds the idea of trans folk has somehow been conflated with the idea of a Drag Queen or King. There is also the assumption that trans folk (particularly trans women) are 'obvious'.

Again this wasn't borne out in my research. What I found out was the trans folk often micromanaged their behaviours so that they did not draw attention to themselves. They were acutely aware of their situation and often accepted 'solutions' to 'problems' such as using disabled facilities rather than gendered ones, or they accepted a ban on leadership and public facing ministry in churches that would have other minorities rightly screaming discrimination.

Those who were part of a regular worshipping community were keen to spare other people feeling 'uncomfortable' and went to great lengths not to endanger their often conditional acceptance in these communities. In one church, where there were a fairly large number of trans folk in regular attendance, they held a separate service once a month to celebrate their identities so as not to overwhelm the larger congregation with 'their issues'.

The people I met and interviewed were not gender rebels. They did not want to overturn binary gender, create a radical theology or challenge church systems and structures. They simply wanted to be unremarkable people worshipping quietly in church communities which valued them as fellow Christians. Their greatest ambition was to blend in, not stand out.

Another assumption was that trans folk are somehow unbiblical. A frequently quoted objection is Deuteronomy 22:5 which is a prohibition against cultic cross-dressing. While this is not the place to discuss this in detail, I would draw the distinction between someone who is wearing clothing appropriate to their identity and those who are not. I would argue that trans folk not wearing clothing appropriate to their preferred gender are more likely to be in contravention of this prohibition than those who are.

Further, I would also argue that unless we took all the Deuteronomic prohibitions seriously, including prohibitions against tattoos, eating shell fish, banking, poly cotton and Freudian therapy, it is difficult to justify this stance even if it is read literally.

The bible is full of gender variant images; women are called brothers (Romans 14:10, 1 Cor. 6:5-6,). We are all brides of Christ (Eph. 5:25-27), all part of the one body (Eph. 5:30), Paul writes of himself as a woman giving birth (Gal 4:19) and Galatians 3:28 asserts that there are no male or female but all are one in Christ Jesus.

There is also a school of thought that the biblical Eunuchs also can be included. They appear in many places in the bible including Esther, Isaiah, Matthew 19 and Acts 8. While they are gender variant folk in the Bible, I feel uncomfortable about this identification. Eunuchs were not folk who suffered gender dysphoria but slavery or childhood poverty. They were often the instruments of powerful people rising to influence and power, while trans folk are some of the most socially and economically disadvantaged people in UK society. By equating mutilated genitals with gender dysphoria this places trans identity entirely in the physical.

I would argue that the book of Job has more in common with what I observed in the narratives of my interview subjects. Job is visited with a series of inexplicable disasters where his social position, his family and his very identity are taken away. He is reduced to sitting in ash mourning his fate while friends speculate on the great sin he has committed that has visited this disaster on him.

Similarly, in the act of coming out, many trans folk I interviewed lost family members and friends. They often needed to leave their homes and their jobs. Employment became more difficult, and while it may be illegal to discriminate, this does not stop employers deciding someone does not have the right skills or are over-qualified. One person recounted that she had applied for 100 jobs in her former profession without gaining one interview. Trans folk often recounted they were asked to leave their places of worship after many years of service, or that congregations and/or ministers created such a spiritually hostile environment that they eventually left.

Just like Job's friends who gather around and speculate and blame, the few documents produced by the Church do the same thing. The two main documents, the Evangelical Alliance's *Transsexuality* and the Church of England's *Some Issues in Human Sexuality* both insist (despite all evidence to the contrary by those working clinically with trans folk and the lived experience of trans folk themselves) that transsexuality is a form of mental illness at best, and sinful wilfulness at worst. They argue that reparative therapies can restore (sic) trans folk to their acceptance of their God given natal bodies, despite every psychological and counselling professional body in the UK explicitly denouncing this practice as abusive and ineffective. Like Job's friends, both reports attempt to apply a rigid theological framework to explain something they do not understand, without once considering the problem is with the framework they are using and not the people that they are discussing (Evangelical Alliance 2000; House of Bishops 2003).

Job, in the face of this onslaught, asserts his innocence. While he professes not to understand why this has happened he continues to believe he is a good person. Just like Job, many of the interviewees continued to assert the integrity of their lives, and their belief that God had not only continued to journey with them, but that their own journeys were blessed. Trans man and theologian Justin Tanis calls transition a sacrament of becoming (Tanis 2003).

And just like Job, many of the interviews had happier endings than may have been expected from some of the difficulties that interviewees recounted. Job does not only experience restoration but abundance. Similarly many of the folk I interviewed felt that their lives were immeasurably better after coming out. Many had found the sense of peace and wholeness they had been seeking and that had prompted them to begin their gender journey. In the process they had gained a deeper, more generous and engaged spirituality.

I completely believe that the Church stands as exposed as Job's friends on the issue of trans folk. Just as this wisdom literature mocks the so-called wisdom of Job's accusers, and their clumsy theological ramblings about why Job has been afflicted, I believe that the Church, in its self-referential musings, is just as exposed. By creating theology that does not reflect on the experiences of trans folk and take heed of those with professional knowledge working with them, the Church is not only being profoundly incurious but attempting to create theology based on assumptions, fears and prejudices that have little basis in reality.

Lastly, I do not believe that trans folk are a threat to the Church. While I acknowledge that rigid interpretation of Genesis becomes impossible, we gain so much more from listening to the experiences of trans folk. The costly act of seeking to become the person that God intended us to be is seen as the aim of a Christian life. Few pay a greater cost than those trans folk in their seeking to follow God's special calling to them to integrity and wholeness. Few others have to continue to believe in a good and beneficent God (and indeed strengthen their faith) through such a time of testing. Few make enormous personal sacrifices to continue to belong to the Body of Christ even when it is refusing to hear or acknowledge the pain it has caused and remains mired in arrogance and wilful denial. And finally, trans folk show us that forgiveness of ourselves and others is the key to freeing ourselves and others from what binds us. These are powerful and profound lessons for all of us to learn. It's time for we cis folk to stop assuming and start listening. There is much to learn and so many wonderful people to meet.

Chapter 10

Taking a Different Path

Susan Gilchrist

This chapter summarises a much larger research study about neurophysiology, psychosocial development, identity, theology and Scripture, which can be found on the author's website (Gilchrist 2015). The reader is referred there to clarify points or references within this text.

Introduction

For nearly two thousand years, attitudes to homosexuality and all forms of gender and sexually variant behaviour, have been framed by the theology of the Church. This is enshrined in article 2357 of the Catechism of the Catholic Church (Catechism 1997). The intent behind this statement presumes that these activities are invariably reward driven and that they always pursue the goals of inappropriate sex[1]. This implies a cognitive continuum which uses perception, intuition, rewarding and reasoning to relate cause to effect. The psychodynamic and social learning theories developed by Freud, Piaget and others also require this framework, as they assume this cognitive continuum too.

A significant transformation in neural processing capabilities takes place at around the age of two years. Before this, development occurs in a fragmented way and without the necessary overall neural co-ordination no cognitive continuum can exist. That led proponents of the psychodynamic and social learning theories to presume that mental development at this time is limited and largely passive or reactive (Freud 1933; 1905/1915; Gruber and Voneche, Ed 1977; Strachey, Ed 1949/1994). This is totally contradicted by the neurophysiological work of Gallese (2003; 2009; 2013; Gallese and

---

1 This conclusion can be implied from the wording. However the distinction can be more clearly observed when it is related to the separate reward driven and identity driven development processes defined in the research study (Gilchrist 2015)

Sinigaglia 2011), Girard (1965/1961; 1977/1972; Girard et al. 1987), Dawkins (1989/1978) and others (Decety and Meyer 2008; Dennett 1987; Diamond 2002; Garrels 2006; Heylighen and Chielens 2009). They show that during this period innate physiologically driven forces impel development by an aggressive and contagious process. The older psychodynamic and the social learning theories of Money (1980; 1995; Money and Erhardt 1996) and others fail because the physiological forces were not acknowledged. In standard psychiatry and psychology the influence of the physiological driving forces is still ignored, and much research and literature is now being produced which assumes that no learning and development can take place without the action of a cognitive continuum at all times of life.

That exclusion is covered in the research study. Gender dysphoria is used as a case study to link the two elements. It shows that this contagious process primarily enforces the core elements of identity and personality. This means that the social learning and psychodynamic theories can only be used as overlays on what has already been formed.

A moral duality is encountered which demands the welcome of same-sex and gender variant relationships that are given in love and faithfulness while condemning those of abusive sex. This contradicts the traditional teaching of the Church, which denies the existence of identity driven conflicts and the physiological driving forces empowering them. From the scientific point of view the traditional teaching of the Church on homosexuality and on gender and sexual variation is shown to be incorrect.

It is also important to determine how the traditional teaching of the Church developed. A theological research study was undertaken using the results of the neurophysiological and psychological study to remove the veil of theological presumptions on gender and sexuality, which have dominated both Church and society for the last two thousand years. On social, scientific and theological grounds, current Church teaching on gender and sexually variant behaviour is demonstrated to be mistaken. It does not derive from the teaching of Jesus himself, coming instead from the need to gain respectability in Greco/Roman society. Why and how this happened is examined in this account.

Science

Research

There are three principal phases involved in early development. The first, which lasts up to about two years of age, is a period when no overall neural co-ordination is present. Development takes place in a fragmented way. No cognitive abilities exist which allow general concepts to be formed. During this time progress is dominated by internally generated strong and contagious forces predicted by Dawkins, Gallese, Girard and others. These involve the physiological processes of empathy, possessive imitation and inhibition. Learning and development is driven with high intensity; the major challenge to be faced is not one of explaining how learning develops, but how it can be managed in an orderly way. No goals are set. It develops through drives of compulsive acquisition and rejecting what is found to be incompatible with the reality that is pursued.

Control starts to come into force during the second phase from around two years of age when a rapid increase in neural capabilities occurs. Distant parts of the brain become linked. Instead of the development of isolated elements, the pre-frontal cortex begins to work as a single unit. There is an explosion in cognitive ability and previously formed fragmented elements of thought coalesce so that core elements of personality and identity are created.

From then on, the externally oriented and cognitively based processes of perception, intuition, rewarding and reasoning take an increasingly active role, but the internally driven physiological forces still remain. The continuing tension between the feed-forward and adventurous forces of physiology and the feedback and restraining forces of cognition provides the stimulation whereby the highest achievements of humanity can be attained[2].

I also identify a third phase, when constancy of personality is created, between the age of two and three years. The connections in the pre-frontal cortex of the brain that are used more grow stronger, and those which are not die back. As a consequence the core elements of personality and identity that have been formed become permanently and physically locked in place. The same person can be recognised over gaps of many years, and this gives the constancy of personality required to pursue an ordered life.

The research study shows that the physiological, neurological and psychological aspects of brain development form a finely tuned system where the maximum amount of individuality, possessiveness,

---

2   The analyisis is given in Gilchrist (2015)

intelligence and inquisitiveness, with the minimum degree of energy expenditure is created.

Struggles

The development of personality and identity is not a peaceful process: it results from a battle between strong opposing drives. In early development the self-reinforcing physiologically driven forces exercise unrestrained power, and their contagion means that the awareness and influence of an initial causative issue may be lost (Girard 1987). Without sufficient powers of cognition to check its direction, development during this period can be misdirected, regarding genuine corrections that should be made as obstacles to overcome; and this further strengthens the drive. The momentum created means that early development is relatively immune from outside pressures. That includes expectations of rearing and it is possible for pre-disposing factors present from birth to have an influence on the outcomes. Advantages are gained when it is part of a tuned process where the greatest possible degrees of individuality and human potential are created. Typical or atypical gender identities can therefore develop, and it is expected that a proportion of people will develop gender or sexually variant identities without any external cause.

Identification

A common process is involved in developing the core senses of identity and personality. The development of everyone's gender identity, atypical or not, proceeds in the same way.

Transsexual people develop a gender identity contrary to their biological sex, which is at least as firmly held as those whose gender identity follows a typical path. The gender identity of transsexual people should be stronger because it has always been fought for. The structural changes in the brain that take place from around the age of two years physically and permanently lock this in place. From this time a constant personality and gender identity is created.

Conventional views that explain gender and sexual variation attribute their development to the influence of pre-natal hormones (Besser et al. 2006; GIRES 2006; 2012) - see Chapter 8; male and female babies have different perspectives from birth, depending on whether testosterone gives the expected result. This pre-natal brain differentiation is taken to be the determining factor in the development of gender identification. However the initially primitive state of the pre-frontal cortex and the absence of neural integration, do not provide the co-ordination required for meaningful concepts of gender to be created at this early time.

The research study shows, instead, that the massive changes in the brain structure and the advances in neural capabilities around the age of two years are the features that enable the core senses of gender identity and personality to form.

Before this happens, two initial formation mechanisms may be involved. One comes from the momentum created by the intensity of physiologically driven forces which involve the mirror neuron system (Cattaneo and Rizzolatti 2009; Iacoboni and Geffen 2009; Keysers and Fadiga 2008; Rizzolatti and Fabbri-Destro 2010). The second is due to endocrinal influences before or near birth (Kerlin 2004; Meriggiola and Gava 2015; Minot Presentation 2005; Rosenthal 2014). Neither excludes the other. Some indication of their relative influences may come from children who have been assigned or reassigned to a gender at or close to birth: (Dessens et al 2005; Diamond and Sigmundson 1997; Diamond and Watson 2004; Kipnis and Diamond 1998; Ochoa 1998; Reiner 2004). A significant but restricted concordance is found. This indicates that gender reassignment of intersex children should never take place until they are able to decide for themselves what is right.

In both cases it is demonstrated that quorum sensing methods may be primarily responsible for creating the core gender identity. This occurs after the brain first becomes able to link the previously un-coordinated elements of thought. When a sufficient quorum of elements has formed, others follow. Identities are set by the direction taken: they are not the product of cognitive thought.

An advantage of this approach is that it can be applied to other aspects of identity and personality creation. The genetic and endocrinal influences are likely to vary according to the nature of the situation: in autism these influences may be high; in gender and sexual variation they may provide a pre-disposition, in tribal identification[3], none may exist.

Conflicts

Two types of conflict are encountered. Reward driven conflicts rely on the existence of later cognitive abilities, and focus on behaviour

---

3   The author is additionally involved in work in this area

that associates desire with reward. Identity driven conflicts arise before cognitive abilities develop, and focus on identity alone. With identity driven conflicts techniques akin to the management of alcoholism must be used. The bipolar nature of identity driven conflicts can promote the highest peaks of human achievement, as well as give rise to intense distress[4].

I indicate that conflicts associated with gender and sexual variation must be classified as identity driven conflicts. Behaviour is not the focus, and as wide a range on moral attitudes, beliefs, inclinations and responsibilities are found amongst gender and sexually variant people as within the general population.

Reward driven conflicts associated with gender and sexual desire also occur. These directly link behaviour to goals and reward. Accurately identifying the type of conflict is important because the correct methods of management are different to each other. Well-intentioned attempts to manage identity driven conflicts as though they are reward driven conflicts can be counterproductive.

Knowledge and interpretation

From the beginning of the twentieth century, psychodynamic and social learning theories came into prominence with the work of Freud and others. About fifty years later, research work on the neurophysiological processes involved in the development of personality and identity began to take effect. Amongst many practitioners and research workers the existence of this neurophysiological research has been completely ignored. That may be because of a lack of suitable case studies to link the two processes; however, gender dysphoria addresses that omission. Or, it could be the resistance due to cultural values ingrained into society by two millennia of Judaic, Christian and Islamic traditions.

What stands out in the research study is the contrast between the results of the different theories. The neurophysiological study predicts a duality. By denying such duality the traditional teaching of the Church condemns gender and sexually variant behaviour as being sinful acts. The possibility that gender and sexually variant behaviour could be engaged in for pure motives is denied by the theological approach.

---

4   See Gilchrist (2015)

Today research is still being undertaken and literature written which relies exclusively on the psychodynamic and social learning theories to interpret their results. It is assumed that no other processes are involved. The research study shows that this assumption is incorrect. It is demonstrated that the social learning and psychodynamic theories are invalid if used to identify the processes that lead up to the creation of the core elements of identity and personality, though they can still act as overlays on what has already been formed. It shows that a pattern of continuous development can be traced from infancy to adult life.

Theology
Traditional teaching
The duality in gender and sexually variant behaviour is denied by many churches where such expression in any form, or for any purpose, is considered to be reward driven and always immoral. This is socially and culturally significant for the societies concerned, which is why the impact of gender and sexual difference in the early and modern Church must be examined.

Transformation and integration
A major challenge overcome by Christianity was its success in transferring the distinctive views of a minority Jewish sect into the dominant culture of the Greco/Roman state. That meant confronting the self-centred moralities of the culture and the sexual values that were characteristic of Greco/Roman male dominated society. It additionally meant challenging and appropriating the power structures within powerful and dominant societies, by placing the concern for the victims and the oppressed first on the religious and the social agendas of their cultures, and by embracing an all-encompassing morality founded on compassion, nurturing and love.

From his identification with the poor, women, the rejected and the outcast, Jesus turned the basis of authority on its head. His rejection of all worldly power led to his sacrifice and death as a scapegoat on a cross. Jesus had applied his radical teaching without compromise to the whole of society, but Peter and Paul sought respect for the Church. The command of Jesus to work within society to change it rather than to destroy it, presented Peter and Paul with a difficult choice.

Continuing with the refusal to compromise would have led the Church to make direct attacks on the power structures of Greco/Roman society. If the early Church chose to compromise with these structures it could gain the influence it needed to take the Gospel message to the wider world. The Letter to Philemon indicates that the early Church sought to fulfil the radical nature of Christ's teaching within the Christian community, while accepting the need to conform to the social structure of society beyond. The admonitions attributed to Peter and Paul in their later writings meant that this separation of the Christian community from the rest of society could never be complete. This need for the Church to gain respectability in the Greco/Roman world is a recurring theme in the writings of Peter and Paul; it also meant that the Church could no longer attack the power structures of Greco/Roman society directly, but it could attack their abuses of sex.

Discussion and argument about what Peter and Paul meant in the writings attributed to them in the New Testament have gone on for years. Paul's statement in Galatians 3:28: 'There is neither Jew nor Greek, there is neither slave nor free, there is no male and female, for you are all one in Christ Jesus', is acceptable today. But, there are conflicting statements by Peter and Paul which define the behaviour that women and men should adopt to obtain respect for the Church. There was pressure on the Church from the start to separate itself from gender disrupting behaviour and its associations with the Goddess cults[5]. It also needed a code of behaviour that did not threaten the power structures of Greco/Roman society. By embracing a form of gender complementarity that originated from and was amenable to that society, the Church could resolve both issues and gain respect.

Power and sex
Paul's condemnations of same-sex activities have to be seen in the light of this duality, the perceptions of sexual moralities, the enforcement of power between subject and dominant societies and the first-century interpretation of certain texts. It is strongly attested from contemporary first century and other sources that Leviticus 18:22 and 20:13 prohibited the act of anal penetration alone. Unlike later interpretations, the rabbis of the first century were very specific about confining the prohibition exclusively to this physical act. It was enforced entirely because of misuse, social disruption and the humiliation it caused, not because of an intrinsic abhorrence of the

---

5   These relationships are described in Gilchrist (2015)

act. In the research study a detailed consideration is therefore given to the relationships between power and sex.

What tends to be ignored completely is the way in which these sex acts enforced subjection and domination in and between gender and socially unequal societies. The prohibitions of Leviticus 18:22 and 20:13 have to be viewed from the perspectives of the teaching of Jesus, this neurophysiological and psychological study, the doctrines of the New Covenant and the Jewish Midrashim traditions. The abuses of power were the major concern, rather than the pleasure of the acts. Thus in loving and faithful relationships where the dynamics of power are not involved, there should be no prohibition of same-sex acts.

Paul outlines the teaching of Jesus in Galatians 3:26-28 and this can be tested both from the scientific and the theological perspectives. The neurophysiological and psychological study demonstrates that as wide a range of moral attitudes exist among gender and sexually variant people as there are in the population at large. Jesus makes exactly the same distinction in his teaching in the Gospels and the New Covenant, where the prohibitions that were previously based on the letter of the Law are now to be interpreted in the context of love and on the intention of the acts[6]. Therefore, judged from both the psychological and the religious criteria the traditional teaching of the Church has no foundation, because of its allegation that every expression of gender and sexually variant behaviour is always a sinful and heinous act.

This biblical research study demonstrates that transgender, transsexual, lesbian, gay, heterosexual and bisexual people who attempt to live their lives in ways that fulfil the love of Christ, and who seek to express their own identities in roles that are true to themselves, should be accepted equally by the Christian community. Sexual behaviour is governed by purity of intention, so there is no automatic condemnation of any same-sex act.

A major feature of gender complementarity comes from the way it separates the male from the female roles. Any form of gender and sexually variant behaviour, for any purpose, challenges this distinction and may threaten the social order. Peter and Paul reflected these concerns by declaring that in public women should submit to men. The more gender inequality there is in society, the greater

---

6   For a full description see Gilchrist (2015)

the threat to the social order of that society. Doctrines of gender complementarity make no allowance for the duality that is inherent in gender and sexually variant behaviour. Contrary to the teaching of Jesus the total condemnation of any expression of gender and sexually variant behaviour has become the doctrine of the Church.

Consequences

The conclusion of the research study is that the traditional doctrines of the Church on sexual and gender variance rest on false foundations. They arose from the need to gain respectability in Greco/Roman society and not from the teaching of Jesus himself. Christianity adopted a form of gender complementarity that was amenable to Greco/Roman society, which led to gender discrimination in the later Church.

Pragmatic and cultural arguments must also be considered. The command for Jews to populate the world in Genesis 1:28 was taken seriously, but Judaism did not define that as the only purpose of the sexual act. Contraception was permitted in certain situations, and Onan was advised to spill his seed on the ground. The pragmatic decision to adapt gender complementarity allowed Peter and Paul to bring Christianity to the world but this has since been interpreted as a doctrine of the Church. The consequences of turning discipline into doctrine are set out in Mark 7:1-23. This may preserve an institution, but at the cost of the teaching itself.

Disruptions occur today in societies embodying gender inequality and polarization because of the social implications of same-sex sexual acts. Denying the moral duality inherent in gender and sexually variant behaviour also leads the Church to make gender and sexually variant people the scapegoats for abusive sex. Translation drift and re-interpretation are further concerns. Many contemporary translations of the bible incorrectly state that Leviticus 18:22 and 20:13 condemns homosexuality; instead of abusive same-sex sex acts. Similar issues involve the interpretation of the Greek words *agape* and *pais*, where changes in meaning have tended to support the traditional theology of the Church[7]. The Church's collusion in these matters has been very harmful. It will continue until the scapegoating stops and these issues are addressed.

---

7   See Gilchrist (2015)

It should be emphasised that in the research study a clear distinction is made between same-sex sex and cross-gender behaviour which is engaged in for pure motives, and that pursued for immoral purposes. This is the basis for the moral duality here considered. There is no toleration of immoral sex, and the same degrees of moral condemnation can still be applied without compromise to those who misuse all same-sex acts

The Church has taught that all forms of gender and sexual variant behaviour are immoral acts. However, from the 1960's onwards and with the de-criminalisation of homosexuality, society's view has diverged from the traditional doctrines of the Church. That moral duality is now available for all to see in the love expressed in same-sex marriage and civil partnerships. It has also become easy for an unbiased observer to separate a same-sex relationship given in faithfulness, love and lifetime commitment from a strong heterosexual friendship, and to discriminate between loving and illicit same-sex acts.

A neurophysiological and psychological approach shows that the traditional teaching of the Church on gender and sexual variation does not match the reality of human development. The behaviour determined by the research study corresponds to would have been known to Jesus, John, Paul and others in first century society where same-sex relationships were widely expressed. Today the conflicts between what society understands as common sense values and the fervent reliance by the Church on its traditional doctrines are believed by the author to be destroying the credibility of Christianity in the eyes of the world. Change is urgently required; but it is not change which departs from the Gospel message: it is change which returns to the Gospel texts.

Part 2: Sibyls' Stories

Section 1: Transsexual Christians

Jay Walmsley

The Story of the Sibyls

It is hard to disentangle the story of the Sibyls from my life story. When the Sibyls was formed, I put masses of my life, love, and experience into the group and the group gave back so much love and experience that the two stories became interwoven.

At the time of the foundation of the Sibyls, I was in my fifties and a senior finance executive with a multinational. My wife had died of a heart condition a few years before. My elder daughter had flown the nest but my younger daughter was still at school and needed my attention. The times were not propitious for transgender people. Society did not understand, Church people were mostly hostile, and, had it been known to my employers, I would certainly have been dismissed. Consequently I lived at home as female, at work as male. Full transition only became possible when I took early retirement. However in my search for myself I had found God and come to the Church.

Very early in my transsexual transition, I realised that I needed a spiritual director. Many decisions had to be taken, with huge effects on my life and on the lives of others. It was apparent that I needed someone who would look at me dispassionately and sensibly, and provide a spiritual health check. That was one of the wisest decisions I ever made. I was greatly blessed to be introduced to the Revd Malcolm Johnson who took me on. To him I owe a huge debt - as do the Sibyls!

From 1988 I was involved with the Beaumont Trust, first on the helpline, and then as Secretary and Treasurer. The Beaumont Trust is a tiny independent charity whose aims are to assist transgender people and to educate the public. I was also involved with the Seahorse Society, a lovely group and the first transgender group I joined. A helpful church course taught me that I could listen to people. From there it was a slow but natural progression to thinking about spiritual direction. I was accepted on the Southwark SPIDIR training course and enjoyed two wonderful years absorbing ideas and skills from Dorothy Nicholson and Gordon Jeffs.

Whilst doing this, I pondered with Malcolm where it might lead and whether I could do anything useful for transsexual people. He suggested that I start a Christian group for transsexual people. The idea was Malcolm's; Sibyls is his inspiration. All I learned about spiritual direction has been channelled into the Sibyls.

Using my contacts in the transgender world, the idea was spread. The very first meeting was on 3rd August 1996 at my house when five of us, Val, the two Kates, Ken and I, got together over a meal and then sat on the patio discussing the way forward. A number of issues were immediately clear:

1. Val was a woman researching for a book involving a transgender person who was a Christian. When she asked if she could join the group, the only possible response was to welcome her. That immediately established that anyone who was transgender and interested was welcome but you didn't have to be transgender. It also foreclosed any debate about whether Sibyls was for people who are transsexual or transvestite, or both. In addition to inadvertently forcing those decisions, Val has been a tower of strength to Sibyls and we certainly took the right decision.

2. The successful basis for future meetings would be a safe place with a sharing of both religious experience and food and drink, preferably with a degree of comfort. Jesus is frequently reported eating with others; his lead often makes sense.

3. Religious services had to be provided, especially communion. The hostility often shown to transsexual people by Christian churches and the consequent lack of opportunity for some to take communion was becoming apparent. Subsequent experience bore this out; many of our members had been thrown out of their own churches.

From that simple start the Sibyls gradually grew. The next meeting was held in October 1996 at The Royal Foundation of St Katharine. Malcolm was then the Master and offered us the use of the housekeeper's flat for lunch and discussion, with a communion service in the chapel. Thereafter numbers grew with a winter dinner meeting at my house and the start of our weekends, when numbers really shot up.

The weekends, firstly at St Katharine's and then at other retreat houses across the country, have been very successful. They provide time and space to come together in safety, to be looked after, be comfortable, and to explore together. Services are held, both communion services with a priest or minister presiding and our own prayer offices. For the morning and evening prayer offices, four in a weekend, we have learned to give a slot to a Sibyl and let them do what they will with it. The results have been astonishing in depth of worship and thought. The intensity of feeling and involvement is almost palpable; they have been incredibly exciting. Would that the same could be said of services in the church at large.

From the first weekend we have held a Saturday night entertainment at which everyone who wishes can do a turn. With a sympathetic and appreciative audience, there have been some wonderful musical and dance experiences, jokes, sketches, stories. While the evenings have been fun in themselves, people gain the confidence that they can perform and that they have talent. And of course the weekends provide meal times and chatty gaps with opportunities to talk. Many a problem has been aired and many a friendship made, which helps through both good and bad times.

We had to learn as we went along. It was quickly agreed that we should accept all denominations and none. It didn't matter what denomination you belonged to or if you didn't. What mattered was that you were somehow on the spiritual road.

There was debate about whether we should admit members of other faiths, Muslim, Hindu etc. We reluctantly decided that we would not. It was hard enough to arrange services etc. for all Christian tastes; to cater for other faiths would make the task almost impossible.

The name Sibyls has caused much comment. In the early days I thought long and hard to find a name and an acronym that would suit the group. Nothing worked. Then inspiration dawned. My dictionary defined Sibyls as wise women who spoke the word of God. That was what we were about. We had a little problem when female to male transsexual people joined us but everyone liked the name Sibyls and it has stuck.

In the early days there were huge problems in trying to define what we were about. There was much anguished debate but nothing was right. Eventually we decided that our purpose was to follow

Christ's instruction to love one another. Not surprisingly that was perfect.

We also had to decide whether we should have a constitution and whether we should seek charitable status. In the event we decided we were better without either. What seemed obvious is that we were all about and for God, and who knows where that would take us and when. A written constitution, a trust deed, would define us and limit that freedom, a denial of what God wanted of us. Not having charitable status meant the loss of tax advantages, a small price to pay for the freedom to be true to our calling.

We did establish our one and only rule. Every member must have a total concern and respect for the security of each and every member. Security rules are common in all transgender groups but are of particular importance to the Sibyls. When Sibyls was most active, society and especially the Church were hostile to 'transgenderism'. The lives of many of our members could have been devastated if their transgender status became widely known. We number among our membership priests and ministers. If information about them had got back to their bishops or congregations, they could have lost home and living, a huge price to pay. It has happened; it is not acceptable, indeed it is outrageous that someone should lose so much for simply being true to themself. Irrespective of whether their transgender condition is public knowledge or not, information about members is something never to be talked about. The Sibyls as a group is not secret; membership details are.

Funding too was the subject of much discussion. Subscriptions were discussed and the idea always rejected. We found it best to ask the membership to donate as they thought fit. Some were living on tiny incomes, State benefit etc. and could not afford to give, whereas others were well off, with shades in between. If each gave as they wished, we as Sibyls have the knowledge of being appreciated; they have the satisfaction of giving. So far it has worked well. Whenever we needed money, somehow it was provided. Annual accounts are always sent to the membership.

The Sibyls is run on a shoestring. The quarterly newsletter is important to keep members informed of what is going on and to give news and views and to simply be a point of contact with the group. That cost money. Our box number took a little more. We like to support members who can't afford to come to the weekends. It then took about £1,000 per annum to keep us running. If push came to shove, some of the wealthier members would have shouldered that. The cost has dropped greatly now that most newsletters go out by email. Financially, there is no way we can be stopped, because we cost so little. Poverty has its advantages, which Jesus knew very well.

There were difficulties and crises along the way. A major issue was denominational difference. Others decried offerings at prayer offices. Some worried about my style of leadership, that I was favouring particular styles of worship. After a great deal of soul searching, we ran Myers-Briggs courses at two weekends to better understand our differences as well as our similarities. In the end it was crystal clear to every Sibyl that others had to be respected, that one might not agree with the beliefs of others but they were real for them, and that a particular office might not be to one's taste but that someone would welcome and gain from it. Above all, the individual, each and every one, had to be respected and their beliefs upheld. It worked. At each weekend we try to provide a variety of styles and denominations to ensure that everyone will find something to their taste. It is important to maintain a balance.

Many of our offices provide debating points that the meeting will pick up. I remember especially one Friday evening when the speaker closed with the words 'That shows God's purpose in action'. There was a silence, you could almost see a collective speech bubble 'Does it?' rise, members gathered their thoughts, and one after another began to speak. Each speaker offered a point of view, often disagreeing strongly, but always with respect for the other speakers, always with total consideration for them. The discussion raged for about an hour and a half with a huge range of thoughts, ideas, and inspirations but with no hint of anything other than a perfect consideration for the others. It was amazing – and lovely.

In addition to weekend meetings we have smaller meetings, usually for a meal and with a service. These again provide the essentials, a religious experience and time together over food and drink to talk and air problems, to ask for help or simply to talk.

We faced a particular challenge with the introduction of the Gender Recognition Bill. As the only specifically Christian transgender group, the onus was on us to talk to the Government and counter the propaganda of hostile Christian groups. It was essential to show that not all Christians think that belief and being transgender are incompatible. We worked closely with the civil servants in the Department of Constitutional Affairs. It was simply disgraceful to hear speakers in the House of Lords trying to introduce legislation to exclude transsexual people from attending the church of their choice and from receiving communion there. The reality is that many Christians are extremely supportive. It is a matter of delight that, despite the efforts of the religious lobby, the bill passed successfully through Parliament to become the Gender Recognition Act 2004. We also intervened in the Civil Partnerships Bill and the proposed identity card legislation. While there are many other transgender groups, none have that unique Christian voice. We did not set up as a campaigning body, did not wish to be one, but someone had to stand up and be counted.

Membership was varied. We had a peak of 200 members but fewer now. The world has changed from the 1990s and society is largely accepting, as are a number of churches. The need for Sibyls has diminished.

Why has Sibyls worked so well? The answer lies in the membership. They are there for each other, the friendship, the love and the support is always given, is almost palpable. That's what keeps it going, that's why it exists. To love each other in God's love.

My task as leader was to nourish and grow that love by providing the welcome, the facilities, food and drink for both body and soul, space to let it all happen, comfort and security for relaxation. No dogma, no certainty, above all no being right; a safe space for each and every one to explore, to find themselves, to grow, to learn to be.

I was greatly aided by the help of a committee. As I moved into my seventies I resolved to step down. Societies are full of founders who won't let go, which can be very unhealthy. It was time to hand over before it became imperative and it is now up to the committee to do the best they can with God's grace.

What of the future? The hope is always that one day there will be no need for groups like this. If society were fully supportive, there would be help for all who need it. Our prayer is that someday, hopefully soon, we will not be needed and can disband. However every indication is that the institutional churches will continue to reject and we will have to be there to pick up the pieces. One day, Dear Lord.

What challenges Sibyls face in the future heaven knows. Nothing stands still. In God's grace, we shall go forward. It's been fun, a marvellous adventure, and I wish the committee as much joy.

Jemma (1921-2015)

Lifting the Veil

An elderly Sibyls' member and a private person, 'Jemma' – the name she wanted used here – is a pseudonym, but she was willing to be interviewed and this chapter is a summary of a longer narrative.

Inveterate traveller, student, transgender campaigner, habitué of meetings and free meals – she has lived her life across three continents and was keen to record her journey around Australia during the 1930s Depression.

At the final interview, Jemma revealed that the *Anne of Green Gables* books of Lucy Maud Montgomery – the story of a precocious, whimsical, accident-prone orphan – offered a clue to her life. Like the eponymous Anne, Jemma was orphaned. Neither was the child their adoptive parents expected. Anne won over hers, and her community; Jemma's progress was more tortuous.

Orphan

Born on 5 May 1921 at Queen Charlotte's Hospital, then in Westminster, London, her birth certificate, which records her sex as 'boy', has no father's name. Despite family disapproval, her mother drove lorries at the Front during the First World War. She conceived, post-war, while in service with Lady Papillion, which prompted the typical rumour that Jemma's father belonged to that family.

Cared for initially by nuns, her mother married a widower with two young sons and they moved to south Harrow. Jemma remembers saying her prayers beneath a reproduction of Holman Hunt's *The Light of the World*.

When she was five, her kindly mother died from a mastoid abscess, and her stepfather sent her, with her two stepbrothers, to an orphanage at Burnt Oak. As in a fairy story, when Jemma's stepbrothers were removed from the orphanage by her stepfather, Jemma lingered there, Cinderella-like, another four years, without explanation.

Her 'fairy-godparent' was her maternal uncle, a former P&O steward, in Brisbane, Australia. He and his wife were childless and Jemma seemed a promising surrogate.

Brisbane

The journey, a great adventure, was headlined in the local Brisbane paper, 'All alone from London'. Her new 'mother' named her 'Ronald' (the first of several name changes) after a perfect little boy she once knew; an unrealistic ideal Jemma could never fulfil. Caught in the crossfire of her aunt and uncle's marital difficulties, their emotional turmoil seemingly reflecting Australia's economic depression, Jemma experienced delayed grief at her mother's death.

Raised in the Bardon suburb of Brisbane, Queensland, she attended Rainworth School, successfully completing four grades/ classes in just two years. Was she girly then? She enjoyed the novels of Lucy Maud Montgomery, and was 'home-maker' when she and friends made cubby homes.

Having edited the school magazine she seemed suited to journalism. At her headmaster's suggestion she spent two years studying typing, short-hand and modern business methods at the State Commercial High School and College, but left to work at the Anvil Book Shop. She had begun to make her own choices.

Beating about the Bush

Thanks to a government farm scheme she left home to enjoy a little freedom in the Bush. Starting from Coalstoun Lakes, she milked cows and hoed cane at Mungar Junction, and then worked on dairy farms at Mount Isa, and later at Melawondi, where she almost killed the farmer while testing her rifle. Aged seventeen, naïve, and barely conscious of her gender identity, she grew her hair long to style it in a pigtail. Her stated plan was to earn her fare to England, and head for Darwin to board a boat there.

At Marion Downs, near the Northern Territory borders, a six thousand square miles station, with ten thousand head of cattle, she became a cowboy. Unlike the 'alpha male' American cowboy, the Australian cowboy was a young man, or elderly male, who milked the cows and helped around the homestead – stereotypical 'feminine' tasks.

At Boulia, the Methodist minister persuaded her that a haircut would make her more employable. He was mistaken. Keen to work, but 'on the road' she lived like a 'hobo' – poor itinerant workers who jumped on and off moving trains dodging the fare – and learned hobo songs, some of which she reprised at a Sibyls' weekend in 2008. Caught 'jumping trains', she was arrested and briefly imprisoned several times in her attempt to reach Rockingham, where she took the train to Ingham, a sugar growing region about a thousand miles from Brisbane.

Daphne's War

When war was declared she returned to Brisbane, and joined the Army. A touch typist, she was promoted to corporal, but at Camp Ingleburn, near Sydney, had difficulty maintaining discipline and returned to the ranks. Now eighteen, a teetotaller, non-smoker, who didn't swear, the men called her 'Daphne',[1] a femme name she disliked as it implied homosexuality.[2] As she observed in retrospect, then there were only three options: male/female/homosexual.

Sleeping on the parade ground to avoid mosquitoes, she dreamt that the car she was travelling in turned into a lady's slipper, followed by a scream: a premonition of gender transition perhaps, or anxiety at her perceived femininity? When the dream recurred, she woke screaming to find a lorry had run over her feet. The injury would assist her army discharge.

Jemma and her comrades left Sydney on the RMS Queen Mary – then the second largest ship in the world – in a convoy of six ships transporting five thousand Australian troops. Apparently headed for the Middle East, they disembarked at Liverpool. The evacuation of Dunkirk occurred at this time.

Her romantic dreams of the English countryside dispelled by the reality of wartime Britain, Jemma still hoped to remain. She tried 'disappearing' before being assigned with the medically unfit to a British troop ship bound for Palestine. There she tried to unsuccessfully re-join her battalion, and then, at Haifa, feigned a catatonic state. Suspecting schizophrenia, the doctors sent her back to Australia, but within six months she had gained special permission to leave again on the Port Adelaide, which joined a fifty-ship convoy.

---

1   Transgender Christian the late Sonia Burgess told the author that Jemma's femininity, and incipient 'transgenderism', was evident from photographs of Jemma from this date which she had shown at church.
2   Unease with, or even distaste for, homosexuality is common in older transgender people's narratives.

Landing in New York, Jemma was spotlit at a film premiere like a celebrity.

Allocated to another large convoy, her ship was battered by a terrific storm. Arriving in Liverpool the police accused her of spying, but released her, and she headed for London.

The next day, at Ealing, she joined the British Navy. Already proficient in Morse code, she trained in wireless and telegraphy at Skegness. Although she scored highest IQ, her aptitude and attitude were questioned when she was found welding with the girls.

In 1942, she achieved top marks in the meteorology examination, and served on the HMS Pretoria Castle, the Navy's largest aircraft carrier as part of the Fleet Air Arm.

Nurse

A meteorological rating for two years, in 1945 Jemma underwent an emotional breakdown. Sent to recover in Scotland, she was discharged BNPS – 'below Naval physical standard' – and began a nursing career. On passing the Royal Medical Psychological Association (RMPA) and the General Nursing Council finals she became a Registered Mental Health Nurse (RMN), and was studying to become a State Registered Nurse when she suddenly resigned and left for Germany.

Germany

She arrived in Hanover, which was swarming with refugees, with nowhere to stay. Advised to learn Esperanto in the Navy, with typical idiosyncrasy she had taught herself German using an Esperanto textbook. Local Esperantists found her accommodation and work as a bilingual telephonist at the British Army Supply Depot, where she attracted suspicion and was arrested and interrogated by MI6 officers and military intelligence. No longer permitted to work – she was on a tourist visa – and unable to access her money, due to British travel allowance restrictions, she returned to the UK and to nursing.

University

Homesick for Australia and being English born she re-emigrated for £10 and worked as a nurse in Sydney. She studied part-time for the School Certificate and after briefly living in Tasmania enrolled at the University of Melbourne, where she met Barry Humphries. Reading Psychology, German, English Literature and Ancient History while earning a living proved too much. She concentrated on German, but imagined visiting Prince Edward Island, and researching Lucy Maud Montgomery while continuing her studies in Vancouver.

Canada

Turning dream into reality, she travelled on the Orient Liner to Vancouver, and enrolled at the University, but there were no jobs, so she visited Calgary and explored the mountains. Hitchhiking on the Canadian Highway in January, without suitable protection, her hands turned yellow with frostbite. She lived on her savings, staying in YMCAs or the local jail, even sleeping in a trench in the snow, travelling by Greyhound Bus to Toronto via Chicago, Hamilton and Guelph, and hitchhiking to Montreal, Quebec and New Brunswick.

Prince Edward Island, immortalised by Lucy Maud Montgomery, was her next destination. There she saw an advertisement for the 'Principal' of what was, in reality, a single teacher school in the rural community of Coleman. Jemma was appointed, and completed her initial teacher training at Prince of Wales College, Charlottetown, which Montgomery herself had attended. Her dreams fulfilled at last, her life mirrored a darker episode in Montgomery's fiction when the Royal Canadian Mounted Police tried to arrest her as an Australian spy. Her innocence established she returned to England, after hitching round Nova Scotia and Boston.

Teacher

After a further two years teacher training at Newland Park College of Education, Chalfont St Peter, Buckinghamshire, she taught for a year at St Paul's School, Canonbury, Islington, but then decided to return to Australia. 'It might be different,' she told a friend, 'if I had a house here', so the friend found her one. She bought it and stayed – except for holidays abroad – for the rest of her life.

In 1960, the tough secondary school near Euston Station where she taught was closed, and she transferred to the newly opened Risinghill School, an early experiment in comprehensive education in Islington. It only lasted five years due to the controversial progressive, non-authoritarian policies of its charismatic Head, Michael Duane, but Jemma flourished there, delivering Religious Instruction to the entire school – six hundred pupils – every week. A shocked inspector sent her to County Hall for teaching Esperanto, but she was commended rather than disciplined.

Transition

Jemma's gender transition commenced in retirement when she grew her hair long again: reviewing her life, her sense of gender dysphoria was, in her own words 'Always ... to do with the hair.' She still sported a beard, as in her Navy days, which is not unknown among pre-transition trans women.[3]

At the Killieser Avenue Nursing Home, where clients' ages ranged from birth to over eighty, her long hair was unremarkable in a job that combined her teaching, nursing and play leadership skills.

A new stage occurred when she became home carer – and eventually, friend and companion – to 'Mary', who lived in North Lambeth. Keen to develop breasts, Jemma began taking Mary's HRT tablets. The results were dramatic, and she had breasts, long hair, and a beard for some time. The photograph in her identity documents showed her with breasts.

Jemma joined the leading organisations for trans people – Gendys, the Gender Trust and the Beaumont Society – but her appearance and documents caused confusion. She became nanny to a family, whom she accompanied to Bangladesh, where she wore the sarong-like longi, and unisex tops. Next she exchanged the longi for the kilt. Both could be perceived as 'men's' garments, but these were women's kilts. She then began to wear women's skirts, and finally, dresses – still with a beard. She recalls travelling 'through the entire Republic of Ireland ... with a beard en femme'.

Eventually her GP issued her with her own HRT prescription, and she was referred to 'Charing Cross' Gender Identity Clinic. Knowing the Clinic's strict protocols she shaved off her beard prior to her appointment. It felt a huge step, a final relinquishing of her masculinity. She conformed, mainly to obtain gender confirmation surgery. Already in her seventies, and having lived in gender limbo for a while, she avoided the NHS waiting list for surgery by going private. Mary, who was still in Jemma's care, was admitted with her.

Migrant/Pilgrim

Jemma's intermediate gender stage resembled the concept of 'blending' genders (Ekins and King 1996). 'Migrating' is a sociological category of transgender experience – along with oscillating,

---

3   Another Sibyl, Bernadette Rogers, had a beard prior to transition, arguing that it meant she didn't need to shave, shaving being a male activity.

negating and transcending – identified by Ekins and King (2006: 34). Problematic as a descriptor of transition, it functions better metaphorically (Beardsley 2015), and resonates with Jemma's story.

Her life has been full of journeys, border crossings and interrogations. Isolated and on the margins during her initial journey in the Bush, there she explored gender roles, including various masculinities.

Jemma exercised dual citizenship during the Second World War, first in the Australian Army, and later, the British Navy, a fondness for duality reflected in her subsequent gender blending, which also caused confusion, like the wartime suspicions that she was spying in Allied-occupied Germany, Liverpool and Canada.

Like Montgomery's 'Anne', Jemma was the expected orphan boy who turned out to be a girl. Jemma's femininity emerged over decades, but was obvious early on – her fellow soldiers were well aware of it. She found the Second World War dislocating, as many did, but her restless toing and froing between England, Australia and Canada, may reflect 'oscillation' between masculine and feminine, male and female, and frustrated desire to transition, which only became widely available in the later twentieth century.

Jemma tried several careers, eventually exchanging the manual and technical for nursing and teaching: caring, nurturing professions at which she excelled, though even here stability proved elusive and she changed jobs often.

Happiest in an intermediate place – living on the borderlands of male and female: feminine in dress, female in upper body, yet bearded – she removed her beard to please the clinical gatekeepers ('border guards'?) in order to complete her physical transition.

She delighted in eccentricity, arcane knowledge and colourful clothing. She was content to be 'different', to be queer: gender queer to be precise.

She worshipped in the Coptic Church, which segregates the sexes, until forbidden to cross the aisle on transition; since when she became a practising Anglican.

Her facility for languages remained to the end of her life – Romanian being the last – and proved invaluable on her travels. At university she undertook specialist level studies in the Brythonic Celtic languages, and used her knowledge of Goidelic on her journey round Ireland. Her explorations continued and she was rescued from remote spots on more than one occasion. Prince Edward Island, through its associations with Lucy Maud Montgomery's life and fiction, remained her spiritual home in a life full of pilgrimage.

[Jemma died on 25 October 2015.]

Michelle le Morvan
(24/10/1932-17/06/2009)[1]

'There's a Long, Long Trail Awinding ....'

I have recently had the report of a second psychiatrist who confirmed the diagnosis of the first that I have the medical condition of Gender Dysphoria. This means that my brain structure and hypothalamus are female rather than male, hence my gender is female and I was born divided with a male body but a female gender. I have come to realise now that the most fundamental aspect of my personality is my female gender rather than my male biology.

The result of this was that I was born with a deep division within me for which there is no psychiatric or psychological cure, and that division has plagued my life. In fact I have lived a double life at a subconscious level for nearly seventy years. In the end this nearly destroyed me. It has also caused much pain to many others, especially my wife, a pain which I can understand but which I could not help inflicting on her and others simply because in the end I had to face the pain within or simply end everything. I spent seventy years denying my real self and actually living a subconscious lie. No one knows how biology comes to be opposite to gender in this condition, it is still one of the unsolved mysteries of medical science. The fact that 20% of gender dysphoric persons attempt suicide and 90% of the rest contemplate it at some time is a testimony to the terrible havoc that the condition causes within the personality.

My long trail...
I was born near the end of 1932 in the midst of the depression (a mental condition which I carried for much of my life). The eldest of three boys with no sisters, I have few recollections of those early years, but

---

1   Michelle Le Morvan died since this collection of narratives began. The diagnosis she refers to was made in about 2001.

am now aware that from early on I was very serious, a trait which has lasted most of my life and has been associated with a passionate desire for approval. Few could have been such an 'approval seeker' as I was. This argues I suppose to a certain insecurity. My parents were very loving and concerned but I feel now, rather sadly, that I never really knew them because there was no deep sharing (after all they had been brought up in Edwardian times where 'stiff upper lip' was the normal way of life). We were a very religious family and I know my life has been for the most part intensely religious (as a good conscientious Catholic always involved in religion in one way or another).

It was in order to get a good Catholic education that the family moved soon after Pearl Harbour. My middle brother and I went to a school run by Brothers who had left Guernsey in 1940. They were kindly men and good teachers and when they returned in 1945 we were sent to another school run by the Brothers of the same religious order. In the meantime I had experienced for the first time 'cross dressing' and was filled with shame and guilt - a shame and guilt which weighed me down for nearly fifty years. Although now free of it I still remember it vividly. I was at this time and for many years to come, ignorant of sexual matters, a situation which is almost inconceivable today. I was terrified, and with the prospect of hell looming large on the horizon. Having a relative who was a priest I felt that here was safety. I remember one of the brothers saying 'a priest is a man of God', and for me the emphasis was, as I now realise, on Man, not on God. Subconsciously I was seeking to be a man and I made myself interested in games and sports though unfortunately I wasn't very good at them. The interest has long since dropped away apart from my love of cricket and my support for the Irish rugby team (more anon). In order to save myself and my sanity I volunteered to become a priest. I was sure that my problems would subside - and they did, for a time. In the summer of 1949, the last year of double summer time, I joined the parish tennis club where I met a lot of young women of about my own age. I felt at home among them. There was no sexual attraction but it was as if I was one of them I was so comfortable in their company.

Then I was away to the Seminary. While at school I had learned to love study, it was something which absorbed my time and energy and gave me immense joy and satisfaction. This developed in these years of further study. Otherwise they were not memorable years but I hung in and was eventually ordained priest. Towards the end of my time I applied to go on to further studies in order to teach rather than work in a parish. Looking back it was a good step for I know that I would have 'blown up' in a parish. The only snag was that I was asked to study science rather than humanities which had always been my strength. At the time this was a heavy burden but was to prove very fruitful in the years ahead. Eventually I went to University in Ireland where I spent what were in some ways the happiest years of my life. Again I was able to feel at home in female company and at the same time enjoyed my studies, especially geology which has always remained a passion - though one which has had to take a back seat in the events of my life. Now as I can take my life at a more leisurely pace it has come back to me so that I may relish it again.

After completing my studies I returned to commence a teaching career, which proved to be a very rewarding way to earn my living and which on the whole I enjoyed for many years. Altogether I taught in schools for thirty one years but was also able to be involved in adult education full time after retiring from secondary education. In the earlier years I had been involved in this on a part-time basis including a number of years with the Open University which were a real joy. Yes I enjoyed my teaching career, though I am glad not to be involved with it today when conditions have changed so drastically.

Anyway I taught in the Diocesan school for nine years but by the end of it I knew that I could no longer remain a priest. I still did not understand what was causing such deep distress within me and I felt that if I was married it (the deep stress and the accompanying depressions) would all go away, and I did love my wife. Many others in the transsexual community have felt the same and made the same mistake. If I had known then what I know now I would never have got married, it was so unfair to my wife. The first years of marriage were good and my troubles subsided and seemed to be over. I had three step-children whom I loved and still do. We moved to the south of England to make a new start. We were both Catholics and continued to practise our faith as normal until we became involved, almost by accident, in the Charismatic renewal. This opened up new opportunities for our faith and in subsequent years my wife was led to develop a whole new way of ministry. It was my job to keep the home fires burning while I carried on teaching.

Towards 1990 my troubles, which I thought had gone away, resurfaced like a new volcano and with greatly increased destructive power. By this time we had become involved in a religious education project which made us locally well known. I was in a terrible dilemma and did not know what to do. I was fortunate to find a counsellor who listened very patiently but to whom I could not reveal my real problems for over two years. At this time (the early 90s) I was referred to the Gender Identity Clinic at Charing Cross Hospital where again one of the psychiatrists gave me support for several years. But by this time I was really ready to end everything. The inner pain and turmoil were unbearable and I seriously began to think of killing myself. I took time away living in our motor caravan in the grounds of a friend's house and again things got a little better. I had received much prayer for healing from many people and for a while matters eased - only to return with increased vigour. But it was causing much pain to my wife and our marriage was disintegrating.

By the end of 2000 I had at last really begun to understand my whole gender problem and could do nothing about it. It wouldn't go away and was getting steadily worse. Through my counsellor I had been able to make contact with a Christian transgender group - the Sibyls. This contact has since developed over the years and flowered into some lovely friendships which have been a great blessing. By this time I needed all the support I could get just to remain sane and human. What saved me in the end though was a religious house which was also a pastoral centre. At the end of 2000 they offered me a cottage in their grounds for three months. This saved my sanity and probably my life. I can never repay that debt but I pray God to bless that truly Christian community.

When I arrived there everything fell apart. My life disintegrated completely and I experienced a total collapse, emotional, psychological and physical. As I realise now, though I did not then, my whole religious life also collapsed. I did remember, however, that Dr Frank Lake had said many years before 'a breakdown can be a breakthrough if handled properly'. So I wrote a journal in which I recorded everything, over 200 pages of A4 size, just externalising all the inner pain. I was nothing but a mess. I had no future and I felt that my life had been totally wasted. The despair was complete.

But in the midst of that pain my life began to revive, and in the first instance it was because I had been able to attend the courses on 'Jesus and the Gospels' and on the Parables, being conducted for the course participants. Although I had done much teaching on the Gospels this hit me like a sledgehammer. Of course all my defences were down and I was like a devastated town in which new flowers appear in the desolate streets between the cracks in the paving. Suddenly I saw afresh the 'Man from Galilee' without all the dogma which had previously surrounded him. His message stood out clearly and unambiguously. In the years since that time of conversion the challenge to try and live fully the Gospel values has changed my life. By the time I left the cottage I was beginning to rebuild my life. With almost no effort I was able to get a flat within driving distance of the Pastoral Centre so I was able to keep in regular touch with those who had been so supportive and who still play a very important supportive role in my life.

The remainder of the story is more briefly told. Though badly let down by the hospital, I was able through a friend in Sibyls to become a patient of a very compassionate and humane psychiatrist who encouraged me to follow my journey. I was also challenged by a priest to make a decision about my life. He pointed out very clearly that I had lived a double life, denying myself and playing a role as a male actor. Shortly after that I made my decision, which had now become much more straightforward, but still with a considerable amount of apprehension as to how it would be received by my neighbours, my family and my friends, as well as more generally in the area in which I now live. I needn't have feared so much for, in general, I was graciously received. By working in a charity shop as a volunteer I have got to know many people and my life has moved forward. By joining a painting class and by membership of a local scientific society I have become further immersed in the local scene. At Easter 2003, after attending the Easter Vigil, I was driving home and suddenly realised what an enormous burden had been lifted off my life. It was a real resurrection experience. Later in 2003 I went to Canada to stay with my middle brother and his family and couldn't have received a more loving and kinder reception. Since then the struggle has been to receive NHS funding for surgery, a struggle which has been strongly supported by my local Member of Parliament. Now, at last, having fulfilled the conditions laid down by the Harry Benjamin rules, I await the decision of the local PCT.

The cost has been heavy as I have already suggested. My marriage collapsed and I appreciate the pain that the condition has caused my wife. I have lost my whole way of life, many of my family and some of my friends. I have had to start again from scratch. Like many others I have had a very long, and very painful, journey of self-discovery. Having been able to accept myself at last, I can now accept where others are and bear none of them any ill will - life is too short and I will always hope for some form of reconciliation. Meanwhile a second life that has been opened up has been with new friends who are themselves transsexual. The Christian transgender group, the Sibyls, has given me a framework in which I have been able to make some new and very caring friends. Some of them have had journeys much more terrible than mine. This friendship, and they are very real friends, is very important because we all go through periods of great fragility, for a variety of reasons. There are many who do not wish us well (and tragically they include many who call themselves Christians but who do not seem to have ever read the Gospels with their message of love, compassion and inclusiveness). So we do support one another and these friendships are deeply treasured. On other occasions we can help to educate others simply through sharing our story, though at times this can be scary.

What lies ahead? Even with hormone treatment and surgery I will be at best a construct woman, even though my gender is female. When I awake at night or feel depressed or lonely (for indeed after all my years in community and in marriage) I know that I will always be alone. In those moments I wish it had been different, and I wish I had been born a girl as I should have been. This wish I actually 'feel' in my body, for my biology will not react as it should to the messages from my brain. I can actually feel the pain in my body, and I understand why so many gender dysphoric people attempt suicide. But in spite of the pain I have never been so content in my life. As I learn to accept myself more completely, so I see with gratitude the way I have been led. As I look back now at the impossible positions I was in, I marvel at the way that so many things have fallen into place. I am a very blest woman. I am still struggling religiously - from having lived my life with a religious intensity, I find that I can no longer do that. I have become a seeker after divine Presence, but the call of the Gospels to a way of life provides me with a clearly marked set of values. The meaning of life can only be found in the present moment and not in some 'heaven' lying ahead. It is the Gospel which leads me into this moment.

It has been 'a long, long trail awinding ...' and I have not yet reached 'the land of my dreams', but continue to journey in hope because I have been led through and delivered from much pain and many shadows and I am sure that one day I will reach the land of dreams.

Helen Belcher

Labels are Odd Things

Evangelical, liberal, heterosexual, transgender, analyst, geek – they all tend to be things applied to you from outside, and you can either learn to conform to the expectations or rebel against them. So when you're labelled as Christian, or I'm labelled as trans, that immediately creates a bunch of perceptions. Their accuracy depends upon people's previous experiences and understandings.

In line with lots of others, I knew I was trans before I knew the term, and also before I fell into evangelical, fundamentalist Christianity as a teenager. Confused by puberty, and desperately hiding my innermost thoughts from my testosterone-driven compatriots, the evangelical message was appealing in its simplicity. I'd never had cause to question the existence of either God or Jesus. The crucifixion and resurrection were presented as historical facts. And the idea of having some kind of communication channel with the creator of all things, so I could find out how I was supposed to live, was comforting.

Except what it did was further reinforce the feelings of shame. Very quickly there was an expectation that I would change fundamentally. While there were some changes, I was left feeling a failure because of all the things that hadn't – amongst which was the struggle over wanting to be female. I kept a diary of events, and marked those specific 'failures' with black circles. Most days had black circles. Most days I felt guilty and ashamed, and most days this self-loathing was driven deeper and deeper into myself.

I wasn't able to tell anyone. I 'knew', from various preachers, that homosexuality was an abomination and, in an all-boys' school, it wasn't hard to understand what homosexuality was – at least in a very crude way. But I didn't know if that applied to me. I didn't know how men were attracted to women, and didn't realise that sexual attraction wasn't wrapped up in wanting to be the object of your desires. If I wanted to be a woman, didn't that automatically mean I was gay? But I didn't fancy men – and my own (non-sexual) experiences of a boys' boarding school meant that I was acutely aware of the shortcomings of men.

Evangelical Christianity held out so much promise. Pray more, because that will cure you. Enter 'healthy' relationships because those will cure you. Date a girl, and that will cure you. Marry someone, because that's the cure.

I got to the point where, aged nearly forty, I had an eighteen-month-old daughter, a happy marriage, a responsible managerial job and a leadership role in my local house church before the edifices started to really crack. I'd come close to a couple of breakdowns in my twenties, but somehow managed to pull through. Dealing with my daughter made me realise I had to sort myself out, because otherwise there was a very real danger that I would hate her as she grew into the woman I could never be.

I knew Deuteronomy 22:5. I knew the exhortations against men sleeping with other men. I 'knew' I needed healing, so I started to investigate Christian sites on the Internet. The sites I was uncovering all peddled denial – such as making the sign of a cross when you started to feel yourself fall, or confiding in your pastor, or repeated fasting and intense praying. Treating women as some kind of vampire didn't seem to me to address the core issue, nor did being made to feel perpetually guilty. I was good at feeling guilty – I'd had years of practice. Instead I wanted to be whole.

But, at the same time, I was uncovering testimonies that I could relate to – this feeling of being different since young, having this itch that you simply cannot scratch away – and alongside those was the revelation that God made you as you are, he knows you intimately, and he wants you to be a whole and complete individual. Suddenly there was a different understanding of the Scriptures. It was possible to be trans and Christian. It was also possible to be a trans woman and not want to sleep with men. The mistake from my teens was to see that my trans-ness should be set apart rather than integrated. I also saw a lot of pain in those testimonies. Pain over wasted time. Pain over broken relationships and rejection. But they rang true.

My training as a teacher had imparted a certain knowledge of psychology, in particular group dynamics and the importance of belonging. For the first time I started to apply that knowledge to my church life as well as my own life. I was encouraged to worship God as a whole person, even when dressed as a woman. That simple act inverted my whole world view. I believed I heard God accept me as I was, not who others wanted me to be. So began the long slow Damascene road of dismantling the religious objections that kept me male.

I had to be honest with my wife as well. When the inevitable questions came, I knew enough to stand my ground – this was who I was; I was starting to understand that I had been created this way, and it was difficult to see that as a mistake, or how it could be excised without dramatically affecting the rest of me. It was hard for her to hear.

The other key wall was destroyed in a matter of minutes. I never believed I would be remotely passable as a woman. I was wrong. Going to a professional make-up artist suddenly showed me me – as female. My world pretty much fell apart at that point, two days before Christmas 2002.

My wife was a star, as usual. She immediately identified that this was bigger than the two of us, and that we needed help together. The obvious place to start was the leadership of our church.

Our church leader's response - denial. Not of the reality of me being trans, but of the need to be a whole person. My trans-ness needed to be controlled, denied, resisted. We were back to the standard evangelical route of 'healing'. The science underpinning diagnosis was flawed, apparently. The stories I had read were unusual and not representative. I disagreed, and was able to cite examples from people I'd actually met by that time. A year later he sat in my front room and forbade me to come to church as Helen, then walked out saying that I needed to deal with my anger problem. The facade of acceptance had been destroyed.

Many, many months later the other leadership apologised. When challenged on their theology, they admitted they hadn't any, but felt they needed to be able to answer to God for how they had acted to protect my children. Nothing about being able to answer to God for how they had protected me.

Church hadn't finished with me yet. A vast number of my friends from university days parked the knowledge on the 'too difficult' shelf – they still do. I met with unbridled arrogance, fuelled by ignorance and a belief that they were hearing directly from God so I must, therefore, be completely deluded. 'Did God make mistakes' I was repeatedly asked. 'No', was my response, 'He made me this way'. The biological evidence underpinning diversity was ignored as inconvenient.

My wife and I moved to another church which seemed welcoming, until I actually wanted to contribute, at which point I was seen as a theological issue rather than a person. Even attending a day away as a guest at my in-laws' church became a problem. It was clear – Church had no place for me.

If I was to remain a Christian outside of church circles, then I had better be sure of what exactly I believed. A 'pick-and-mix' set of beliefs had been condemned early in my evangelical youth. The only sure ground was the Bible.

Except it wasn't. All those contradictions that had been neatly side-stepped for over 25 years now reared their ugly heads. I started to understand that the Bible had actually been compiled in a series of political meetings, or had been conveniently 're-translated' or edited to bring out or adapt particular points. I was faced with questions about the basic morality of a God who refuses to intervene except in particular circumstances. I started to understand how humanity had worked out the vastness of the universe we inhabited - vastness of space and time most of us simply cannot begin to comprehend. It became untenable to believe that humans, however you defined them, were special in the light of that understanding, added to which we were discovering that animals and birds could do pretty much everything we viewed as 'human'. Beyond all this, I was faced with the reality that many Christians only operated within the boundaries of their own comfort. If a relationship with God was truly life changing, then it seemed to be very limited in its scope. I couldn't maintain my faith in the face of this onslaught.

So it was actually a relief when, in the autumn of 2009, I was finally able to say to myself that I no longer believed in any of it. The world didn't fall in. My underpinning values didn't change. Eight years of struggle had ended.

When a trans person transitions, those around them also have their own transition process. The trans person has wrestled with thoughts, often for many years. It's unreasonable to expect those around them to process those same thoughts within a matter of minutes. It can take months, years even. But it also requires proper listening. Psychology tells us that people are generally afraid of difference, and someone changing their gender presentation is about as different as it comes. That's why it's so often seen as comic.

But churches' reactions to trans people are very slow to change. That's fundamentally why I see a lot of churches as arrogant. That arrogance is generally fed by a belief that the individual or group knows God's thoughts, but this usually means an expression of discomfort. There tends to be a requirement placed onto the trans person to explain, often at a time of high vulnerability when the thought process isn't clear to the individual concerned, and in high-pressure situations. So the trans person falls back on media clichés, which are usually inaccurate and simplistic, and easily countered. The reality is usually more nuanced, more holistic, more complex than most want to deal with. Our perceptions have been challenged, compliance is key, so the trans person must be wrong to want to step out of our box.

I think it's true to say that we all have a choice in how to deal with certain things. I don't have a choice about being trans, but I did have a choice about what to do with it. But that choice wasn't between transition and the status quo as most people understood it to be. Instead it was between transition and suicide. I felt I owed it to my children to try to be the best parent I could be – me alive and female would be better than me dead and male. One verse that kept me going throughout 2004 was 'I lay before you today life and prosperity, death and destruction. ... Now choose life' (Deut. 30:19) If I was wrong, I could revisit that decision. I've had no need to do so in the last eleven years.

In the last two years I've been campaigning on legalising equal marriage. The response of most religious leaders has, once again, fallen into a simplistic and unscientific world view. And, sadly, although predictably, it is the Church from which the most vocal opposition has come. If you are going to say, as many Church leaders do, that marriage is between one man and one woman, then you must define what you mean by 'man' and 'woman'. And I can guarantee that every definition you come up with will be wrong.

This pharasaical insistence on English translations of some verses of the Bible while ignoring the key message of love and wholeness is baffling to those outside religion. The inconvenience to you of investigating the diversity within human societies and across nature is surely worth doing, to avoid the daily pain caused to those who don't fit neatly into your world view. There's only one word for the insistence that such a viewpoint is right based upon a theory while ignoring physical evidence – arrogance.

I was taught for years that real freedom is in Christ. My experience tells me the exact opposite is true. In walking away from religion and faith, and accepting myself as I am, flaws and all, I found myself freed from society's expectations, and empowered to challenge society. My wife, children and colleagues have stood beside me and life is now rich, colourful, exciting and precious. I am me. The labels you attach to me no longer define me.

Carol Nixon

The Problem of Being too Definite

Many objections to transsexualism base themselves on what is claimed to be 'the revealed Word of God'. It would be easy enough to counter these criticisms by disputing the interpretation of that Word, but this would imply some level of agreement with the objectors over their use of the Word in this way at all. It would accord to the words on the page an absolute level of inflexible authority that reduced moral enquiry to determining the 'real' meaning of a segment of language.

For me it is preposterous to assert that God can be comprehended in human language - that way one person's revelation becomes another person's heresy, for which they should be burnt alive or bombed. Much of the religious persecution and slaughter that has so degraded European history might be blamed on obsession with the Word. I have heard misguided clergy describe this as the 'working out of God's purpose in the world'. Who says? It would be laughable if it were not so tragic. Those people who are really possessed by the love of God do not persecute, degrade, torture, maim and kill. Nor even condemn. They cannot. How could such actions be derived or justified from the texts of revelation without proving the texts to be counter to the love of God? I want none of it. Truth is experienced, not spoken; true religion is practiced, not believed. Therefore all I can do here is to describe what I have experienced.

First, an example of the kind of painful thing that happens only too often - though I am glad to say I have suffered it only once. When I decided to change my gender presentation, to live the rest of my life in a way that felt true, I told those who knew me what I was doing, and, to the best of my ability, why. I was attacked and abused by a 'born-again' Christian for my irresponsibility. I hadn't even considered the religious implications, she stormed. (In actual fact, I had wrestled with the conflict between what I had been told and what I actually experienced for forty years.) Where, I wondered rather sadly, was the 'Christian Love' in that response? On further investigation, I learnt that Christian love was to be regarded as a sentimental aberration if it was extended to those who 'broke the law'. So much for her.

What have I learnt since then? Well, starting to live in the gender to which my whole being cried out was a mystical experience in itself. The flood of euphoria caused a state of mind that I think I can validly compare with the ecstasy of the meditative, or the 'trip' of the drug-user. This effected a permanent increase in the amount of energy available for caring about, and for, other people.

There was also a change in perception, rather like getting one's glasses on straight. Freed from the need to check my thoughts and behaviour at all times to ensure their masculinity, I could observe and behave as a whole person. At the time, friends told me they saw this as a transcending of gender (which reminded me of the special role transsexual people are allotted in several non-Western cultures), but I would simply call it feeling (at last) at home with oneself in the Universe, which is not a specifically transsexual phenomenon. The only specialty is that one has a comparatively unusual base of experience from which to intuit.

And God began to come much, much closer ... I have hesitated about using the word 'God', as may be explained in a moment. This movement began years ago with a sudden clear certainty one Sunday morning that I was to drive some 17 miles to the nearest town and go to church. I had not been to church for decades, never having resolved the intellectual issues raised for me by the study of anthropology. But I acted on this certainty, without knowing when the services might be, nor where the churches were. I simply got up, had breakfast and went. On reaching the town, I heard a bell ringing from a small church that I had never noticed before, with people going in. This was it. I joined them, received a warm welcome, and have been going there ever since.

The next eruption of wordless communication occurred in October 2000, when I suffered a pulmonary embolism at 11p.m. at home. I could hardly breathe, and the idea of going to the phone was beyond me. I sat in bed, propped against the wall, and fought for breath. I suspected a heart attack, and thought I hadn't long to live; but there welled up in me a kind of acceptance which could only be expressed verbally as 'I don't want to die, but if that is the way it is to be, I am yours ... I accept what You will'. Instantly, equally non-verbally, as it were a hand closed gently round me and I was soothed with the message 'You're safe. Don't worry'. I fell asleep within minutes, and did not wake till 8 in the morning, not cured, but well enough to make my own way to a (very alarmed) doctor.

Over the next two years I visited a terminally ill lady in our remote village quite late every evening, to make her laugh and to put her to bed. Often, as I set out from home, I felt overpoweringly weary, because I never used to get enough sleep; but I soon discovered that the energy (and the ability) to make her laugh would flood in as I walked into her house. You are given the energy to do what is laid before you to do - if you accept. Two interesting footnotes to this:

1. I could not easily have been of as much service to her in my old male persona
2. It was granted to me that she actually died in my arms.

The climax of this learning journey so far occurred early in 2004, while taking Communion in church. I had been greatly angered by someone's thoughtlessness the previous day, and was praying for humility, so as to step away from pride and judgmentalism. I certainly needed it. By chance I was the last at the altar rail, and having a cold, I had kept the bread in my hands to dip into the wine rather than spread germs on the cup. I suddenly became aware that I held - symbolically - the whole of Christ in my hands, and there were just the two of us. Not being fond of formulae, I inwardly just said 'Hi!' I could not have been more shaken by the response if the church had blown up. A roaring, vibrating, glowing stream of - what? - pure energy? - appeared to pour out of my hands into my face, making me tremble and burst into tears; and letting me 'know' things. There was so much communication in this energy that I have never succeeded in verbalising it, except, rather oddly, for a 'statement' which was invested with huge emotional emphasis, 'I have no name.' (That is why I hesitate to say 'God'). The flow was totally benevolent, but much more than personal. In one infinite instant I was shown my minuteness beside this hugeness, and yet transfigured by the privilege of being shown it. I weep whenever I recall it, and especially at Communion.

Have I strayed indulgently from the issue of gender? I think not. The dialectic whereby nothing can be both A and B (where A is defined by the absence of B), applied equally in my earlier life both to religion and to gender. I had not been able simultaneously to worship God and not believe in Him/Her; I had not been able to conceive of being simultaneously female and male; for in those days I had abhorred the Zen-like concept of believing contradictory ideas. It threw into doubt my whole basis of knowledge; much as I imagine that ambiguous gender expression threatens the world view of some conventional thinkers.

But like a physicist forced to accept the contradictory characteristics of light despite her logical objections, I have had to learn that we cannot understand all things, and that we cannot impose verbal schemata upon experience without deleting some of it. Through being compelled eventually to accept the way I am, I have been shown how to keep the door open to what the modern educated mind rejects as illogical. This is not blanket credulity - it is the opposite. It is the realisation that the most dangerous and untrue claim anyone can make is that they can express the truth in words.

Abigail

I am a Christian. I seek to follow Christ. I am also antinomian: I do not accept human moral law, or human interpretations of God's law. I try to live a good life, so am interested in what people say about morality, but do not accept any person or institution as my guide,

I have had a lot of psychotherapy over the last six years. I believe I have also had the gentle but insistent prompting of God, leading me from a tense, angry and frightened denial to acceptance of my true self. Before I transitioned, I wanted to die - I remember looking longingly up at tall buildings. Only since my GRS have I begun to appreciate my body - my thighs, fingertips, earlobes and eyelashes - and delight in it

Because I am good with words, I tried to use words to help me make my decision - words like 'manly', 'feminine', 'selfish', 'truth', 'reality', 'good'. I finally made my decision to transition when I was driven to it, when there was nothing else I could do: without words or argument, because words and argument were no longer any use.

A paradox: I reach wholeness through mutilation. Yet although I could probably have fathered a child in the narrow sense of fertilizing an ovum, while pretending to be a man I could not have formed relationships within a family and brought up that child.

Last year, I went with friends to a garden open to the public. I expected to be bored, but I was captivated. As I have come fully to life, I have come to appreciate the beauty of Creation. What used to be just a tree, and so dull, is now light and shadow, shape and movement, wonder and life. I feel that I know and fit my place within God's creation.

Stephanie

My Journey of Faith as an Evangelical Trans Woman[1].

Even the Darkness

My name is Stephanie, I am a trans woman in my fifties, and this is my story.

I was born on 27 May 1958 in London. I was the smallest surviving baby in the ward, so perhaps God does have a sense of humour.

I was brought up in a traditional English family where anything different was frowned upon and brought up with strong beliefs of right and wrong and trans was definitely wrong.

My first intimation that I was different was at the age of six when choosing my favourite colour I went instinctively to pink. However, knowing that was wrong chose red instead - as the nearest I could get to it.

I had a number of thoughts like this as I was growing up, however things went crazy at the age of twelve when instead of being attracted to girls I was attracted to boys, I had a deep need to dress in girls clothes and had a deep need for girls' company. I tried to repress these thoughts as I had been told they were wrong, my nickname at school was 'Steph' so perhaps I didn't hide them so well.

However when you repress something as strong as your sexual identity it comes out in a different way that is not always good, and at the age of sixteen I became a compulsive gambler. I think it was my way of hiding from my gender dysphoria.

I was destroying my life gambling up to £200 a day on fruit machines, and although I had some happy times in my twenties the gambling blighted my life in that period.

By the age of twenty-seven my life was in ruins and I was seriously thinking of suicide when I was invited to a mission. Most of the talk

---

1   This is a version of a talk originally delivered at a seminar on and led by trans people of faith, held at the Lambeth Conference Fringe in 2008.

went over my head; however, one sentence caught my attention that 'Whoever is in Christ is a New Creation'. God was offering me a fresh start and I took it because I wanted to stop gambling so much and needed a new start to my life.

I joined a fundamentalist church where we were taught very strict values of right and wrong which was exactly what I had been taught as a child. This strengthened my denial of my feminine nature because now not only were my feelings wrong, they were also of the devil.

But God was true to me in that my need to stop gambling brought me to Christ and with the help of GA [Gamblers Anonymous] and my active involvement in the church I stopped.

I was very active in the church but was very wary about sharing my faith and once said to God 'Watch my lips, I will do anything for you except evangelism', as it frightened me. One night I went to what I thought was a praise meeting in a church but it was actually a launch meeting for a Billy Graham mission (silly me). They asked for volunteers and being at the front row of a church with 200 evangelical Christians I thought they would all volunteer so I put my hand up, because I felt I could at least make coffees or knock in tent pegs.

The problem was that in that hall I was the only volunteer, but sitting at the front I didn't know this so I was co-opted onto the leadership team being one of only 2 un-ordained people on that board. It was a successful mission with over five hundred people giving their lives to Christ and my life of evangelism had truly started.

About this time I started going out with a lovely woman called Roz who had always been a good friend but things developed and she turned into my soul mate. We were married in 1990, and we embarked on a life of Christian ministry together.

We became prayer coordinators for the main mission organisation in West Berkshire called 'Mission Together', and led a prayer meeting of up to seventy people; there was a great desire for God to move at that time. We then led a mission, which was again successful and together with our active witnessing and my preaching were well regarded by the fundamentalists in the town

However, my gambling was a coping mechanism to avoid my underlying feelings, and they were bound to surface. At the age of thirty-six, one day I had a sense that deep down I was a woman and in realizing this I found a deep sense of peace, and being close to my wife I went home and told her. She was very upset, which was understandable, and caring for her I tried to repress my feelings. I found I couldn't do that, became unstable and ended up in a psychiatric hospital, where I was diagnosed as transsexual and discharged. But as a Christian I couldn't accept myself as I knew and had been told it was evil, so I became unstable again and was readmitted. When I was discharged I parted from my wife. Because of all of the strain of the loss of my job due to my illness, and the strain of living with such uncertainty, my wife had a total breakdown, was sectioned and was admitted to a psychiatric hospital.

For me as a Christian husband my first thought was for my wife, so we reunited and I gave up work to look after her and tried to bury my feelings. I don't regret this because I feel that although she couldn't (not wouldn't) accept my need to live as a woman we became closer. In choosing to remain true to our vows our love deepened.

I tried everything to be healed from my feelings, we used to make weekly five hours round trips to London for one hour of counselling. I even tried exorcism to cast out the demon of transsexualism and my wife used to pray for about an hour a day for God to heal me, but nothing worked and the feelings persisted.

We threw ourselves into ministry and spent a great deal of time witnessing and saw many people come to Christ (it is testimony that even though I was living a lie Christ honoured our faith). In one week we led seven people to Christ, which was a wonderful experience.

However, in my mind I became more and more intense, more and more like a pent-up spring and more fanatical; I went from a called person to a driven person, constantly trying to achieve more for God and yet becoming more and more unhappy. I hated myself, I was constantly angry with my wife (although not violent) and resented God (how could God make me like this when all I wanted to do was follow Him). I think the truth was though that as time went on I became less a servant of God and more a servant to my own fears.

As I wasn't working we became more and more behind with our mortgage until in the end we decided to sell the house and move to Huddersfield.

A year after we moved, Roz became ill, was diagnosed with cancer and died within three weeks. God was so close to us in that time, I remember Roz saying 'you know this is a terrible situation but God has been so close to me I wouldn't have missed it for the world'. I share those sentiments because it was like walking in hell watching my soul mate die, but God was so close to me in that time; for me it was a time of walking with one foot in hell and one foot in heaven.

Before Roz became ill I had made an appointment to see a psychiatrist for him to diagnose me, he diagnosed me transsexual and said that I was so ill that I had either to accept gender reassignment or go insane, but for me as a Christian I felt it would be against God so replied 'I'll go insane then because I will not disobey my God'. This promptly happened and the next 3 years were a time of great pain and instability.

But God is a faithful God who stayed with me during that time, and one day I felt Him speak in my heart three words: 'Live in Truth'. Then I asked myself the questions who am I and who does God really see? I saw that God looked into my heart and saw me as I was in my heart, as in my heart I was a woman, and that is who God saw. I felt so stupid.

In my heart I was a daughter of God trying to be his son and wondering why I felt so unhappy. I could almost hear the angels sing 'at last SHE'S got the message', I couldn't come to God as anything other than myself, and yet God by His grace had stayed with me until I had learnt that lesson.

I started to attend an LGBT church in Manchester called MCC and at last started to live in truth. I changed my name to Stephanie, got diagnosed again and went into transition.

I have now been living as Stephanie for three years and in that time I have changed so much: I had a chronic stammer which has almost gone; I am a lot more relaxed, and I am starting to rediscover my disciple's heart; I am starting to rediscover that love for God. I am a member of the Methodist Church and have just co-authored a report for them on the LGBT situation in West Yorkshire, and by the time you read this the service will have been up and running for a period of time. I am now also a worship leader in my church, which holds many challenges.

I still have many inner conflicts and am only now learning to grieve the loss of Roz; you do not spend your life in denial and put it right overnight. For me transition is a pilgrimage of becoming me and the operation is only part of that; for me that pilgrimage will last the rest of my life.

I do not know what the future holds, but I do know who holds the future, I walk towards it with a living God at my side.

Suzanne's Story

I'm not sure when the unease arose, but I know I had begun to think of myself as wrong inside before I was four years old. I still remember bits of a television spy adventure I somehow watched at that age where I found the leading lady riveting, and especially her final triumph, dressed in an evening gown! That it is one of the few things I recall from that age and that I identified so closely with the heroine strongly suggests that it must have been significant to me.

I felt incredibly guilty that I had these 'unboyish' feelings, and yet they wouldn't go away. They came and went as the years went by: at seven I sewed a long 'dress' from some old slips my mother had thrown out; at nine I burnt my eyebrows off with a homemade napalm bomb while disposing of a model 'Graf Spee'; at eleven I started working with a former marine sergeant to toughen me up; yet at thirteen I stole a cocktail dress from some jumble to wear secretly at home, although I returned it after a couple of days.

When I joined the Royal Navy I wasn't much further forward. I did hope it would solve my problem. I found I was attracted to girls but nothing ever came of it. I suspect I mainly wanted to be friends and share their life and interests. On the other hand I enjoyed naval life and worked hard at my studies. I had made a definite Christian commitment in my late teens but it began to drift a bit as time went on.

Then two important things happened. I fell in love, and I was nearly killed in a military 'confrontation'. It put my faith back on track since I felt I had survived for a purpose. I also found my feelings for the person who became my wife partly pushed my need away. I tried to explain how I felt to her, but didn't understand much myself since I deliberately ignored the subject as much as I could. (Not that there was much help or information around — mostly weird stories in the tabloids that didn't resemble the way I felt.) I assumed that in time the new relationship would get me back to 'normal', which was strange since I wanted to excel, not be 'average' in anything else!

Marriage was a wonderful experience of sharing. I also found for the first time that I could function in every way as a man. Yet within six weeks the old feelings were back as strongly as ever. It wasn't my wife's clothes, although proximity and her being roughly my size did exert a pressure. I wanted to be what they gave visible expression to — a woman. Dressing up did this in part, so I did from time to time, accumulating a wardrobe of clothes to avoid using my wife's. Having children was wonderful. I was able to be present for the births, feeling a bit jealous, even. Not that I wanted the pain of course! I was good with babies - bathing and changing them was a joy. I still have exceptionally good relationships with my adult daughters who both knew about Suzanne from their teens and took me clothes shopping and to 'weepies' at the cinema, as well as still wanting me for all the 'dad' things.

After I had left the navy, in my mid-thirties my wife and I became involved with a couple in our neighbourhood who were having problems in their marriage. Part of it was that the husband was transvestite. He wasn't like the newspaper stories I had read and seemed more like me. Through his help and information I started to attend one of the many support groups. It did help, but the secrecy cut into me, and to be fair a good many of those attending were just men dressed up. That of course was what I was too, but it wasn't where my needs lay. Through the group I learned a lot, and was eventually able to discuss my situation with a couple of relevantly experienced psychiatrists. They both diagnosed me as 'gender dysphoric' (i.e. transsexual).

Over the following years I worked to keep a balance. With my wife's knowledge I lived in a woman's role for half my annual leave allowance well away from home, staying with various friends. Mostly I did the everyday things I did the rest of the time, but with so much more joy. I also took the occasional chance to 'glam up' which was fun. The rest of the time I was a leader in my church, and worked as a carer, which gave me some outlet for my feelings. I don't doubt the diagnosis I was given — it is still with me whenever I am not busy. But I believe I am obeying God's call not to change over, and I made promises to my wife I intend to honour, particularly now as she comes up to retirement. Even so, the first time I took communion as Suzanne at a Sibyls meeting I cried my heart out. It was so wonderful to acknowledge all of me before God even though I couldn't in my own church and town.

I tried to find a cure in a number of ways. I have also been counselled, and prayed with for healing. (I no longer believe that I'm ill, though, just different.) The odd weeks I spent away kept me going, although it was so very hard to return to my male role afterwards. The energy I put into suppressing this need I'm sure has caused health problems in my retirement, and yet being as I am has helped me grow as a person and care for outsiders. I also understand more about the anger and pain that was within me as a young man as I tried to burn 'It' out.

Even in my late sixties I would still gladly go forward into transition. I would not relish the surgery, but there is something very seductive about not having to constantly fight an inner war, and spend so much of my life playing a role which I feel is untrue. A number of my friends have made this transition, not always easily, but with so much inner peace that I am sometimes quite jealous. I no longer pray for God to take my difficulty away — who would want to lose so much of themselves? I do continue to ask God to use me, and help me to grow in love and wisdom. For me my difference helps me to be a gender bridge. I am just sad that it is a pain and problem to others.

Raymus's Testimony

I do not have any trouble with my transition from a Christian point of view. As I was not 'whole' before, I used to (sometimes) start on the vodka too early in the day.

Also the New Testament itself is full of ideas of new beginnings.

Section 2: Christians who Cross Dress

Janet

Experiences of a Christian Transvestite

Early Years

I was born (male) during World War II in one of the British colonies. At the time of my birth my parents' marriage was breaking up, and I think my mother saw me as an extension of my father. Years later I found out that after my birth she hadn't touched me until I was six weeks old: I had been left in the charge of a nanny. Whether this influenced my later behaviour, I know not. At age six months my mother brought me back to Britain, and at first we lived in my father's home town. I suppose Mum hoped for some sort of reconciliation. But this didn't happen, and when I was four we moved and went to live with my maternal grandmother on Tyneside.

It was then that I first cross-dressed. At about age five, I used to go up to my mother's bedroom and put on some of her clothes. This ended in disaster, as one day, a neighbour from across the road - a doctor - obviously saw me through the window, and reported this to my mother. She was very angry (and no doubt embarrassed), and I got a scolding and a spanking, and after that I didn't dare play with her clothes: well, at least not for a long time afterwards. But there were two other influences at this time.

The first was some of our girl neighbours. In those days it was common practice to have very grand birthday parties to which you went dressed in your best clothes. As a boy, I loathed this, but was rewarded by the sight of some of the girls in their best clothes. There was one girl, called Brenda, who had the most wonderful russet-coloured taffeta party frock with many layers of petticoats, and which swished and rustled noisily, which enthralled me. And there was Helena, a Norwegian, who used to come to parties in a Norwegian folk costume: a laced bodice worn over a frilly white blouse, a brightly coloured skirt, and stiffly starched apron. These two girls and their dresses were the highlight of the parties as far as I was concerned, and I used to dream of being able to wear such clothes.

Generally I was very unhappy, being bullied a lot by other boys (I had a very low threshold at which I started crying – I believe that this is a hereditary thing as one of my sons and my daughter are exactly the same), and I was not very happy at home either. Also I was useless at all forms of sport, not being able to catch balls, and so on. Although I much preferred girls' company to boys', it was more their clothes that I dreamed of, although sometimes I did dream of being a girl. One of my favourite occupations at this time was going to the station and watching the trains - very much a boy's thing. On the other hand I did like the girls' serials on the radio - things like *Ballet Shoes* by Noel Streatfeild; and some of the girls' books, like the Ameliaranne series.

The second thing that was a strong influence was the dress of one of the teachers at school. The French teacher, Miss Marshall, was nicknamed Fanny, and I adored her, and wished that she was my mother. I was good at French (we started this when I was seven), and Fanny was kind to me. But the thing that really attracted me to her was that she was always most impeccably dressed. She often wore suits that had tight-fitting jackets showing off her figure to good effect, and usually had skirts with very sharp pleats, whether accordion pleats or box pleats. Her favourite colour was a soft red, and she usually wore lipstick to match. She went home from school on the train, and soon I had a new reason to hang around the station, watching out for Fanny on her way home. She always had a fetching hat, a neat handbag, high-heeled shoes and gloves. Thinking back, I realise that she was more like a fashion model than what we nowadays expect from female teachers. But that was 1949!

A few years later, when I was eleven, we moved to Yorkshire and I started a new school.

Teenage Years

Somewhere about 1956 petticoats and full skirts came into fashion. The first person that I really noticed was the headmaster's secretary at school. She was a buxom lady, in her thirties I think. She usually wore a crisp blouse, and a very full skirt much distended by voluminous petticoats. We sometimes had study periods in the main hall if one of the teachers was absent, and this lady used to walk between the headmaster's study and the school office quite frequently. In the silence of the hall you could hear her very loud rustlings as she walked along. I think it was with her that I first realised that this interest in female clothing turned me on sexually.

I went to the local church youth club which met every Saturday night, where we danced rock 'n' rollfashion to the latest pop music, but also older dances like waltzes, quicksteps, and the veleta. The girls all wore very full-skirted dresses with lots of petticoats, and dancing with them, or watching them, was great fun. I had various girlfriends, but these relationships were usually short-lived as my mother got quite jealous; and when I had a relationship with one particular girl called Anne that became serious, she tried to interfere and went to see Anne's mother. I was very upset as I had fallen in love with Anne - it wasn't just the dresses she wore - but I couldn't bear my mother's nosiness.

My time at school was certainly not the happiest time of my life. I loathed it: particularly having to play sport. I still find most forms of sport very boring, and much prefer music, poetry and art as hobbies.

Early Adulthood

I went to university in Manchester and had a great time, having various girlfriends unhindered by my mother, and going to the Hallé concerts conducted by Barbirolli. And one wet day I went into the City Art Gallery and discovered 'art' - the Pre-Raphaelites particularly appealing to me. But I was still interested in female clothes, and I remember one time going into a corset shop in Hale and attempting to buy a corselette. But the elderly shop assistant was so embarrassed that I hurriedly left.

After leaving college and into my second job, I met the woman who became my wife. I adored her, and I still love her greatly. After a while I bought a few petticoats and hoped that she might wear them, but, not surprisingly, she wasn't interested. In due course she recognised my interest in women's clothing - I was chided for watching 1950s films, and costume dramas where Victorian crinoline dresses were worn, and opined that this was 'wrong'. This led me to pretending to myself that I wasn't really interested in clothes: at that stage I never told my wife my childhood history, and I suppressed these feelings.

We went to a Methodist Church. My wife told the minister and a friend about my unnatural interest in female clothes. The four of us then had an interview where I was made to renounce all interest and all thoughts to do with female clothes, and had to promise to destroy any books, photographs, etc., that had pictures that I found attractive. I hoped that all this would work. I loved my wife, and I just wanted to be 'normal'. If someone could wave a magic wand (as it were) over me and convert me into a 'normal' being then I would be very pleased. But it wasn't long before I was again caught watching a 1950s film with full-skirted dresses. So this time it was arranged that we should go to a Christian Healing Centre – Ellel Grange, near Lancaster. We went for a weekend, and during this time, two people prayed for me, and laid hands on me, exhorting 'the spirit of a woman' to leave me. This went on for what seemed a very long time, and I felt as if I was being put through a mangle: it was a dreadful experience, one of the most traumatic experiences of my life. Anyway, I thought that I must have been healed: God surely wouldn't put you through an experience like that for nothing. So when it was all over, I was on a high: I thought I had been 'healed'.

In Middle Age

I am no longer sure of the true order in which the following events actually happened: it probably doesn't make any difference, anyway.

At some stage my wife said to me that she believed that I wasn't just interested in petticoats, but that I wanted to wear them myself. I was still refusing to accept myself as I really was, and so I denied this, but she was insistent, and said that as this was so, why didn't I get myself a skirt and some petticoats? I was amazed, and couldn't really believe it. But some time later I bought a cross-dressing magazine, and saw an advert from a dressmaker who made petticoats. I contacted this lady, and it turned out that her husband was a cross dresser and that sometimes they came up to the Northern Concord[1] in Manchester. We met there, and she brought a skirt that she had made for me. I remember trying it on in a bedroom in The Rembrandt[2]. I was very deeply moved: in fact I was overwhelmed by a great sense that God loved me just as I was. Afterwards I skipped and danced down Whitworth Street on my way back to Oxford Road station to go home.

I gradually acquired a few more female clothes. At first things went all right with my wife. She prayed to know whether this dressing up was right. Her gut feeling was that it wasn't. But within a week of her praying to know if this was okay, she read about four

---

1   Northern Concord is a support group for people who cross dress or are transsexual.
2   The Rembrandt Hotel is where Northern Concord used to meet.

different newspaper and magazine articles about cross-dressing, and so she concluded that it must be right. Furthermore she was puzzled by the effect that the cross-dressing was having on me: I was much calmer, more relaxed - it made me a much nicer person to be with.

But this didn't last. After a while we had another row. In desperation one day I sat down at my desk. I wrote God or Jesus a letter, imploring him to change me – to make me 'normal'. But then I had this amazing 'religious experience' – it was as if Jesus was standing next to me at the desk: he said 'Don't worry, Ian, I know that you like petticoats and women's clothes. That's how you are, and I like you that way. Stop fighting against it, wanting to be someone else all the time. I love you, so why shouldn't you love yourself as you are?' I was amazed. This wasn't the answer to my prayer that I had expected. I went and told my wife. She didn't believe it, but said, 'Of course you imagined that – that is the answer that you wanted to hear.' It was to be some years before she accepted that for me it was a very real experience. At the time she was very scornful.

About this time I got a PC and discovered an American website that was for cross-dressers who liked full-skirted dresses and petticoats. On the opening page was a statement that said something like. 'God has created you in a very special way. Give thanks for your love of female dress and full skirts, and rejoice in it.' This seemed to be the same message that I'd got sitting at my desk. It still seemed to me novel, and it was still taking me by surprise. I had spent so many years thinking my interest was wrong, and feeling very guilty about it. It was taking time to re-adjust.

But things were still very fraught between my wife and myself. I thought that I would try and stop dressing – to show willing. I took all my clothes, including a beautiful blue taffeta dress that I really loved, and put these in the Oxfam bin – I often wonder what they made of them!

After a while it became obvious to both of us that I was much worse off without my clothes, and so I started all over again. A thing that helped was that my wife realised that she had a problem of her own that she could do nothing about, although she desperately wanted healing in the same way that I had done with my 'problem'. We came to an understanding that I was allowed to dress on two evenings a week, and go away to a couple of weekends a year.

Concluding Thoughts about Cross-Dressing.

One of the things that my wife and I both wasted a lot of time on was asking the question: 'Why?' As if by understanding where the cross-dress phenomenon had come from, one might be able to cure it. There are some clues, I think, in the history of my early childhood. But even if one did fully understand 'Why', it's a delusion to think that the problem will go away. In the end one has to face up to the situation as it is, and make the best of it: discover which ways it can be put to positive use, if at all possible.

Another thing that 'wasted time' is what I call the 'Jekyll and Hyde' theory. The idea that when I am in female guise as Janet that I am a different person from when I am the male Ian. My wife was fearful that Janet might do unpredictable things, and she was rather frightened of her. But to me it became clear that Janet and Ian were one and the same person, and that there was a synergistic effect. The whole personality is greater than the sum of the two. To deny one lessens the other. My wife now understands this as well.

For a long time I had thought that my interest in female clothes, and my desire to dress up in them was purely a form of sexual fetishism. After all I was 'turned on' sexually by them. But when I came to dress seriously I found that I wanted to wear a wig, to put on make-up – in fact to become a woman. There was something deep inside my personality that seemed to want to be female. And it remains that I am at my happiest, my most relaxed when I am in female mode. As I write this I am wearing a white blouse, woollen box-pleated skirt, and court shoes, and I am wearing a firm corselette, and I know what hair-style (wig) suits me, and what jewellery: it feels that I am really 'me', and I don't feel anything particularly erotic about this.

Self-discovery is a long and difficult process, requiring us to be honest with ourselves, which is often painful. And being able to do this in an unselfish way that doesn't hurt others is not always easy. And this process has to be followed by self-acceptance. I once read that the greatest work of healing that the Holy Spirit can do is to show us ourselves as we really are - to remove any façades that we may build, and then to show us how we might be. The healing that I experienced was in fact the opposite of what I had once hoped for - to learn to accept myself as I was, and to learn to love myself, instead of expecting some magic cure. We are told to 'love our neighbour as ourselves' - it's difficult to do that if we don't love ourselves in the first place. There have been other areas where I have only discovered myself quite late on in life. A few years ago I discovered the Quakers and their silent worship, and I left the noisy Methodists, and in my case the judgemental Conservative Evangelicals. For me, it was like discovering the true living water that Jesus talked about. It was a 'coming home' experience.

This business of perceptions is important: whether they are real or not. When I first started going regularly to the Northern Concord in Manchester, and I met other transgender people for the first time, my reaction was to try and categorise them: Was she (a) a 'real woman'; (b) transsexual; or (c) transvestite? I think this is probably what many people do: they want to put people in the appropriate 'box', and for many out there, there are only two boxes available, and if you don't fit adequately into one of those boxes, then there's a very negative reaction. For some 'transsexual' is also an acceptable 'box', but few find 'transvestite' to be an acceptable answer. After a while with dealing with transgender people, I realised that I was no longer categorising them; I just accepted them as they were, as a person, and it no longer entered my head to try and decide what their gender status was. And I hope that's what they did with me. I began to realise that what was more important for me was their behaviour and their values. I am 'turned off' by loud and raucous people telling bawdy jokes, or talking incessantly about football, as if it is the only thing that matters in life; much preferring quiet and gentle people who are thoughtful, and who have some spiritual awareness, and so on. And this has not much to do with gender: there are some loud and raucous women about.

For some people who cross dress, the most important goal is to be able to go out and about, and not be 'read', i.e. for the public at large not to realise that it's a man under there. I quite understand this: people want to be accepted, not rejected, and as I've explained, if you don't fit in the right 'box', you're liable to be rejected. I rarely go out 'dressed', and for a number of reasons: although at one time I would have liked to go out and about locally sometimes as Janet, my wife was scared stiff that I'd be recognised; and maybe she's right - that I'd be 'read' and the chances of being stared at doesn't appeal. But it is more than that: I just want to be 'me' whatever that means. I have had enough of building a façade and pretending to be something that I'm not, and going to great lengths to convince the outside world that I am really a woman would be another pretence. For me, this is more of the same, but the other way round. I look forward to the day when I can be accepted by the world at large for what I am. But I am doubtful whether this will happen in my lifetime. So I dress at home, and away from home at transgender house-party weekends.

It probably follows from the above that I wouldn't want to be a woman all the time – to be transsexual. Why not? Well, there are a number of answers to this. First, for quite a lot of the time (in fact most of the time), I am quite happy to be a man: I like pottering in my shed doing woodwork; building a model railway; tinkering with electronics; taking things to pieces and mending them. Second, I don't think that I have the patience or the courage to be transsexual. I have a number of good friends who are transsexual, who have gone down that road, and I know what is involved: it's not easy.

Loving my wife is a very important reason that I stay as I am; she is my best friend. I don't like hurting her. She has found it difficult enough to get to where we are now. I have now got to the point where my love for my wife is so strong that it pains me to hurt her. It's obvious from her body language that she much prefers me to be a man in men's clothes than wearing a skirt. So now I often wait for her to suggest that it's about time I 'dressed'. And in any case I know that I couldn't get on living by myself; that I need a female partner. When I was a teenager I was very lonely, and I used to dream of having a wife, and that still matters a lot to me.

But in all this I have become a much more 'whole' person: and that is what God wants for us. As whole people we can love others much more successfully, and do a little more about making the world a better place to live for our neighbours, than otherwise would be the case. And I think that I am doing that. And I give thanks for who I am.

Elaine Sommers

Faith, Gender and Me (Self-Interview)

Elaine is the femme name of a transgender Christian living in SW England.

Q: Elaine, you describe yourself as transgender. Can you explain this term?
A: I use transgender as an umbrella term. I don't really identify as a cross-dresser or transsexual. I think dual-gendered is the best way to describe how I see myself.

Q: Does that mean you are gay?
A: No, I am heterosexual, and have no confusion about that. Transgender is about gender identity, not sexual orientation. It is estimated that the incidence of homosexuality in the trans community is similar to that of the general population. My own observation in the trans world bears this out. Confusion may arise because of the publicity given to drag queens (such as Lily Savage and the like) most of whom are gay. They tend to caricature and satirise women in an exaggerated and sometimes crude way. Further confusion arises because trans people may frequent gay venues, simply because these are places where they feel safe and accepted.

Q: When did you start dressing as Elaine?
A: I guess I must have been about twelve or thirteen. I got this urge to dress in women's clothes and experimented in secret. I thought I was the only person in the World who had these feelings. I dressed on and off as I grew up, but never dared to let anyone else know about it. I hated myself for being this way. I just wanted to be the same as everyone else. I became a Christian at 18, and thought that my trans side would go away, but it didn't. However, my spiritual life developed and flourished and I have been a follower of Jesus ever since.

Q: Did you keep the secret from your wife?

A: No, I told her on about our third date. She was quite taken aback, but we were in love, and it didn't stop our friendship blossoming. A year later we married. We were both convinced that, as time went on, my transgender feelings would go away. How wrong we were. We discovered later that for most trans people, this part of their identity lasts for a lifetime. I was no exception.

When we started having children, we felt it was important that my trans side was kept secret. Opportunities to dress were few and far between. When I did grab the chance, it caused friction between us, as my wife was very unhappy about my covert dressing activities.

Q: Did you seek God's healing?

A: If I had thought I was sick, then I would have sought for healing. If I had thought I was demon possessed, I would have prayed for deliverance. If I had thought I was indulging in a sinful act, I would have repented and asked for God's forgiveness. At varying times over the years I did believe those things, and tried my hardest to deal with them appropriately. At other times I managed to abstain from dressing for months at a time, even years. But deep down I knew that the female side of me was still there. In spite of much advice, counselling and prayer, I remained a troubled and confused person. God had answered so many of my prayers concerning other things, so why not this? Why had I been dealt such a tricky card?

Q: What's happened since then?

A: Once the children had grown up, I got to thinking, why am I so mixed up about all this? I started searching the Internet and discovered that there were thousands of people just like me, coming from all walks of life. Maybe it would be helpful if I could meet some of them and talk things over. So, calling myself Elaine, I ventured forth to a trans weekend function. It was a real eye-opener. For the first time in my life I found that other people, who understood exactly how I felt, accepted my female side. That led me to be able to accept myself for the first time, no longer ashamed, or feeling I was a freak. I also began to sense that God accepted me too, just as I was. I was able to be in His presence, freed from the burden of guilt that had surrounded me for so long. It was life changing.

Q: What do you actually do when you are dressed?

A: Initially, my time as Elaine was spent at trans events and weekends, where hotels are group booked for the purpose. These are wonderful times for making friends, supporting each other, chatting, laughing a lot, themed costume evenings, meals together, discos, etc. They are incredibly well behaved gatherings and the hotels often comment what a pleasure it is to have groups to stay.

Nowadays, my Elaine time has diversified to include everyday activities, like driving, walking, shopping, sightseeing, eating out, going to the theatre, etc. I also enjoy singing in a choir and a female voice trio, and solo singing. I love travelling to visit friends and have discovered the joys of cruise ship holidays. I am on the steering group of a Christian charity, with the aim of encouraging churches and Christian groups to fully accept trans people into their midst. This involves me in giving talks and seminars, and writing blogs and articles.

Q: But I thought cross-dressing was all about sex!

A: That's how many perceive it. Early on in one's development, there is often some sexual arousal associated with dressing, but as time goes on that is usually replaced with a feeling of peace, wellbeing and pleasure, as one expresses the feminine feelings inside. As far as sexual encounters with other trans people are concerned, I have never been propositioned by anybody. If I were, I wouldn't be interested.

Q: Have you met other trans Christians?

A: For a long time I thought that I must be the only trans person who was also a Christian. But once I started attending events, I came across others, from every denomination, ministers, deacons, lay readers and lay people. I also discovered Sibyls, a trans Christian group, which holds retreats twice a year and has its own email network and newsletter. I get the impression that many trans people have more spiritual awareness than the general population.

Q: Do you intend to live as a woman full-time?

A: No, I don't. I am happy in my male role, at work, as a husband, father and grandfather. I don't have a yearning to transition into the female role permanently. I just love to be able to express the two sides of me, which brings a breadth to life that most people cannot imagine.

Q: Why did you decide to 'come out' as transgender?

A: In the end, after a lifetime of subterfuge and deception that I had to employ to keep this side of me secret, I grew tired. I realised that I couldn't face the rest of my life doing that, looking over my shoulder all the time and wondering if I was about to be 'outed'. This, and the fact that I had become much more comfortable with being Elaine, convinced me that I should be more open. After all, what did I have to be ashamed of?

It took a lot of deliberation, heart-searching and prayer to make the decision to come out. We knew it would be risky, and my wife and I had to weigh up the possible outcome. She had strong reservations about it, but in the end she assured me that if I felt it was the right thing to do, she would support me, whatever the outcome.

Having made the decision to go ahead, we realised that we would have to tell people in a specific order, and the place to start was with our grown up children and their partners. Then, it would be our respective siblings and their partners, followed by our friends. Going wider, I would inform my work colleagues, and finally our church minister, elders and members of the church would be told. We feared that it would be this last group that would react the most strongly. We were right.

Q: And what was the response from each of these groups?

A: As far as our children, families, friends and work colleagues were concerned, the general reaction was very positive. This level of support meant an awful lot to us. When it came to church members, it was a bit like lighting a tinder box. A few of them tried to assure us that we were still friends and that they loved us. But most were shocked by the revelation, and that I had accepted my 'chosen lifestyle'. Some of the letters we received were hostile and judgmental. It hurt.

After many months of discussions and negotiations with the church leaders, I was informed that, while I was permitted to attend the church, I would not be allowed to participate in any kind of ministry, including worship-leading, which I had enjoyed doing for many years.

Under these circumstances we felt we couldn't carry on, as I was unable to play an active role in the church. So, with great sadness we decided to leave. There were no thank yous, no farewells. And we also had the problem of how to find a new church family? Would any church accept us? Would we be spiritual outcasts? It was our bishop who came to the rescue. He listened to our story and put us in touch with a local church, one that was happy to take us in, just as we were. We were quite open about my background, and we were accepted on those terms. At last I was able to contribute to church life again; it was a real privilege.

Q: Do you attend your church as Elaine?

A: Initially, it wasn't in my mind to do that, but as the years have passed my feelings have changed. I now enjoy worshipping as Elaine in a number of venues and settings, so it is a little odd that I have not done the same in my home church. It's something that I long to do; I think it would help the congregation to understand me more, and hopefully learn to accept me at a deeper level. As with everything about our journeys of faith, we all need to be moving forward to a better place.

Q: What are the downsides about being a male who cross dresses?

A: Almost all of the problems of being trans relate to people's attitudes towards the subject and towards trans people themselves. This can result in the trans person internalising everything, which leads to feelings of shame, inadequacy and rejection, and the thought of being regarded as abnormal or a freak. It can also have a devastating effect on personal relationships, as wives or partners may be unable to come to terms with their other half's female identity and their need to dress. Sometimes wives only find out about their husbands' secret after many years of marriage, which can bring feelings of betrayal and deceit into the situation.

The trans person may be driven into extreme secrecy, with the constant fear of discovery, and this may produce great tensions, anxiety or depression. In desperation, the person may try total abstinence, involving ritual purging of all female clothes and the decision to 'give it all up'. It rarely works, and may lead to frustration, misery, upset and the inevitable sense of failure when the need to dress starts all over again. The stresses and strains of this can lead to mental health problems, even suicide attempts.

Q: Is there a good side?

A: Yes, definitely. If one could eliminate all the negative attitudes towards transgender, what remains is really quite positive. The transgender community is made up of an interesting and diverse group of people, and I feel privileged to be part of it. I have gained many close and trustworthy friends. I meet genuinely caring people, and times sharing together are relaxed and enjoyable. Many partners attend these socials, and the degree of love and support they show to their loved ones is touching. A past president of the Beaumont Society (the national organisation for trans people) told me that she felt privileged to be 'gender gifted,' able to experience the best of both worlds.

The challenge of transforming a male appearance and behaviour into a female one requires a lot of creativity, ingenuity and perseverance. For some it is a nigh on impossible task, requiring all the skills and craft that clothing and makeup can provide. But in the end, it's not so much about whether you can 'pass' in public, but whether you feel comfortable in your female gender role. If one manages to pass in public, then that's an added bonus.

Q: Isn't that a recipe for confusion?

A: The blurring of gender may confuse those who encounter a trans person. Are you male? Are you female? What is going on? It's made worse as we're used to seeing everything in watertight compartments, and we must squeeze everyone into one of them. Learning that life isn't as black and white as one thought may help to lose the stereotypes and see that there are more varieties and shades of gender than we had realised. For the trans people themselves, there can be some interesting dilemmas, but on the whole, this extra dimension to our lives enriches them.

You might also think that my female side erodes my maleness, turning me into an emasculated man. In my own situation, it seems to do the opposite. Being Elaine is energising and refreshing, which spills over into my male life as well.

Q: So what about Deuteronomy 22.5?

> A woman must not wear men's clothing, nor a man wear women's clothing, for the Lord your God detests anyone who does this (New International Version).

A: Ah yes, that verse... Well, it haunted me for most of my life, but I now see it in a different light. Read the verse in the context of the laws around it, considering the historical context of the time. Explore it with an open mind. Realise that the verse is directed to women as well as men. Did you know that there are still conservative Christian groups in the UK that do not permit women to wear trousers, because they are 'men's clothes'? That's an awful lot of women out there who need to stop sinning! I am now clear in my mind that this verse, addressed to the Israelites, has no bearing on transgender people, then or now. I fail to see anything morally wrong in being trans.

Q: But surely it is not honouring God?

A: If it was not honouring God, then it must be dishonouring God, which would be wrong. That to me would be sinful, and something in need of repentance. I believe that God has given us a conscience to help us through life. If we as Christians think or do anything which disturbs that conscience, then we need to question whether it is right or wrong, together with reading the Bible and prayer. If we listen to His voice and follow Him day by day, He will tell us when something is wrong. I've learned this over the years, in all aspects of my life. There have been many times when God has had to get me back into line.

Q: Why don't you just stop being trans?

A: If you asked me if I could stop drinking tea and coffee, I would say yes. I would miss the good feeling that a nice cuppa brings, but I could do it without much hassle. If you asked me to stop engaging in any form of music, playing, singing or even just listening, I would also say yes, but it would a much harder task, as music is an important part of my life, expressing very deep feelings and emotions. If then you were to ask me to stop expressing any part of my female side, it would be really hard, because it goes even deeper into my being. Many trans people have been down the road of abstinence and denial and it usually ends in tears, or worse. I have no desire or leading to go down that road again. I have now come to accept the way I am, without self-hate or shame. I am at last free from the great burden of guilt (I would actually say it is false guilt) that dogged me for most of my life. I can walk with God in total honesty and thank Him for loving me just as I am.

Q: How do people react to your telling them you are trans?

A: There's no way I can dictate or demand how they respond. I have found that people react in a wide variety of ways. Some people have no problem with it at all, some are uncomfortable to begin with but come round to it, but there are those who firmly believe that this is totally against God's will and who say they will pray for my healing and/or deliverance. By being open about my trans nature, I hope that it will help people to think through the issues at a deeper level. Whilst their initial responses may be negative, I hope that in time, and with further reflection, a more open attitude may develop, so that transgender people can be accepted as they are, 'different', but in many ways the same.

Q: How should the Christian Church address transgender issues?

A: There has been a lot of discussion in the C of E General Synod and in the Evangelical Alliance (EA) about homosexuality, but there's been very little about transgender. The EA has produced a booklet on transsexuality, focusing mainly on the rights and wrongs of gender reassignment. I believe that the debate on trans is much wider than this and that more aspects should be considered. People like myself, who have come out into the open, may have something to contribute to the discussion and to help church leaders understand some of the problems which trans Christians have to face. If the Church could discover a more conciliatory and accepting stance in relation to trans, then much of the bitterness and anger which many transgender people feel towards their fellow-believers and towards God could be ameliorated. Some of the experiences I've heard about from trans Christians concerning rejection and condemnation make me weep. Can we not get alongside them, demonstrating God's love and care, instead of racking up guilt and anguish for them? This is the approach that I believe the Church should be adopting.

Q: Where do you see your transgender journey going in the future?

A: It's always difficult to be sure. I hope to be able to continue to express and enjoy my femininity, rather than struggling, fighting and denying it. I want to show that trans people can be responsible members of Society, who do not deserve to be feared, avoided, ridiculed or despised.

Q: You talk a lot about acceptance. How can people be more accepting?

A: It has taken me most of my life to come to terms with my transgender nature. At long last I have been able to accept myself fully. I do not have all the answers, but I am content and at peace.

With that in mind, it would be unrealistic of me to expect those around me to accept my transgender side without difficulty. In fact, I can't demand anything of them. However, I do encourage friends and family to consider travelling along what I have called the Road to Acceptance.

Q: So how does someone start to move on this road?
A: I've identified four levels of acceptance, though in truth they are really part of a continuum. But these levels do highlight how someone might proceed.

Level One: Intolerance.   At this level transgender people are regarded as sick, warped or perverted, and are looked on with a high degree of suspicion or disgust. They should be avoided, and might be a risk to children. The Press may expose or 'out' them and present them in a negative light, with ridicule and scorn. I have personally been the subject of this sort of exposure (in *The Sun* newspaper), and it was a distressing and traumatic time for my family and me. Fortunately, we had wonderful support from friends, work colleagues and people we hardly knew, which helped us to weather the storm.

In some Christian circles any expression of the opposite gender is seen as sinful and in need of repentance, healing, or both. Church leaders may ban a trans person from all forms of leadership and ministry, and even exclude them completely from the church. Such experiences are hard to bear. Some never get over it, remaining bitter and alienated from the Church, and sadly, sometimes from God.

Level Two: Tolerance. The common response of many British people when considering transgender (or any other group of people who are different from the norm) is an uncomfortable tolerance. They have a gut feeling that it 'isn't quite right' (rarely based on a moral or Christian argument), but they are not going to make a big deal about it. They would rather not talk about it, but if they do it is in hushed tones and with considerable embarrassment. Think how many pub jokes or remarks in sitcoms refer to men in bras, stockings, etc.? Such humour is often met with a good laugh too. But this approach usually avoids facing the issues. Life goes on much as before and friendships seem to be unaffected by the knowledge that I am trans. I'm reluctant to raise the subject with them, for fear of causing embarrassment. Christian friends may adopt this approach too, without seriously considering whether there is any scriptural reason to do otherwise.

Level Three: Acceptance. This level may require some homework, making an effort to try to understand more about transgender, facing lifelong prejudices and, where possible, listening to trans voices. They will begin to see that here is a person who needs love, rather than a person with a problem. However, there will still be limits and some awkwardness when addressing trans matters. It remains something talked about as little as possible.

Level Four: Inclusion. There is I believe a level beyond acceptance where the trans person is seen as somebody to be embraced and affirmed by those around him or her. This is a fuller acceptance, or inclusion.

The person is valued and welcomed, in whatever way they choose to present. Any confusion that this may cause friends or family is dealt with by the individual, which may require time and effort. Transgender is no longer seen as an enemy, or something to discourage. The friends I have who have come to this point are worth their weight in gold.

Q: How can someone move along the road towards Inclusion?

A: There are some for whom trans is no big deal and who are inclusive from the start. Others have major problems, be they social, moral or theological. The question is, are they open minded enough to consider change? If so, then their journey towards acceptance and inclusion can begin. If not, they may never be able to find a way forward from an intolerant position. This brings heartache for all, and can result in marriage break up, loss of friends, or church exclusion.

Q: Can the trans person do anything to help a person along that road?

A: For those who are prepared to explore the issues, and challenge their initial reactions, I would first encourage reading around the subject. It would be helpful to chat with anyone with specialist knowledge on the subject, including trans people themselves, and preferably in their adopted gender role. This provides a more personal perspective than the drier academic approach.

Q: What is your hope for the future?

A: My hope and prayer is that more transgender people will decide to come out, and encourage those around them to travel down the road to towards inclusion.

Q: Surely this is going to take a very long time?
Possibly, but things seem to change more rapidly these days. The picture is rosier now than it was just ten years ago. I have seen so many transgender friends living secret lives in misery and loneliness that I will do all I can to change that, and make the world a better place for those who follow.

Section 3: Allies

David Horton

A Journey of Discovery

I am a retired minister of the Church of England from the Evangelical tradition. I learned the gospel as a child along with stories of my mother's work in the bad parts of Deptford and New Cross with the Salvation Army between the World Wars. I made my personal commitment to the living Christ after a Youth for Christ meeting, and had my first overwhelming encounter with the Holy Spirit back in 1968 under the ministry of Dennis Bennett, a visiting Episcopalian minister, at Church House, Westminster.

Some years ago I gained a certain amount of notoriety when I wrote a booklet on the subject of transvestism and transsexuality. It was called *Changing Channels*. In writing terms I must have done well as it sold out fairly quickly, although Grove Books still sell copies as an e-book. I cherish the fact that in the same week shortly after it was published I had a seventeen-page letter full of vitriol from a Midlands cleric for my temerity in trying to help 'those persons' and a letter from a transgender person that started 'it is obvious that you do not like us very much'. I tend to feel that this indicates I did something right!

My personal journey into this world of transgender people began in 1987 with a 'tranny' who came for help in understanding his behaviour. Over the years I have now met and talked with several hundred so-called 'transgendered' people and many of those who work with them. I have been with some of them through surgery and watched them blossom into whole people. I have also known three people full of potential become so low through rejection and lack of treatment that they have committed suicide. I was honorary chaplain to the Sibyls for some years. I have to say the duty was not onerous! The group members help each other, with the support of an increasing number of ministers and others who come to learn as well as to minister.

Down the years I worked with transgender people, their loved ones, and their churches I reached several conclusions. This seems like a good place to air them.

My first conclusion is that to be transgender is at heart a biological variation. Many cultures have experienced in-between people down the ages and handled it in various positive and negative ways. The term 'transsexual' originated in the work of a medical journalist in 1949, and 'transvestite' was imported from Germany in about 1910, but the practical reality much precedes medical involvement, possibly going back to early Biblical times or even before. If it touches so many differing cultures from around the world it cannot be fundamentally social. Equally, transgender people have been seeking psychological help in this country for over a century. Despite claims to the contrary, and a variety of approaches, transgender orientation does not seem to respond to such treatments. More importantly from my point of view I have met literally dozens of Christians who have sought spiritual healing or deliverance with no change in their inner need. (I had thought I had come across one such person in evangelical church life, but like a number of other less prominent instances I have known, the return to the original gender role was only an effort to please others, and ultimately failed.) Since I have known several remarkable healings and deliverances in my general ministry I conclude that, of itself, it cannot be a spiritual problem. That leaves only biology, although I do not discount the social, psychological and spiritual dimensions.

I believe the work of Professors Gooren and Swaab and their team in the Netherlands in the two published reports of autopsies (in 1996 and 2000) has shown that transsexual people have an important part of their brain structure that matches their desired sex and not that of their birth. In prenatal hormonal research in mammals there is a 'brain sex' mechanism that can account for this condition and there are also parallels from some intersex conditions. GIRES is an organization that has continued my education. I conclude that there is a biological element in much transgender behaviour.

Research clearly remains inadequate. There are no knighthoods for transgender research! Yet it is clear that what research there is has convinced many of those actively involved in medical and psychiatric care that it is not a lifestyle choice, and if so it is not a willful sin.

My second conclusion is that many Christians have shown a very great lack of humanity, far less agape, in their approach to this condition. How can Deuteronomy 22.5 be applied solely to male transvestism when so many women have moved into male clothing styles even as they have moved into previously male roles and activities in the West? Whatever the verse may mean it is clear that it applies as the prime case to women! It also angers me when fellow evangelicals welcome transsexual people into churches (do they?) and then reject them if they cannot agree with the conclusion they are living a lie. I do not believe it is a sin to disagree with a diagnosis (especially one often given by people with no real knowledge of the subject), and yet it is often treated as such and hurting people are rejected. We are all damaged in the sight of a perfect God, and yet Christ receives us and leads us on willingly. Is our love and our faith in Christ's power to transform so weak?

To my shame, the first time I went to meet a group of transgender people to whom a doctor had opened her home I was half-afraid that I might be assaulted by Danny La Rue look-alikes! It was a disgrace that I still feel. Transgender people are people, with an extraordinary problem, loved and cherished by God. I hope after reading this book you will be able to remember that.

My third and most important conclusion. These people are not just problems. The difficulties they have faced, and the way some have had to fight to survive means that many are admirable. Down the years many Christians alive or gone before have helped me. But a few have been central to my spiritual growth and development. I suppose the first was Commissioner S. L. Brengle of the Salvation Army through his 'Helps to Holiness'. Another was the woman deaconess/deacon/priest with whom I worked in my first parish. But three of those seven or eight people have been transgender. One was Lee Frances - a former U.S. Marine who ran a skid-row mission for many years before founding the 'Grace and Lace Letter' and who became a pen friend. The second was Grace, a former Methodist Minister who changed over in the 1960's in the South West and with whom I also corresponded for many years. The third was a prominent Pentecostal minister who never did come out and whose wisdom was inspiring: 'Peggy'. Each was unique. I would be a lesser person without having known them.

Appendices

Appendix 1

Glossary and Terminology

Note on use of terminology:

Trans is an adjective: as in *trans man, trans woman, trans folk, trans people,* etc. - by implication the same applies to *cis* as for *trans*. Using compound words, such as *transman, trans-man, transwomen, transfolk,* etc. as nouns implies that there is something intrinsically different about a *transman* rather than a *man* (i.e., a 'real' man) which implies less authenticity. We say 'black woman', we do not say 'blackwoman'. A *trans person* is not *a trans*.

People are not called *transsexuals*: a person may be *transsexual*, but is not *a transsexual*; that reduces them to a single attribute, that of being a transsexual. *Transsexual* is an adjective, not a noun; *transsexual people* is preferred to *transsexuals*.

People are not *transgendered*, they are *transgender* (and not *a transgender*). *Transgendered* suggests some action or process that makes someone *transgender*. *Transgender people* is preferred to *transgenders*.

MtF (male-to-female) and **FtM** (female-to-male) are also avoided, in favour of **trans woman** and **trans man**.

Intersex people usually remain in their childhood gender assignment, but many reject and choose to change that assignment later in life; a few prefer not to identify as any specific gender.

People can born be *intersex*, but are not *intersexed* (they are not made intersex). *Intersex people* are not referred to as *intersexes* or *intersexuals*, and individuals are not an *intersex* (nor an *intersexual*). *Intersex* is a state of physiological sex variation present from birth, and should not be confused with *transgender, intergender, third-gender* or *non-binary gender*. People who are born clearly male or female, but go on to express themselves in such ways do not become *intersex*.

Words may be used in inverted commas, to make a particular point or as a quote. So, *tranny, trannie,* and *trannies* are not used unless in quotation marks.

Labelling is very important, as Foucault notes; the labels we use give or withhold power from subjects. Developing a coherent and consistent style across these chapters was important, helping eliminate a lot of disparate usage which has developed within and outside the community (such as the media, for example).

GLAAD have a page that explains this quite clearly:
http://www.glaad.org/reference/transgender
We have tried to be consistent in imposing this usage throughout the book.

Glossary of Terms:

Cisgender: someone who is not transgender, but who expresses and identifies with the gender assigned at birth.

Cross dress: wearing the clothes appropriate to a different gender (preferable to the term *transvestite*, which has origins as a pathological category)

DSM: the **Diagnostic and Statistical Manual of Mental Disorders** produced by the American Psychiatric Association (APA). The current version is **DSM-V**, which replaced the version that was predominant from 2000-2013: **DSM-IV-TR**. The diagnosis of *Gender Identity Disorder (GID)* was dropped in DSM-V in favour of *Gender Dysphoria*. Intersex adults and children with gender dysphoria were included within that diagnosis explicitly for the first time.

Gender: the state of being male or female.

Gender Dysphoria (GD): discomfort with one's birth/assigned gender

Gender Expression: the external presentation and appearance of gender.

Gender Identity: the internal sense of gender, who one is.

Gender Incongruence (GI): mismatch between sex characteristics, gender role and gender identity, term proposed for use in ICD11

Gender nonconforming: where gender expression is different from conventional expressions of maleness, femaleness, masculinity and femininity.

Genderqueer: having a gender expression that falls outside, or between, those normally expected for men and women.

Gender Recognition Certificate (GRC): the certificate that is issued in the UK which confirms the recognition of the gender transitioned to; this is accompanied by a revised birth certificate that reflects the gender now expressed. This became law through the **Gender Recognition Act (GRA)**, and is supervised by the **Gender Recognition Panel (GRP)**.

Gender Role: the social roles customarily expected for people of a given gender.

ICD: International Statistical Classification of Diseases and Related Health Problems. This is the international classification that covers all medical conditions, including intersex, as well those mental health conditions covered by the USA APA's **DSM**. The current version, **ICD-10** has been in place since 1994, and **ICD-11** is currently being constructed. This is the system that is referred to by UK psychiatrists, rather than DSM (which is American, not international). It has been proposed that **GID** will be replaced by **Gender Incongruence** in **ICD-11**.

Intersex: being born with sex characteristics that are not fully male or female, or with medical conditions that entail atypical sex development.

Non-binary: not identifying with either of the two compulsory genders, male and female (or identifying with aspects of both at the same time)

Sex: the assignment from birth, as male or female, as recorded on birth certificate. Birth Sex - the sex assigned at birth, as male or female.

Sex/Gender Reassignment Surgery (SRS/GRS): surgery that conforms the sex characteristics of a transsexual person to appear as expected for somebody of their expressed gender. Sometimes referred to as Gender Confirmation Surgery. In the UK, GRS is more usual, in the USA, SRS is usually used.

Sexual Orientation: the form of sexual attraction to people of a specific gender.

Trans: abbreviation of 'transgender' (should only be used as an adjective)

Trans man: a transsexual or transgender man, a man who was assigned female at birth (preferred term to *FtM*).

Trans woman: a transsexual or transgender woman, a woman who was assigned male at birth (preferred term to *MtF*).

Transgender: an umbrella term, which includes people who are described as 'transsexual'; it describes the expression of, or identification with, gender in a way that differs from the sex assigned at birth, and which in some cases may be affirmed through 'transition'. Also included are people who do not identify with a gender ('non-binary'), people who identify as 'third gender', and people who cross-dress, amongst others.

Transition: the process through which somebody moves from the gender assigned at birth to living in a way that matches their gender identity.

Transsexualism or (**Transsexuality**): when somebody identifies as the opposite sex to that which they were assigned at birth, wishes to permanently live as a member of that sex, which usually involves some form of 'transition', and can include surgical reassignment and/or sex-hormone replacement, both of which alter sex characteristics so they match gender identity, and aid living in that gender. The term 'transsexual' is still often used to describe such people. These terms are problematic due to their historic pathologising associations; as a diagnosis, they are being replaced by 'gender dysphoria'.

Transvestite: original term for someone who cross dresses. Some people who cross dress prefer to use this term.

Chapter 1: Outline of the Workshop

The Sibyls'   'Gender, Sexuality and Spirituality' Workshop
Introduction: Welcome to your Workshop!   • Who are we, where do we come from?   • History of the Workshop   • Your expectations of the Workshop   • Confidentiality/safety (see next section).
The Workshop is a safe space – Confidentiality is essential   • Only share what you feel safe with   • The more open, the more benefit   • People's stories are personal   • Do not repeat people's stories outside.   If we write on these issues, we will not use anything personal that people have said in the Workshop.
The Workshop begins with two or three (depending on the number of presenters) short presentations which encompass: • Gender   • Sexuality   • Spirituality.   Any questions?
PART 1:1   Working alone to begin with consider how you would define or describe your   • GENDER   • SEXUALITY   • SPIRITUALITY.

PART 1:2

In small groups discuss what you discovered about yourself, or the issues that this posed, especially:

- Were you aware of changes over time?
- Were there reasons for celebration or areas of conflict and, if so, why was this?

Feedback to the large group

PART 2:1

In the large group, one or more of the presenters introduces the interplay model using themselves as an example:

Gender

identity – role – presentation

Sexuality

Identity – role – practice/attraction

Spirituality

identity – role – practice

An example of a completed interplay model:

- Gender identity – female (trans history); gender role – wife, nurturer; gender presentation – classic skirts, tops and shoes (Jigsaw), occasional stylist's help
- Sexual identity – attracted to males/androgynous females; sexual role – partner/wife; sexual practice – monogamous + infatuation
- Spirituality identity – Christian/shaman/dancer; role – priest/chaplain; practice – dance/contemplation/reading.

PART 2.2

Working alone consider yourself in terms of the interplay model:

Gender

identity – role – presentation

Sexuality

Identity – role – practice/attraction

Spirituality

identity – role – practice

PART 2.3
Working in small groups – thinking about role, identity and practice/
presentation:

- Do these interplay with one another in our lives?
- Do some make more sense to us than others?
- What happens when there is a mismatch?
- Is there any conflict between these?
- Are there parts we would change, or have different?
- If so, Why?

Feedback to the larger group

Michelle Le Morvan: A Spiritual Path (January 2009)

Now, at the age of 76, I look back on my journey. I can distinguish five aspects of what seems to me the path along which I am still moving, and which will lead me to the end of the road. They are not chronological, but interwoven with one another.

Awareness

Becoming aware of myself and of my life and of the world in which I move. This involves listening to my body – emotionally as well as physically and mentally. The divine presence lives within and without, and it is the only way it can speak to me.

Acceptance

Life is what it is, whether we like it or not. It is *what it is* and we cannot change it. There is actually no such thing as good or bad luck. If we wish to learn and grow up, our only teacher is life – what is. We cannot change it, only learn from it and work with it.

Surrender

To know what is, and accept it, leads to a surrender to something greater than ourselves. This is not the same as 'giving up', and passively lying down; it is a positive acceptance of reality and a working with the reality to the utmost of our powers to fulfil our destiny in life. Each of us has a task to fulfil, no matter how small it may be. Only I can fulfil my destiny. It is personal to me.

Gratitude

Meister Eckhart said that if we were only to say one prayer, it should be one of thanks. Even when days are bad – and some can be awful, full of pain and despair, I have learnt to say 'Thank you'. There is always something, no matter how small, to say 'Thank you' for, even through gritted teeth. Often it is the only prayer I can now say, especially when I look back on my journey, and see the 'impossible' path along which I have travelled, and all the wonderful people who have walked part of my journey with me.

Love

This aspect of the journey envelops and enfolds all the others. As these earlier aspects come together they are bonded in love. As Richard Rohr writes, 'The greatest command is not "you shall be right" but "you shall be in love"'. From my own experience I know I have disliked and detested myself because I could not live up to the ideal of religious perfection demanded of me. Then I slowly began to see that it was all irrelevant, and that I was loved exactly as I was – there's no earning this lover. As the judgemental me began to fade, I began to see others in a new way, and this is helping me to be less judgemental of others, and to begin to open out to them. This has changed my openness to the Divine Presence. It has also freed me from the religious chains which had bound me for seventy years – with all their 'shoulds' and 'oughts', doctrines and dogmas. For me it is the freedom that Jesus came to bring, and which lies at the heart of the Gospel.

All my life I had sought *Approval*, and it was a powerful drug. It was only at the age of sixty-eight, when I was living alone in a rented cottage that I became free – I had a complete breakdown which lasted three months at the beginning of 2001. Coming through this pain, I was finally able to face myself and then begin to move on. It was awful, but it was the healing I needed, and my life changed forever. Be prepared to face the pain and loss, if you want to be free.

Together with the Gospels, I have been helped especially by two wonderful books I have read and reread, viz. *Awareness* by Anthony de Mello, and *Everything Belongs* by Richard Rohr. They have been great companions for the journey.

There are two blessings which I love – one Jewish and one Celtic; I wish them upon all who read this:

> 'The Lord bless you and keep you;
> the Lord make his face to shine upon you
> and be gracious to you;
> the Lord lift up his countenance upon you
> and give you his peace.'
>
> *Numbers 6:24-26*

> May the road rise to meet you,
> may the wind be always at your back,
> may the sun shine warm upon your face,
> and the rain fall soft upon your fields,
> and until we meet again,
> may God hold you in the palm of his hand.'
>
> *Celtic Blessing*

I can identify with Anthony de Mello:

> I am satisfied to do my thing, to dance my dance ... and have done with it.
> According to a nice sentence I read somewhere,
> 'A bird does not sing because it has an answer.
> It sings because it has a song.'
> I am content to sing my song,
> Even though often the whole thing seems meaningless.
>
> Anthony de Mello,
> *We Heard the Bird Sing*

Bibliographies

Foreword Bibliography

Beardsley, C. (2004/2000), *The Transsexual Person is my Neighbour: Pastoral Guidelines for Christian Clergy, Pastors and Congregations*, Brighton: Gender Trust [Online] http://changingattitude.org.uk/resources/publications/the-transsexual-person-is-my-neighbour [Accessed 30/10/2015]

Beardsley, Christina (2005), 'Taking Issue: The Transsexual Hiatus in *Some Issues in Human Sexuality*', *Theology* 58.845, 338-346

Cornwall, Susannah (2010), *Sex and Uncertainty in the Body of Christ: Intersex Conditions and Christian Theology*, London: Routledge

Cornwall, Susannah (Ed.) (2015), *Intersex, Theology, and the Bible: Troubling Bodies in Church, Text, and Society*, New York, NY: Palgrave Macmillan

O'Brien, M. (2004) 'Intersex', in Beardsley, C. (Ed.) *The Transsexual Person is my Neighbour: Pastoral Guidelines for Christian Clergy, Pastors and Congregations*, Brighton: Gender Trust [Online] http://changingattitude.org.uk/resources/publications/the-transsexual-person-is-my-neighbour [Accessed 30/10/2015]

Office for National Statistics (2013), '2011 Census, Detailed Characteristics for Local Authorities in England and Wales' [Online] http://www.ons.gov.uk/ons/rel/census/2011-census/detailed-characteristics-for-local-authorities-in-england-and-wales/index.html [Accessed 15/10/2015]

Reed, Bernard, Stephenne Rhodes, Pietà Schofield and Kevan Wylie (2009), *Gender Variance in the UK: Prevalence, Incidence, Growth, and Geographic Distribution*, Gender Identity Research and Education Society (GIRES) [Online] http://www.gires.org.uk/assets/Medpro-Assets/GenderVarianceUK-report.pdf [Accessed 15/10/2015]

Introduction Bibliography

Savage, H., (2006), *Changing Sex? transsexuality and Christian Theology*, Durham E-Theses: [Online] http://etheses.dur.ac.uk/3364/1/185.PDF?DDD32+ [Accessed 30/10/2015]

Chapter 1 Bibliography

Beardsley, C., O'Brien, M. and Woolley, J. (2010) 'Exploring the Interplay: The Sibyls' 'Gender, Sexuality and Spirituality' Workshop', *Theology & Sexuality*, 16(3): 259-283.

Althaus-Reid, M. and Isherwood, L. (2009) *Trans/formations*, SCM Press.

Foucault, M. (1998/1981) *The History of Sexuality Vol 1: The Will to Knowledge* (trans Hurley R.), London, New York: Penguin.

Mollenkott, V.R. (2001) *Omnigender: a trans-religious approach*, Cleveland, Ohio: The Pilgrim Press

Mollenkott, V. R. (2009) 'We Come Bearing Gifts: Seven Lessons Religious Congregations Can Learn From Trans People', in Althaus-Reid, M. & Isherwood, L. (Eds.) *Trans/formations*, London: SCM Press.

Money, J. (1998) *Sin, Science and the Sex Police*, Prometheus Books.

O'Donovan, O. (2007/1982) *Transsexualism: Issues and Argument*, Cambridge Grove Books.

Stoller, R. (1985) *Presentations of Gender*, Yale University Press.

Stuart, E. (2007) 'Sacramental Flesh', in Loughlin, G. (Ed.) *Queer Theology: Rethinking the Western Body*, Oxford: Blackwell Publishing.

Stuart, E. and Thatcher, A. (1997) *People of Passion: What the Churches teach about sex*, London: Mowbray.

Sullivan, N. (2015) 'The Matter of Gender', in Downing, L., Morland, I. & Sullivan, N. (Eds.) *Fuckology: Critical Essays on John Money's Diagnostic Concepts*. Chicago and London: The University of Chicago Press.

Chapter 2 Bibliography

Ashley, A. (with D. Thompson) (2006) *The First Lady*, London: John Blake.

Apuleius, L. (1950) *The Transformations of Lucius*, otherwise known as, *The Golden Ass*, trans. R. Graves, Harmondsworth: Penguin.

Bray, A. (1982) *Homosexuality in Renaissance England*, London: Gay Men's Press.

Butler, J. (2008 [1990]) *Gender Trouble: Feminism and the Subversion of Identity*, Abingdon, Oxon: Routledge, 2nd edn.

Carter, P. (1997) 'Men about town: representations of foppery and masculinity in early eighteenth-century urban society', in Barker H. and Chalus E. (Eds.) *Gender in Eighteenth-Century England: Roles, Representations and Responsibilities*, Harlow: Addison Wesley Longman: 31-57.

Coles, R. (2014) *Fathomless Riches: Or How I Went from Pop to Pulpit*, London: Weidenfeld & Nicolson.

Cornwall, S. (2009) 'Apophasis and Ambiguity: The 'Unknowingness' of Transgender', in Althaus-Reid M. and Isherwood L. (Eds.) *Trans/Formations*, London: SCM: 13-40.

Dawson, A. Web review of Stephen Orgel, *Impersonations: The Performance of Gender in Shakespeare's England* [Online] http://extra.shu.ac.uk/emls/03-2/rev_daw2.html [Accessed 1/12/11]

Designing Shakespeare – Character and Representation: [Online] http://www.english.heacademy.ac.uk/designshake/design/character.htm [Accessed 24th March 2010]

DeFranza, M.K. (2015) *Sex Difference in Christian Theology: Male, Female, and Intersex in the Image of God*, Cambridge: Eerdmans.

Durova, N. (1990) *The Cavalry Maiden: Journals of a female Russian Officer in the Napoleonic Wars*, London: Paladin Grafton Books.

Epictetus, (1928) *Discourses Books 1-4, Fragments, The Encheiridion*, trans. W.A. Oldfather, Harvard University Press.

Farrer, P. (1987) *Men in Petticoats: A Selection of Letters from Victorian Newspapers*, Liverpool: Karn Publications.

Farrer, P. (1992) *In Female Disguise: An Anthology of English and American Short Stories and Literary Passages*, Liverpool: Karn Publications.

Farrer, P. (1998) *The Life of Maurice Pollack 1885-1912 a Birmingham Actor*, Liverpool: Karn Publications.

Farrer, P. (2000) *Cross Dressing Between the Wars: Selections from London Life 1923-1933*, Liverpool: Karn Publications.

Foucault, M. (1990) *The Care of the Self: The History of Sexuality*, vol. 3, trans. R. Hurley, London: Penguin Books.

Foucault, M. (1992) *The Use of Pleasure: The History of Sexuality*, vol. 2, trans. R. Hurley, London: Penguin Books.

Foucault, M. (1998) *The Will to Knowledge: The History of Sexuality,* vol. 1, trans. R. Hurley, London: Penguin Books.

Garber, M., (1998) 'Dress codes, or the theatricality of difference', in Goodman, L. and de Gay, J. (Eds.) *The Routledge Reader in Gender and Performance,* London and New York: Routledge: 176-81.

Gilbert, O.P. (1926) *Men in Feminine Guise: Some historical instances of female impersonation,* trans. R. B. Douglas, London: John Lane.

Gilbert, O.P. (1932) *Women in Men's Guise,* trans J. Lewis May, London: John Lane.

Gill, A.A. (2007) 'Oh yes he did!' *The Sunday Times Culture Magazine,* 16 December: 4-6.

Green, R. (1998) 'Mythological, Historical, and Cross-Cultural Aspects of Transsexualism', in Denny, D. (Ed.) *Current Concepts in Transgender Identity,* New York & London: Garland Publishing Inc.: 3-14.

House of Bishops (2003) *Some Issues in Human Sexuality: A guide to the debate,* London: Church House Publishing.

House of Bishops, (2013a) *men and women in marriage,* London: Church House Publishing.

House of Bishops, (2013b), *Report of the House of Bishops Working Group on human sexuality,* London: Church House Publishing.

Howard, J.E. (1998) 'Cross-dressing, the theatre and gender struggle in early modern England', in Goodman L. and de Gay, J. (Eds.) *The Routledge Reader in Gender and Performance,* London & New York: Routledge: 47-51

Ind, J. (2003) *Memories of Bliss: God, Sex, and Us,* London: SCM.

Maas, H. Duncan, J.L. and Good, W.G. (Eds.) (1970) *The Letters of Aubrey Beardsley,* London: Cassell.

Meyerowitz, J. (2002) *How Sex Changed: A History of Transsexuality in the United States,* Cambridge MA & London: Harvard University Press.

Nicol, D. '*Twelfth Night,* performed by the Company of Shakespeare's Globe at the Middle Temple Hall, London, February 2002' [Online] http://extra.shu.ac.uk/emls/08-1/nicolrev.htm [Accessed 24th March 2010]

Norton, R. (1992) *Mother Clap's Molly House: The Gay Subculture in England, 1700-1830,* London: Gay Men's Press.

O. O'Donovan, O. (2007) *Transsexualism: Issues and Argument,* (Cambridge:

Grove Booklets) a reprint of his (1982) *Transsexualism and Christian Marriage*, Nottingham: Grove Booklets.

Paglia, C. (1991) *Sexual Personae: Art and Decadence from Nefertiti to Emily Dickinson*, London: Penguin Books.

Shaw, F., (1998) 'Foreword', in Goodman L. and de Gay, J. (Eds.)*The Routledge Reader in Gender and Performance*, London & New York: Routledge: xxiii-xxv.

Thatcher, A., (2012) 'The One Sex Theory and Why It Still Matters' [Online] http://www.adrianthatcher.org/data/resources/one%20sex%20 theory%20-%20research%20paper.pdf [Accessed 29/10/2015]

Thomas, M. (2008) *The Diary: Sex, God and Death in the Affairs of a Victorian Clergyman*, Bloomington, Indiana: AuthorHouse.

Torr, D., and S. Bottoms (2010) *Sex, Drag and Male Roles: Investigating Gender as Performance*, University of Michigan Press.

Trumbach, R. (2003) 'Sex and the Gender Revolution', in Weeks, J., Holland, J. and Waites, M. (Eds.) *Sexualities and Society: A Reader*, Cambridge: Polity Press, Cambridge & Oxford: Blackwell Publishing: 14-21.

Woolf, V. (1984/1928) *Orlando: A Biography*, London: Granada Publishing: Panther Books.

Yonge, C.M. (1893/1873) *The Pillars of the House or Under Wode, Under Rode*, London: Macmillan.

Yonge, C.M. (1905/1886) *Chantry House*, London: Macmillan.

Oxford English Dictionary (1979/1971) Compacted edn., London: Book Club Associates.

Chapter 3 Bibliography:

Assalian, P., Wilchesky, M. and Cote, H. (1997) *Do children of transsexuals also show gender dysphoria?*, XV HBIGDA Symposium, Vancouver. International Journal of Transgenderism.

Bornstein, K. (1994) *Gender Outlaw*, New York: Routledge.

Butler, J. (1999/1990) *Gender Trouble (Feminism & the Subversion of Identity)*, Routledge.

Califa, P. (1997) *Sex Changes: The Politics of Transgenderism*, Cleis Press.

Crown (2004) *Gender Recognition Act 2004*, United Kingdom: OPSI/TSO.

Davies, B. (2003) *Frogs and snails and feminist tales: preschool children and gender*, London: Allen & Unwin.

Glover, D. and Kaplan, C. (2000) *Genders*, London: Routledge.

Herdt, G. (1996) *Third Sex, Third Gender: Beyond Sexual Dimorphism in Culture and History*, New York: Zone Books.

Mallon, G. (1999) *Social Services with Transgender Youth*, Binghampton: Harrington Park Press.

Mollenkott, V. (2001) *Omnigender: a trans-religious approach*, Cleveland: Pilgrim Press.

Morris, J. (1987/1974) *Conundrum: An Extraordinary Narrative of Transsexualism*, London: Penguin.

Nuttbrock, L., Rosenblum, A. and Blumenstein, R. (2002) 'Transgender Identity Affirmation and Mental Health', *The International Journal of Transgenderism*, 6(4).

O'Keefe, T. (1999) *Sex, Gender & Sexuality. 21st Century Transformations*, London: Extraordinary People Press.

Savage, H., (2006), *Changing Sex? transsexuality and Christian Theology*, Durham E-Theses [Online] http://etheses.dur.ac.uk/3364/1/185. PDF?DDD32+ [Accessed 30/10/2015]

Sexton, P. (2005) *Greater Manchester Police Policy: Dealing with Transsexuals and Transvestites*, Manchester: GMP.

Tanis, J. (2003) *Trans-gendered: Theology, Ministry and Communities of Faith*, Cleveland: Pilgrim Press.

Thorne, B. (1993) *Gender Play. Girls and Boys in School*, Buckingham: Open University Press.

Whittle, S. and More, K. (1999) *Reclaiming Genders: Transsexual Grammars at the Fin de siecle*, London: Cassell.

Chapter 4 Bibliography

Adams, J. M., Adams, T. M., Dunn, K. A. and O'Hara, S. M. (2003) 'An Uncommon Finding: Ovotestes in a True Hermaphrodite', *Journal of Diagnostic Medical Sonography*, 19(1): 51-54.

Beardsley, C., O'Brien, M. and Woolley, J. (2010) 'Exploring the Interplay: The Sibyls' 'Gender, Sexuality and Spirituality' Workshop', *Theology & Sexuality*, 16(3): 259-283

Billings, D. B. and Urban, T. (1996) 'The Socio-medical Construction of Transsexualism: an Interpretation and Critique', in: Ekins, R. & King, D. (Eds.) *Blending Genders: Social Aspects of Cross-dressing and Sex-changing*. London, New York: Routledge.

Chase, C. and Hegarty, P. (2000) 'Intersex activism, feminism and psychology: Opening a dialogue on theory, research and clinical practice', *Feminism & Psychology*, 10(1): 117-132.

Colapinto, J. (2001) *As Nature Made Him: The Boy Who Was Raised as a Girl*, New York: Harper-Collins Perennial.

Cornwall, S. (2015) 'Introduction: Troubling Bodies?', in Cornwall, S. (Ed.) *Intersex, Theology, and the Bible: Troubling Bodies in Church, Text, and Society*. New York: Palgrave MacMillan.

Creighton, S. and Minto, C. (2001) 'Managing intersex - Most vaginal surgery in childhood should be deferred', *British Medical Journal*, 323(7324): 1264-1265.

Cull, M. (2002) 'Treatment of intersex needs open discussion', *British Medical Journal*, 324(7342): 919-919.

Diamond, M. P. D. and Sigmundson, K. (1997) 'Sex Reassignment at Birth: A Long Term Review and Clinical Implications', *Archives of Paedriatric and Adolescent Medicine*, 151(3): 298-304.

Diamond, M. P. D. and Kipnis, K. (1998) 'Pediatric Ethics and the Surgical Assignment of Sex', *Journal of Clinical Ethics*, 9(4): 398-410.

Diamond, M. P. D. (1999) 'Pediatric Management of Ambiguous and Traumatized Genitalia', *The Journal of Urology*, 162: 1021-1028.

Diamond, M. P. D. and Beh, H. G. (2000) 'An Emerging Ethical and Medical Dilemma: Should Physicians Perform Sex Assignment Surgery on Infants with Ambiguous Genitalia?', *Michigan Journal of Gender and Law*, 7(1): 1-63.

Diamond, M. P. D. (2002) 'Sex and Gender are Different: Sexual Identity and Gender Identity are Different', *Clinical Child Psychology and Psychiatry*, 7(3): 320-334.

Diamond, M. P. D. and Beh, H. G. (2006) 'The Right to be Wrong: Sex and Gender Decisions', in: Sytsma, S. (Ed.) *Intersex & Ethics*. Kluwer Academic Publishers.

Fausto-Sterling, A. (1985) *Myths of Gender – Biological Theories about Men and Women*, New York: Basic Books.

Fausto-Sterling, A. (2000) *Sexing the Body – Gender Politics & the Construction of Sexuality*, New York: Basic Books.

Halberstaum, J. (1998) *Female Masculinity*, Durham, London: Duke University Press.

Harding, J. (1998) *Sex Acts: Practices of Femininity and Masculinity*, London, Thousand Oaks (CA), New Delhi: Sage Publications.

Hird, M. J. (2000) 'Gender's nature: Intersexuality, transsexualism and the 'sex'/'gender' binary', *Feminist Theory*, 1(3): 347-364.

Hird, M. J. (2002) 'Out/Performing Our Selves: Invitation for Dialogue', *Sexualities*, 5(3): 337-356.

Hird, M. J. (2002) 'Welcoming Dialogue: a Further Response to Out/Performing Our Selves', *Sexualities*, 5(3): 362-366.

Hrabovszky, Z. and Hutson, J. M. (2002) 'Surgical treatment of intersex abnormalities: A review', *Surgery*, 131(1): 92-104.

Hughes, I. A. (2002) 'Intersex', *Bju International*, 90(8): 769-776.

Kim, K. R., Kwon, Y., Joung, J. Y., Kim, K. S., Ayala, A. G. and Ro, J. Y. (2002) 'True Hermaphroditism and mixed gonadal dysgenesis in young children: A clinicopathologic study of 10 cases', *Modern Pathology*, 15(10): 1013-1019.

Lancaster, R. N. (2003) *The Trouble with Nature: Sex in Science and Popular Culture*, Berkeley, Los Angeles, London: University of California Press.

Lee, P. A. and Witchel, S. F. (2002) 'Genital surgery among females with congenital adrenal hyperplasia: Changes over the past five decades', *Journal of Pediatric Endocrinology & Metabolism*, 15(9): 1473-1477.

Lerman, S. E., McAleer, I. M. and Kaplan, G. W. (2000) 'Sex assignment in cases of ambiguous genitalia and its outcome', *Urology*, 55(1): 8-12.

Liao, L.-M. (2005) 'III. Reflections on 'Masculinity-Femininity' based on Psychological Research and Practice in Intersex', *Feminism & Psychology*, 15(4): 424-430.

McCulloch, G. (1994) *Using Sartre*, London, New York: Routledge.

Meyer-Bahlburg, H. F. L. (2001) 'Gender and sexuality in classic congenital adrenal hyperplasia', *Endocrinology and Metabolism Clinics of North America*, 30(1).

Migeon, C. J., Wisniewski, A. B., Gearhart, J. P., Meyer-Bahlburg, H. F. L., Rock, J. A., Brown, T. R., Casella, S. J., Maret, A., Ngai, K. M., Money, J., et al. (2002) 'Ambiguous genitalia with perineoscrotal hypospadias in 46,XY individuals: Long-term medical, surgical, and psychosexual outcome', *Pediatrics*, 110(3): art. no.-e31.

Minto, C. L., Liao, L. M., Woodhouse, C. R. J., Ransley, P. G. and Creighton, S. M. (2003) 'The effect of clitoral surgery on sexual outcome in individuals who have intersex conditions with ambiguous genitalia: a cross- sectional study', *Lancet*, 361(9365): 1252-1257.

O'Brien, M. (2006) 'How to Define a Term without Defining the Person', 1ères Universités d'été des Intersexes et Intergenres d'Europe, 18/08/2006 Paris. [Online] https://mishmich.wordpress.com/2006/08/10/how-to-define-a-term-without-defining-the-person [Accessed 23/10/2015].

O'Brien, M. (2007) 'Intersex', in Beardsley, C. (Ed.) *The Transsexual Person is my Neighbour: Pastoral Guidelines for Christian Clergy, Pastors and Congregations*, 2nd ed. Brighton: Gender Trust, [Online] http://changingattitude.org.uk/resources/publications/the-transsexual-person-is-my-neighbour [Accessed 30/10/2015]

O'Brien, M. (2015) *Mish's Matters* [Online]. Available: https://mishmich.wordpress.com/ [Accessed 23/10/2015].

Sartre, J.-P. (1958/2003) *Being and Nothingness*, London, New York: Routledge.

Sax, L. (2002) 'How common is intersex? A response to Anne Fausto-Sterling', *Journal of Sex Research*, 39(3): 174-178.

Schweizer, K., Brunner, F., Handford, C. and Richter-Appelt, H. (2014) 'Gender experience and satisfaction with gender allocation in adults with diverse intersex conditions (divergences of sex development, DSD)', *Psychology & Sexuality*, 5(1): 56-82.

Sultan, C., Paris, F., Jeandel, C., Lumbroso, S. and Galifer, R. B. (2002) 'Ambiguous genitalia in the newborn', *Seminars in Reproductive Medicine*, 20(3): 181-188.

Tauchert, A. (2002) 'Fuzzy Gender: between female-embodiment and intersex', *Journal of Gender Studies*, 11(1): 29-38.

Van Lenning, A. (2004) 'The Body As Crowbar: Transcending Or Stretching Sex?', *Feminist Theory*, 5(1): 25-47.

Vilain, E. (2002) 'Anomalies of human sexual development: clinical aspects and genetic analysis', *Genetics and Biology of Sex Determination*. Chichester: John Wiley & Sons Ltd.

Vilain, E. (2006) 'Genetics of Intersexuality', *Journal of Gay and Lesbian Psychotherapy*, 10(2): 9-26.

Vilain, E. (2008) 'Genetics of Sexual Development and Differentiation', in Rowland, D. L. & Incrocci, L. (Eds.) *Handbook of Sexual and Gender Identity Disorders*, John Wiley & Sons.

Weeks, J. (1991) *Against Nature: Essays on history, homosexuality and identity*, London: Rivers Oram press.

Wilton, T. (2000) 'Out/Performing Our Selves: Sex. Gender and Cartesian Dualism', *Sexualities*, 3(2): 237-254.

Wisniewski, A. B. and Migeon, C. J. (2002) 'Long term perspectives for 46,XY patients affected by complete androgen insensitivity syndrome or congenital micropenis', *Seminars in Reproductive Medicine*, 20(3): 297-304.

Wisniewski, A. B., Migeon, C. J., Meyer-Bahlburg, H. F. L., Gearhart, J. P., Berkovitz, G. D., Brown, T. R. and Money, J. (2000) 'Complete androgen insensitivity syndrome: Long-term medical, surgical, and psychosexual outcome', *Journal of Clinical Endocrinology and Metabolism*, 85(8): 2664-2669.

Chapter 5 Bibliography

Althaus-Reid, M. (2000) *Indecent Theology: Theological Perversions in Sex, Gender, and Politics*, Abingdon, Oxon: Routledge.

Althaus-Reid, M. (2003) *The Queer God*, Abingdon, Oxon: Routledge.

Althaus-Reid, M. (2004a) *From Feminist Theology to Indecent Theology: Readings on Poverty, Sexual Identity and God*, London: SCM Press.

Althaus-Reid, M. (2004b) 'Queer I Stand: Lifting the Skirts of God', in: Althaus-Reid, M. & Isherwood, L. (Eds.) *The Sexual Theologian: Essays on Sex, God and Politics*, London & New York: T&T Clark.

Althaus-Reid, M. (2008a) 'Mutilations and Restorations: Cosmetic Surgery in Christianity', in Althaus-Reid, M. & Isherwood, L. (Eds.) *Controversies in Body Theology*, London: Hymns Ancient & Modern Ltd.

Althaus-Reid, M. (2008b) 'On Queer Theology and Liberation Theology: The Irruption of the Sexual Subject in Theology', in Althaus-Reid, M., Quinn, R. A., Borgman, E. & Reck, N. (Eds.) *Homosexualities, Concilium*, London: SCM Press.

Althaus-Reid, M. and Isherwood, L. (2007) *Controversies in Feminist Theology*, London: SCM Press.

Althaus-Reid, M. and Isherwood, L. (2009) *Trans/formations*, London: SCM Press.

Bujnowski, K. (2009) 'Through the Wilderness', in Althaus-Reid, M. & Isherwood, L. (Eds.) *Trans/Formations*, London: SCM Press.

Green, J. (2006) 'Look! No, Don't! The Visibility Dilemma for Transsexual Men', in Stryker, S. & Whittle, S. (Eds.) *Transgender Studies Reader*, New York & London: Routledge.

Kolakowski, V. S. (2000) 'Throwing a Party: Patriarchy, Gender, and the Death of Jezebel', in Goss, R. E. & West, M. (Eds.) *Take Back the Word: A Queer Reading of the Bible*, Cleveland, Ohio: Pilgrim.

Llewellyn-Jones, L. (2002) 'Eunuchs and the Royal Harem in Achaemenid Persia', in Tougher, S. (Ed.) *Eunuchs in Antiquity and Beyond*, Classical Press of Wales / Duckworth.

Mollenkott, V. R. (2008) *Sensuous Spirituality: Out From Fundamentalism*, Cleveland, Ohio: Pilgrim Press.

Quero, M. H. C. (2008) 'This Body Trans/Forming Me: Indecencies in Transgender/Intersex Bodies, Body Fascism and the Doctrine of the Incarnation', in Althaus-Reid, M. & Isherwood, L. (Eds.) *Controversies in Body Theology*, London: Hymns Ancient & Modern Ltd.

Reay, L. (2009) 'Towards a Transgender Theology: Que(e)rying the Eunuchs', in Althaus-Reid, M. & Isherwood, L. (Eds.) *Trans/Formations*, London: SCM Press.

Chapter 6 Bibliography

Bailey, D.S. (1955) *Homosexuality and the Western Christian Tradition*, London: Longmans, Green.

Beardsley, C. (2013) 'Nudging Towards Serendipity: The Church of England and Transsexual People', *Crucible: The Christian Journal of Social Ethics*, July-September 2013: 17-24.

Boswell, J. (1980) *Christianity, Social Tolerance and Homosexuality: Gay People in Western Europe from the Beginning of the Christian Era to the Fourteenth Century*, Chicago & London: University of Chicago Press.

Bray, A. (2003) *The Friend*, Chicago: University of Chicago Press.

Coleman, P. (1980) *Christian Attitudes to Homosexuality*, London: SPCK.

Countryman, L. W. (1988) *Dirt, Greed and Sex: Sexual Ethics in the New Testament and their Implications for Today*, London: SCM Press.

Everingham, (2000) G. W. *Gender Reassignment and the Bible*, 2nd edn. Privately printed.

Fletcher, B. (1990) *Clergy Under Stress. A Study of homosexual and heterosexual clergy in the Church of England*, London: Mowbray.

House of Bishops (2003) *Some Issues in Human Sexuality: A guide to the debate*, London: Church House Publishing.

House of Bishops (2013) *Report of the House of Bishops Working Group on human sexuality*, London: Church House Publishing.

Johnson M. (1994) *Outside the Gate*, London: Stepney Books.

Kruijver, F.P.M., Zhou, D. J.-N., Pool, C.W., Hofman, M.A., Gooren, L.J.G. and Swaab, D.F. (2000) 'Male To Female Transsexual Individuals Have Female Neuron Numbers In The Central Subdivision Of The Bed Nucleus Of The Stria Terminalis', *Journal of Clinical Endocrinology & Metabolism*, Vol 85(No: 5): 2034-2041.

Meyerowitz, J. (2002) *How Sex Changed. A History of Transsexuality in the United States*, Cambridge, Mass: & London: Harvard University Press.

Reid, R., di Ceglio, D., Dalrymple, J., Gooren, L., Green R. and Money, J. (January 1996a) *Transsexualism: The Current Medical Viewpoint*, 2nd edition [Online] http://www.gendercentre.org.au/resources/fact-sheets/old/transsexualism-the-current-medical-viewpoint.htm [Accessed 30/10/2015]

Reid, R. (1996b) Medical Report on the Affidavits of William Jenkins. As submitted to the judicial review of the cases of 'P'and 'G' vs H.M. Govt., March 1996 [Online] http://www.zoominfo.com/CachedPage/?archive_id=0&page_id=1916775622&page_url=//www.pfc.org.uk/node/615&page_last_updated=2008-12-20T00:58:35&firstName=Russell&lastName=Reid [Accessed 30/10/2015]

Robertson, F.W., (1874) *Expository Lectures on St Paul's Epistles to the Corinthians*, London: Henry S. King.

Thatcher, A. (2005) 'Some issues with *Some Issues in Human Sexuality*', *Theology & Sexuality*, 11(3): 9-30. [Online] http://www.adrianthatcher.org/data/resources/some%20issues%20with%20human%20sexuality.pdf [Accessed 30/10/2015]

Thinking Anglicans: 'Report to the House of Bishops on Homosexuality' [Online] http://thinkinganglicans.org.uk/uploads/osborne_report.pdf [Accessed 30/10/2015]

Vasey, M. (1995) *Strangers and Friends: a new exploration of homosexuality and the Bible*, London: Hodder & Stoughton.

Zhou, J.N., M.A. Hofman, L. Gooren & D.F. Swaab, (1995) 'A sex difference in the human brain and its relation to transsexuality,' *Nature*, vol. 378: 68-70.

Chapter 7 Bibliography

My Mums Used to be Men, (2007) Terrestrial & Digital TV, Directed by Beanland, J., ITV.

Beardsley, C. (2007), *The Transsexual Person is my Neighbour: Pastoral Guidelines for Christian Clergy, Pastors and Congregations*, 2nd ed. Brighton: Gender Trust, [Online] http://changingattitude.org.uk/resources/publications/the-transsexual-person-is-my-neighbour [Accessed 30/10/2015]

Brown, M. L. and Rounsley, C. A. (1996) T*rue Selves: understanding transsexualism - for families, friends, coworkers, and helping professionals*, San Francisco: Jossey-Bass Publishers.

Brown, R. E., Fitzmyer, S. and Murphy, R. E. (1990/1989) *The New Jerome Bible Commentary*, London: Geoffrey Chapman.

Crown (2004) 'Gender Recognition Act 2004', OPSI/TSO.

Crown (2005) 'The Gender Recognition Act 2004 (Commencement) Order 2005', Statutory Instrument 2005 No. 54 (C.2) OPSI/TSO.

di Ceglie, D. (2000) 'Gender Identity Disorder in Young People', *Advances in Psychiatric Treatment,* 6(6): 458-466.

DoH (2007) *An introduction to working with Transgender People – Information for health and social care staff,* COI for Department of Health. [Online] http://webarchive.nationalarchives.gov.uk/+/www.dh.gov.uk/en/publicationsandstatistics/publications/publicationspolicyandguidance/dh_074257 [Accessed 30/10/2015]

Horton, D. (1994) *Changing Channels? A Christian Response to the Transvestite and Transsexual,* Nottingham: Grove Books.

House of Bishops (2003) *Some Issues in Human Sexuality: A guide to the debate,* London: Church House Publishing.

Hyde, J. S. and DeLemater, J. (1997) *Understanding Human Sexuality,* New York: McGraw-Hill.

Money, J. and Ehrhardt, A. (1972) *Man and Woman – Boy and Girl,* Baltimore: The Johns Hopkins University Press.

Reid, R., di Ceglie, D., Dalrymple, J., Gooren, L., Green, R. and Money, J. (1996) *Transsexualism: The Current Medical Viewpoint,* Press for Change.

Rooke, A. and Gooch, B. (2006) *Sci:dentity Evaluation Report: Evaluating Phases One and Two,* Goldsmiths College (University of London). [Online] http://www.gold.ac.uk/media/sciidentevalu.pdf [Accessed 30/10/2015]

Rooke, A. and Gooch, B. (2006) *Executive Summary: An Evaluation of the Sci:dentity Project, Phases One and Two,* Goldsmiths College (University of London). [Online] http://www.gold.ac.uk/media/sciidentevalu.pdf [Accessed 30/10/2015]

Trans youth group from Sci:Identity, G. I. a. G. (2007) *A guide for young trans people in the UK,* Department of Health. [Online] http://webarchive.nationalarchives.gov.uk/+/www.dh.gov.uk/en/Publicationsandstatistics/publications/publicationspolicyandguidance/DH_074258 [Accessed 30/10/2015]

Whittle, S. and Turner, L. (2007) *Bereavement: a Guide for Transsexual, Transgender People and their loved ones,* Department of Health. [Online] http://www.gires.org.uk/assets/DOH-Assets/pdf/doh-bereavement.pdf [Accessed 30/10/2015]

Chapter 8 Bibliography

Bao, A.-M. and Swaab, D. F. (2011) 'Sexual differentiation of the human brain: Relation to gender identity, sexual orientation and neuropsychiatric disorders', *Frontiers in Neuroendocrinology,* 32: 214–226.

Burglund, H., Lindstrom, P., Dhejne-Helmy, C. and Savic, I. (2008) 'Male-to-female transsexuals show sex-atypical hypothalamus activation when smelling odorous steroids', *Cerebral Cortex,* 18(8): 1900-1908.

Clark, T. C., Lucassen, M. F. G., Bullen, P., Denny, S. J., Fleming, T. M., Robinson, E. M. and Rossen, F. V. (2014) 'The health and well-being of transgender high school students: Results from the New Zealand Adolescent Health Survey (Youth '12)', *Journal of Adolescent Health,* 55: 93-99.

Connolly, P. (2003) 'Transgendered Peoples of Samoa, Tonga and India: diversity of psychosocial challenges, coping, and styles of gender reassignment', Harry Benjamin International Gender Dysphoria Association *Symposium XVII,* 10-13/09/2003 Ghent, Belgium.

Dessens, A. B., Cohen-Kettenis, P. T., Mellenbergh, G. J., van der Poll, N. E., Koppe, J. G. and Boer, K. (1999) 'Prenatal exposure to anticonvulsants and psychosexual development', *Archives of Sexual Behavior,* 28: 31-44.

Dessens, A. B., Froukje, M. E., Slijper, F. M. E., Stenvert, L. S. and Drop, S. L. S. (2005) 'Gender dysphoria and gender change in chromosomal females with congenital adrenal hyperplasia', *Archives of Sexual Behavior,* 34(4): 389–397.

Dewing, P., Shi, T., Horvath, S. and Vilain, E. (2003) 'Sexually dimorphic gene expression in mouse brain precedes gonadal differentiation', *Molecular Brain Research* 118: 82-90.

Diamond, M. and Hawk, S. T. (2003) 'Transsexualism among twins has a high concordance for GID among monozygotic twins and a strong but lesser concordance among dizygotic twins with the effect more noticeable among males than females', Harry Benjamin International Gender Dysphoria Association Symposium XVII, 10-13/09/2003 Ghent, Belgium.

Diamond, M. and Sigmundson, K. (1997) 'Sex Reassignment at Birth: A Long Term Review and Clinical Implications', *Archives of Paediatric and Adolescent Medicine,* 151: 298-304.

Diamond, M. and Watson, L. A. (2004) 'Androgen insensitivity syndrome and Klinefelter's Syndrome', *Child and Adolescent Psychiatric Clinics of North America (Sex and Gender),* 13(3): 591-607.

EU, F. R. A. (2014) *Being Trans in the European Union - Comparative analysis of EU LGBT survey data*, European Union Bookshop. [Online] http://fra.europa.eu/en/publication/2014/being-trans-eu-comparative-analysis-eu-lgbt-survey-data [Accessed 30/10/2015]

Garcia-Falgueras, A. and Swaab, D. F. (2008) 'A sex difference in the hypothalamic uncinate nucleus: relationship to gender identity', *Brain: a journal of neurology*, 131(12): 3132-3146.

Glen, F. and Hurrell, K. (2012) *Technical note: Measuring Gender Identity*, Equality and Human Rights Commission.

Gooren, L. J., Sungkaew, T. and Gilta, E. J. (2013) 'Exploration of functional health, mental well-being and cross-sex hormone use in a sample of Thai male-to-female transgendered persons (kathoeys)', *Asian Journal of Andrology*, 15: 280–285.

Govier, E., Diamond, M., Wolowiec, T. and Slade, C. (2010) 'Dichotic listening, handedness, brain organisation and Transsexuality', *International Journal of Transgenderism*, 12(3): 144-154.

Green, R. (2000) 'Family co-occurrence of gender dysphoria: ten sibling or parent-child pairs'', *Archives of Sexual Behavior*, 29: 499-507.

Green, R. and Young, R. (2001) 'Hand preference, sexual preference, and transsexualism', *Archives of Sexual Behavior*, 30: 565–574.

Hare, L., Bernard, P., Sanchez, F. J., Baird, P. N., Vilain, E., Kennedy, T. and Harley, V. R. (2008) 'Androgen receptor repeat length polymorphism associated with male to female transsexualism', *Biological Psychiatry*, 65(1): 93-96.

Henningsson, S., Westberg, L., Nilsson, S., Lundström, B., Ekselius, L., Bodlund, O., Lindstrom, E., Hellstrand, M., Rosmond, R., Eriksson, E., et al. (2005) 'Sex Steroid Related Genes and Male to Female Transsexualism', *Psychoneuroendocrinology*, 30(7): 657-664.

Hines, M. (2004) *Brain Gender*, New York: Oxford University Press.

Kipnis, K. and Diamond, M. (1998) 'Pediatric Ethics and the Surgical Assignment of Sex', *Journal of Clinical Ethics*, 9(4): 398-410.

Kruijver, F. P. M., Zhou, J.-N., Pool, C. W., Hofman, M. A., Gooren, L. J. and Swaab, D. F. (2000) 'Male To Female Transexual Individuals Have Female Neuron Numbers In The Central Subdivision Of The Bed Nucleus Of The Stria Terminalis', *Journal of Clinical Endocrinology & Metabolism*, 85(No: 5): 2034-2041.

McNab, C. (2000) *Bellinger versus Bellinger (High Court)*, Press for Change. [Online] http://www.pfc.org.uk/caselaw/Bellinger%20v%20Bellinger.pdf [Accessed 30/10/2015]

Ochoa, B. (1996) 'Trauma of the External Genitalia in Children: Amputation of the Penis and Emasculation', *Journal of Urology*, 160(3): 1116-1119.

Rametti, G., Carrillo, B., Gómez-Gil, E., Junque, C., Segovia, S., Gomez, A. and Guillamon, A. (2011a) 'White matter microstructure in female to male transsexuals before cross-sex hormonal treatment. A diffusion tensor imaging study', *Journal of Psychiatric Research*, 45(2): 199-204.

Rametti, G., Carrillo, B., Gómez-Gil, E., Junque, C., Zubiarre-Elorza, L., Segovia, S., Gomez, A. and Guillamon, A. (2011b) 'The microstructure of white matter in male to female transsexuals before cross-sex hormonal treatment. A DTI study', *Journal of Psychiatric Research, 45(7): 949-54*, 45(7): 949-954.

RCPsych (2013) *Good Practice Guidelines for the assessment and treatment of adults with gender dysphoria*, Royal College of Psychiatrists. Available: www.rcpsych.ac.uk/files/pdfversion/CR181.pdf.

Reed, T., Curtis, R., Levy, A., Playdon, Z., Reed, B. and Wylie, K. (2008) *Guidance for GPs, other clinicians and health professional on the care of gender variant people: Transgender wellbeing and healthcare*, GIRES. [Online] http://www.nhs.uk/Livewell/Transhealth/Documents/gender-dysphoria-guide-for-gps-and-other-health-care-staff.pdf [Accessed 30/10/2015]

Reiner, W. G. (2004) 'Psychosexual development in genetic males assigned female: the cloacal exstrophy experience', *Child and Adolescent Clinics of North America (Sex and Gender)*, 13(3): 657–674.

Snaith, R. P., Penhale, S. and Horsfield, P. (1991) 'Male to female transsexual with 47 XYY karyotype', *Lancet*, 337: 557–558.

Thorpe, L. J. and Walker, L. J. R. (2001) *Judgement in the Case of Bellinger v. Bellinger (Appeals Court, 2001)*. [Online] http://www.pfc.org.uk/caselaw/Bellinger%20v%20Bellinger%20_Appeal_.pdf [Accessed 30/10/2015]

Whittle, S., Turner, L. and Al-Alami, M. (2007) *Engendered Penalties: Transgender and Transsexual People's Experiences of Inequality and Discrimination*, London, H.M. Government Equalities Review, Manchester Metropolitan University, Press for Change. [Online] http://www.pfc.org.uk/pdf/EngenderedPenalties.pdf [Accessed 30/10/2015].

WHO (2006) *International Statistical Classification of Diseases and Related Health Problems*, 10th Revision, Version for 2006, Geneva: World Health Organisation.

WHO (2013) *Improving the health and wellbeing of lesbian, gay, bisexual and transgender persons. Report by the Secretariat*, World Health Organisation, Executive Board. Available: www.ghwatch.org/sites/www.ghwatch.org/files/B133-6_LGBT.pdf.

WPATH (2012) *Standards of Care for the Heath of Transsexual, Transgender, and Gender-Nonconforming People, Version 7*, World Professional Association for Transgender Health. [Online] http://www.wpath.org/uploaded_files/140/files/Standards%20of%20Care,%20V7%20Full%20Book.pdf.

Zhou, J.-N., Swaab, D. F., Gooren, L. J. and Hofman, M. A. (1995) 'A sex difference in the human brain and its relation to transsexuality', *Nature*, 378: 68-70.

Zucker, K. J., Beaulieu, N., Bradley, S. J., Grimshaw, G. M. and Wilcox, A. (2001) 'Handedness in Boys with Gender Identity Disorder', *Journal of Clinical Child Psychology and Psychiatry*, 42(767-776).

Chapter 9 Bibliography

Conroy, M. (2010) 'Treating transgendered children: clinical methods and religious mythology', *Zygon*, 45(2): 301-316.

Dietert, M. and Dentice, D. (2013) 'Growing up Trans: socialization and the gender binary', *Journal of GLBT Family Studies*, 9(1): 24-42.

Evangelical Alliance (2000) *Transsexuality*, Carlisle: Authentic Media.

Forcier, M. and Johnson, M. (2013) 'Screening, identification, and support of gender non-conforming children and families', *Journal of paediatric nursing*, 28(1): 100-102.

Futty, J. (2010) 'Challenges posed by transgender - passing within ambiguities and interrelations', *Graduate Journal of Social Science*, 7(2): 57-75.

Grossman, A. and D'Augelli, A. (2006) 'Transgender youth: invisible and vulnerable', *Journal of Homosexuality*, 51(1): 111-128.

House of Bishops (2003) *Some Issues in Human Sexuality: A guide to the debate*, London: Church House Publishing.

Kennedy, N. and Hellen, M. (2010) 'Transgender children: more than a theoretical challenge', *Graduate Journal of Social Science,* 7(2): 25-43.

Parakleo (2008) 'Our Mission' [Online] http://www.parakaleo.co.uk/mission [Accessed 30/10/2015]

Tanis, J. (2003) *Trans-gendered: theology, ministry and communities of faith,* Cleveland: Pilgrim Press.

Chapter 10 Bibliography

Besser, M., Carr, S., Cohen-Kettenis, P.T., Connolly, P., De Sutter, P., Diamond, M., Di Ceglie, D. (Ch and Adol.), Higashi, Y., Jones, L., Kruijver. F.P.M., Martin, J., Playdon, Z-J., Ralph, D., Reed, T., Reid, R., Reiner, W.G., Swaab, D., Terry, T., Wilson, P. and Wylie, K. (2006) 'Atypical Gender Development – A Review', *International Journal of Transgenderism,* 9(1):29-44, [Accessed 15/10/2015]: http://www.gires. org.uk/assets/Research-Assets/atypical-gender-development.pdf.

Catechism (1997) *Catechism of the Catholic Church,* Homebush, NSW, Strathfield: Pauline Books.

Cattaneo, L. and Rizzolatti, G. (2009) 'The mirror neuron system', *Arch Neurol,* 66(5): 557-60.

Dawkins, R. (1989/1978) *The Selfish Gene,* Oxford University Press. 3rd edition 2006.

Decety, J. and Meyer, M. (2008) 'From emotion resonance to empathic understanding: A social developmental neuroscience account'. *Development and Psychopathology,* 20: 1053-1080.

Dennett, D.C. (1987) 'Reprint of Intentional systems in cognitive ethology: The Panglossian paradigm defended', *The Brain and Behavioral Sciences,* 6: 343-390.

Dessens, A.B. Froukje, M.E., Slijper, F.M.E. Stenvert, L.S. and Drop S.L.S. (2005) 'Gender dysphoria and gender change in chromosomal females with congenital adrenal hyperplasia', *Archives of Sexual Behavior* 34(4): 389–397.

Diamond, A. (2002) 'Prefrontal Cortex Development and Development of Cognitive Function', in *International Encyclopedia of the Social and Behavioral Sciences*: 11976–11982.

Diamond, M. and Sigmundson H.K. (1997) 'Sex reassignment at birth. Long term review and clinical implications', *Archives of Pediatrics and Adolescent Medicine* 151: 298-304.

Diamond, M. and Watson, L.A. (2004). 'Androgen insensitivity syndrome and Klinefelter's Syndrome', in Diamond, M. and Yates, A. (eds.) *Child and Adolescent Psychiatric Clinics of North America (Sex and Gender)*, Philadelphia: W.B. Saunders, 13(3): 623–640.

Freud, S. (1905/1915). 'Three Essays on the Theory of Sexuality', in *The Standard Edition of the Complete Psychological Works of Sigmund Freud*, Volume VII (1901-1905), Hogarth Press: 123-246.

Freud, S. (1933/1991) *New Introductory Lectures on Psychoanalysis*, Penguin Books.

Gallese, V. (2003) 'The Roots of Empathy: The Shared Manifold Hypothesis and the Neural Basis of Intersubjectivity', *Psychopathology*, 36(4): 171–180.

Gallese, V. (2009) 'The Two Sides of Mimesis: Girard's Mimetic Theory, Embodied Simulation and Social Identification', *Journal of Consciousness studies*, 16, No 4.

Gallese, V. and Sinigaglia, C. (2011) 'How the body in action shapes the self', *Journal of Consciousness Studies*, 18((7–8): 117–143.

Gallese, V. (2013) 'Bodily self, affect, consciousness and the cortex', *Neuropsychoanalysis*, 15(1): 42-45.

Gilchrist, S. (2015) *Personal Writing and Research*, [Online]. [Accessed 15/10/2015]: http://www.tgdr.co.uk/sourcesA/index.htm

Girard, R. (1965/1961) *Deceit, Desire, and the Novel: Self and Other in Literary Structure*, Baltimore: Johns Hopkins University Press.

Girard, R. (1977/1972) *Violence and the Sacred*, Baltimore: Johns Hopkins University Press.

Girard, R., Oughourlian, J.-M. and Lefort, G. (1987) *Things Hidden since the Foundation of the World*, Stanford CA: Stanford University Press.

Garrels, S.R. (2006) 'Imitation, Mirror Neurons, and Mimetic Desire: Convergence Between The Mimetic Theory of Rene Girard and Empirical Research on Imitation Contagion', *Journal of Violence, mimesis and Culture*, 12-13, 2006: 47-86.

GIRES (2006) 'Atypical Gender Development: A critique of the review', [Online]. [Acessed 15/10/2015]: http://www.gires.org.uk/assets/IJT-Assets/IJTresponse.pdf

GIRES (2012) 'Diagnosis and Aetiology: an update', [Online]. [Acessed 15/10/2015]: http://www.gires.org.uk/assets/Research-Assets/ Diagnosis%20and%20Aetiology%20update%202012.pdf

Gruber, H.E. and Voneche, J.J. eds. (1977) *The Essential Piaget*, New York: Basic Books.

Heylighen, F. and Chielens, K. (2009) 'Evolution of Culture, Memetics', in B. Meyers (ed.) *Encyclopedia of Complexity and Systems Science*, Springer [Acessed 15/10/2015]: http://pespmc1.vub.ac.be/Papers/ Memetics-Springer.pdf

Iacoboni, M. and Geffen, D. (2009), 'Imitation, Empathy and Mirror Neurons', *Annual Review of Psychology* 60: 653-670.

Kerlin, S.P. (2004) 'The Presence of Gender Dysphoria, Transsexualism, and Disorders of Sex Differentiation in Males Prenatally Exposed to Diethylstilbestrol: Initial Evidence from a 5-Year Study', *6th Annual E-Hormone Conference, October 27-30, 2004, New Orleans*, [Access date 10/10/2015]: http://www.gires.org.uk/documents/Kerlinpaper.doc

Keysers, C. and Fadiga, L. (2008), 'The mirror neuron system: New frontiers', *Social Neuroscience*, 3 (3-4): 193-198.

Kipnis, K. and Diamond, M. (1998) 'Pediatric ethics and the surgical assignment of sex', *Journal of Clinical Ethics*, 9(4): 398-410.

Meriggiola, M.C. and Gava, G. (2015) 'Endocrine care of transpeople part I. A review of cross-sex hormonal treatments, outcomes and adverse effects in transmen ', *Clinical endocrinology*, Wiley Online Library [Accessed 15/10/2-15]: http://onlinelibrary.wiley.com/doi/10.1111/cen.12753/full

Minot Presentation (2005) in *The Prague Declaration on Endocrine Disruptors meeting, June 2005* [Accessed 10/10/2015]: http://www.gires. org.uk/documents/BeyerMinotPresentation2005.doc

Money, J. (1980) *Love and Love Sickness: the Science of Sex, Gender Difference and Pair-Bonding*, Johns Hopkins University Press, 1980. ISBN 0-8018-2317-X, ISBN 0-8018-2318-8 .

Money, J.(1995) *Gendermaps: Social Constructionism, Feminism, and Sexosophical History* Continuum International Publishing Group; October 1995, ISBN-10: 0826408524, ISBN-13: 978-0826408525.

Money, J. and Erhardt, A.A (1996) *Man and Woman, Boy and Girl: Gender Identity from Conception to Maturity* (Masterwork Series) New Edition 1 Jan. 1996, Jason Aronson Inc. ISBN-10: 1568218125 ISBN-13: 978-1568218120.

Ochoa, B. (1998) 'Trauma of the External Genitalia in Children: Amputation of the Penis and Emasculation', *Journal of Neurology* 160(3-11): 1116-1119.

Reiner, W.G. (2004) 'Psychosexual development in genetic males assigned female: the cloacal exstrophy experience', in Diamond, M. and Yates, A. (eds.) *Child and Adolescent Clinics of North America (Sex and Gender)*, Philadelphia: W.B. Saunders, 13(3): 657–674.

Rizzolatti, G. and Fabbri-Destro, M. (2010) 'Mirror neurons: from discovery to autism', *Exp Brain Res*, 200(3-4):223-37.

Rosenthal, S.M. (2014) 'Approach to the Patient: Transgender Youth Endocrine Considerations', *Clin Endocrinol Metab*, 99(12):4379-89.

Narrative No. 3: 'Jemma' Bibliography

Beardsley, C. (2015) 'Metamorphosis & (trans)migration: spiritual dimensions of gender transition', in Scherpe, J. (Ed.) *The Legal Status of Transsexual and Transgender Persons*, Cambridge: Intersentia Publishers: 77-99.

Ekins R. and King, D. (Eds.) (1996) *Blending Genders: Social Aspects of Cross-dressing and Sex-changing*, London: Routledge.

Ekins, R., and King, D. (2006) *The Transgender Phenomenon*, London: Sage Publications.